About the editors

Dr Francisco Dominguez is Senior Lecturer in Latin American Studies, Middlesex University. His publications include: 'The Latin Americanization of the politics of emancipation', in G. Lievesley and S. Ludlam (eds), *Reclaiming Latin America: Experiments in Radical Social Democracy* (2009); 'Violence, the left and the creation of *Un Nuevo Chile*', in W. Fowler and P. Lambert (eds), *Political Violence and Identity in Latin America* (2008); 'The rise of the private sector in Cuba', in A. I. Gray and A. Kapcia (eds), *The Changing Dynamic of Cuban Civil Society* (2008); and *Mercosur: Between Integration and Democracy* (2003).

Dr Geraldine Lievesley is a senior lecturer and teaches Latin American and Cuban Politics at Manchester Metropolitan University. Among her recent publications are: *Reclaiming Latin America: Experiments in Radical Social Democracy* (2009, with Steve Ludlam); *In the Hands of Women: Paradigms of Citizenship* (2006, with Susan Buckingham); and *The Cuban Revolution: Past, Present and Future Perspectives* (2004).

Dr Steve Ludlam is a senior lecturer and teaches Cuban and Latin American Politics at the University of Sheffield. His recent publications include 'Cuba at 50 – what about the workers?', *Bulletin of Latin American Research* (2009); *Reclaiming Latin America: Experiments in Radical Social Democracy* (2009, with Geraldine Lievesley); and *Labour, the State, Social Movements and the Challenge of Neo-liberal Globalisation* (2007, with Andrew Gamble, Andrew J. Taylor and Stephen Wood).

RIGHT-WING POLITICS IN THE NEW LATIN AMERICA

reaction and revolt

edited by Francisco Dominguez, Geraldine Lievesley and Steve Ludlam

Zed Books
LONDON | NEW YORK

Right-wing Politics in the New Latin America: Reaction and Revolt was first published in 2011 by Zed Books Ltd, 7 Cynthia Street, London N1 9JF, UK and Room 400, 175 Fifth Avenue, New York, NY 10010, USA

www.zedbooks.co.uk

Set in OurType Arnhem and Futura Bold by Ewan Smith, London
Index: ed.emery@thefreeuniversity.net
Cover designed by Rogue Four Design
Printed and bound in Great Britain CPI Group (UK) Ltd, Croydon, CR0 4YY

Distributed in the USA exclusively by Palgrave Macmillan, a division of St Martin's Press, LLC, 175 Fifth Avenue, New York, NY 10010, USA

A catalogue record for this book is available from the British Library
Library of Congress Cataloging in Publication Data available

ISBN 978 1 84813 812 4 hb
ISBN 978 1 84813 811 7 pb

Contents

Acknowledgements

We thank Ken Barlow at Zed Books for his support and patience. We also thank the UK Society for Latin America Studies for facilitating discussion of some of the chapters. Special thanks are due to Guy Burton for checking Portuguese spellings and to Jose Camean for translating material used in the chapter on Brazil. We are deeply indebted to many friends, colleagues and students in the UK and in the Americas for educating and inspiring us. As ever, we thank our friends and families for their support and forbearance. We dedicate this book to the tens of thousands of Latin Americans who have been murdered by right-wing forces, and are still being murdered today, above all in Colombia, for their commitment to democracy and equality, in the hope that it may make a tiny contribution to ending the continent's periodic history of violent oppression.

Francisco Dominguez, Geraldine Lievesley
and Steve Ludlam

Abbreviations

ACyS	Acuerdo Cívico y Social, Social and Civic Agreement (Argentina)
AD	Acción Democrática, Democratic Action (Venezuela)
AFL-CIO	American Federation of Labor and Congress of Industrial Organizations
ALBA	Alianza Bolivariana para los Pueblos de Nuestra América, Bolivarian Alliance for the Peoples of Our America
AP	Acción Popular, Popular Action (Peru)
APC	Alianza para Cambio, Alliance for Change (Paraguay)
APRA	Alianza Popular Revolucionaria Americana, American Popular Revolutionary Alliance (Peru)
APS	Asociación de Productores de Soja, Association of Soya Producers (Paraguay)
ARENA	Acçao Nacionalista Renovadora, National Renewal Party (Brazil)
ARENA	Alianza Republicana Nacionalista, Nationalist Republican Alliance (El Salvador)
ARP	Asociación Rural del Paraguay, Paraguayan Rural Association
AUC	Autodefensas Unidas de Colombia, United Self-Defence Units of Colombia
BCB	Banco Central de Bolivia, Bolivian Central Bank
CANF	Cuban American National Foundation (US)
CCPSC	Comité Civico Pro-Santa Cruz, Civic Committee of Santa Cruz (Bolivia)
CEPRA	Coordinadora Ejecutiva para la Reforma Agraria, Executive Coordinating Committee for Agrarian Reform (Paraguay)
CIA	Central Intelligence Agency (US)
CNE	Consejo Nacional Electoral, National Electoral Council (Venezuela)
COPEI	Comité de Organización Política Electoral Independiente – Partido Social Cristiano de Venezuela, Committee of Independent Political and Electoral Organization – Social Christian Party of Venezuela (Venezuela)
CTV	Confederación de Trabajadores de Venezuela, Confederation of Venezuelan Workers
DEA	Drug Enforcement Agency (US)
ELN	Ejército de Liberación Nacional, National Liberation Army (Colombia)

FARC	Fuerzas Armadas Revolucionarias Colombianas, Revolutionary Armed Forces of Colombia
FBI	Federal Bureau of Investigation (US)
FDI	foreign direct investment
FEDECAMARAS	Federación de Cámaras y Asociaciones de Comercio y Producción de Venezuela, Venezuelan Federation of Chambers of Commerce
FREDEMO	Frente Democrático, Democratic Front (Peru)
GDP	gross domestic product
IDB	Inter-American Development Bank
IFE	Instituto Federal Electoral, Federal Electoral Institute (Mexico)
IMF	International Monetary Fund
IRI	International Republican Institute (US)
M-19	Movimiento Revolucionario M-19, 19 April Revolutionary Movement (Colombia)
MAS	Movimiento al Socialismo, Movement towards Socialism (Bolivia)
MAS	Muerte a Secuestradores, Death to Kidnappers (Colombia)
MDI	multilateral development institution
ML	Movimiento Libertad, Liberty Movement (Peru)
NAFTA	North American Free Trade Agreement
NED	National Endowment for Democracy (US)
NGO	non-governmental organization
OAS	Organization of American States
OPEC	Organization of the Petroleum Exporting Countries
PAN	Partido Acción Nacional, National Action Party (Mexico)
PDT	Partido Democrático Trabalhista, Democratic Labour Party (Brazil)
PDVSA	Petróleos de Venezuela, Venezuelan Oil
PEMEX	Petróleos Mexicanos, Mexican Oil
PFL	Partido da Frente Liberal, Liberal Front Party (Brazil)
PJ	Partido Justicialista, Justice Party (Argentina)
PLRA	Partido Liberal Radical Auténtico, Authoritarian Radical Liberal Party (Paraguay)
PMDB	Partido do Movimento Democrático Brasileiro, Party of the Brazilian Democratic Movement
PODEMOS	Poder Democrático Social, Social Democratic Power (Bolivia)
PPC	Partido Popular Cristiano, Popular Christian Party (Peru)
PRD	Partido Democrático de la Revolución, Party of the Democratic Revolution (Mexico)
PRI	Partido Revolucionario Institucional, Revolutionary Institutional Party (Mexico)

PSDB	Partido da Social Democracia Brasileira, Social Democratic Party of Brazil (Brazil)
PT	Partido dos Trabalhadores, Workers' Party (Brazil)
RCTV	Radio Caracas Televisión Internacional (Venezuela)
RN	Renovación Nacional, National Renovation (Chile, Peru)
TNC	transnational corporation
UCR	Unión Cívica Radical, Radical Civic Union (Argentina)
UDI	Unión Demócrata Independiente, Independent Democratic Union (Chile)
UN	Unidad Nacional, National Unity (Peru)
UNACE	Unión Nacional de Ciudadanos Eticos, National Union of Ethical Citizens (Paraguay)
UNASUR	Unión de Naciones Suramericanas, Union of South American Nations
USAID	United States Agency for International Development
YPFB	Yacimientos Petrolíferos Fiscales Bolivianos, Bolivian State Petrol Reserves (Bolivia)

Introduction: reaction and revolt

GERALDINE LIEVESLEY AND
STEVE LUDLAM

The challenge from the left

In researching and writing *Reclaiming Latin America* (Lievesley and Ludlam 2009a), which investigated the rise of the left-leaning or 'pink tide' governments in the early twenty-first century and their achievements, we and our colleagues realized how important it was to evaluate the nature and strength of right-wing opposition and of the forces supporting it, and how they have gone about resisting the 'pink tide'. As we pointed out in that study, quite apart from anything else, some of the 'pink tide' presidencies relied on narrow majorities – or even, in the case of Nicaragua, on a minority of the popular vote (2009a: 3–5). The main dynamic behind the 'pink tide' was the intensity of popular mobilization across the region against the political and socio-economic policies known collectively as the 'Washington Consensus' (liberal-democratic politics going hand in hand with neoliberal economics). These policies were strongly endorsed by the US and gave succour to right-wing forces in the form of governments, political parties, think tanks, corporations, religious institutions and the media, all of which overwhelmingly and enthusiastically embraced neoliberalism. As many countries moved from military to civilian rule after 1980, the Washington Consensus provided the ideological ballast and justification for attempts to establish elitist and exclusive governments that aimed to block movements for redistributory and socially just reforms. Governments embarked upon massive economic restructuring and the privatization of natural resources, selling off the national patrimony (including public services and utilities) to domestic and international capital, and opening up previously protected sectors (notably agriculture) to competition from the industrialized producers of North America.

The social consequences were massively debilitating for the mass of people, who responded over time with demonstrations that eventually coalesced into a repudiation of neoliberalism and the narrow political regimes it sponsored. Aspects of the neoliberal programmes directly triggered revolts that led to left-wing electoral victories: for example against the impact of tax increases driven by minimalist fiscal policy, as in the *Caracazo* riots in Venezuela; against the consequences of severe and non-discretionary fixed exchange-rate regimes, as in Argentina; or against the privatization of public utilities, as in Bolivia's 'water wars'. In the final two decades of the twentieth century, the widespread popular association of poverty and exploitation with neoliberalism left the right – both its populist forces and the more traditional party-based forces – with its core policy appeal in ruins and with no obvious alternative political economy to offer. And while the endorsement by much of the right in Latin America of the so-called 'third wave' of democratization was evidently important, its narrow conception of democracy as a set of constitutional and legislative processes brought it increasingly into conflict with a mass electorate, much of which was expecting its material poverty to be redressed through a broader conception of the purpose of democracy, and much of which was expecting to participate in a democratic culture that was far more inclusive and participatory than was envisaged by the right (Lievesley 1999; for extensive survey material see UN Development Programme 2004). Hence, while the impact of neoliberalism explained many popular revolts, including some that clearly resulted in left-wing election victories, others were revolts against aspects of the limitations of really-existing democracy, against corruption, against ruling-class interference with constitutions and courts, against electoral fraud, for indigenous rights, and so on (for a graphic overview, see Inter-American Development Bank 2006: 113–14). So even if (as surveys found) over half of the electorate of Latin America was prepared to opt for authoritarian government if it solved its economic problems (UN Development Programme 2004: 80), there was no obvious incentive to look for an authoritarian alternative on the right! And, given the context of a worldwide depression from 2008 that was so clearly linked to the market fundamentalism of the neoliberal order, why, apart from disenchantment with the performance of the left in office, would the popular vote move to the right?

Elements of right-wing advantage

Against that background, what does emerge in this book is a set of elements that can sustain the power of right-wing politics, and to which we return in our concluding chapter. The intrinsic, historically conditioned variety of national right-wing politics in Latin America, and the contrasting condition of the right being in government in some states and in opposition in most, has not inclined us in this book to attempt a thematically organized comparative study. The book is structured around chapters on continental themes – an overview, studies of US hard and soft power in the region – and on studies of states where the right is in office, and of states where it is in opposition (in one case in exile). This structure is outlined further below. Nevertheless there are some core themes that emerge from these studies and that are worth drawing attention to in this introduction. We will return to them in our conclusions.

A first and critical question is how far and how deeply has the Latin American right become democratic? By the time you have finished reading this book, you may well conclude that the answer is 'not very far and not very deeply'. There is an underlying hypocrisy at the heart of the Washington Consensus: if a choice had to be made between democracy and stability, the latter would undoubtedly win. Lip service is paid to democratic governance, but only in so far as that provides the environment in which US security concerns are pursued. Stability and security are understood as the necessary conditions for the US, its Latin American allies and the multinationals and international institutions (such as the International Monetary Fund – IMF – and the World Bank) to do business, accrue profits and prevent the introduction of radical social programmes. In its efforts to undermine and subvert contemporary left-leaning governments, the Latin American right has masked its intentions behind such words as 'freedom' and 'democracy', but in practice has gone in for media demonization, street violence, murder, sedition and – *in extremis* – military coups (Livingstone 2009). That final recourse of right-wing forces was used in 2002 (unsuccessfully) in Venezuela, in 2009 (successfully) in Honduras and in 2010 (unsuccessfully) in Ecuador; and there have been rumours of impending military intervention in a number of other countries, including Paraguay and Bolivia. Clearly many right-wing forces wear their democratic clothes very loosely. Indeed, the right identifies with democracy only when it suits its economic and ideological purposes. As one scholarly study recently concluded: 'Latin America's armed forces have not stepped entirely out of politics. They stepped aside. In most countries they retained the option of deciding whether, when, and how to return' (Smith 2005: 106).

Secondly, the right retains formidable resources that enable it to exercise political power even when out of office. The support of key national economic sectors – the core of the ruling class – is an immeasurable force, whether exercised directly in capitalist 'strikes' in Venezuela from 2002 and in Argentina in 2008; in armed sub-national breakaway movements, as in Bolivia in 2008; or indirectly, by constraining policy choices through threats of disinvestment. The supranational powers of US-based international financial institutions, of course, continue to exercise constant influence over national policymakers. The political power of the news and current affairs media in Latin America is, notoriously, overwhelmingly at the service of right-wing politics. The support of other members of the ruling-class elites embedded in the judiciary and other institutions of the state has been another crucial instrument for obstructing left-wing presidencies, as illustrated in this book, for example, in the cases of Argentina and Paraguay. And, while neoliberalism may have changed the form of private profiteering from the corrupt control of public contracts and resources to the direct sale of public services, enterprises and natural resources, structures of informal right-wing power persist in networks of clientelism, patronage and corruption. These networks in some areas sustain a mass electoral machine for the right, as in Brazil. But, thirdly, right-wing politics also retains a broad mass appeal based in deep-rooted conservative social attitudes, not least in areas such as power in the family, state policy on contraception, abortion and gay rights, and generally the processes of socialization based around family, Church and education and cultural discourses shaped by the old explanations of deference, false consciousness and fear of modernity. And in this respect the right enjoys a great deal of support in its campaigns from religious centres of power, not only those of traditional Catholicism, but increasingly also those of well-resourced Evangelical Protestantism. Having lost the ability it enjoyed during the Cold War to pose as the national defender against subversion, and now damaged by its neoliberal internationalism, to what extent the right is capable of wrapping itself in the flag and occupying the nationalist high ground is a question of vital importance. Fourthly, the right enjoys the support of supranational political forces, notably the machinery of would-be full-spectrum dominance by the US – not just in military and security spheres, but also in the deployment of soft power through US-funded non-governmental organizations (NGOs) that directly fund right-wing political groupings throughout the continent. Fifthly, just as it suffered in electoral terms from the errors it made while in government, so the right can profit from the mistakes of others in government. The behaviour of the left in office, especially if it disappoints its core supporters as it reaches across the political centre for votes, can empower right-wing opponents.

The structure of the book

This book, as was noted above, is not a comparative text in political science or a theoretical intervention. Nor have we sought to represent just one ideological approach, since that would have been a thankless and intellectually constrained task. The country case studies demonstrate that particular and distinctive historical and cultural traits must be taken into consideration in assessing the right's influence and its ability to shape the region's politics. The first chapters below, though, address the continental and international context in which the right operates. In his chapter, Guy Burton provides a typology of the right in government and opposition, identifying a power spectrum ranging from political dominance (Colombia), to an inability to govern but an ability to exercise indirect influence (Peru), to a provocative but ultimately non-hegemonic status (Venezuela and Bolivia). Even in countries where its political influence is limited, it is able to block the legislative programmes of left-leaning governments and so impede their general strategies. Central to Burton's argument is the question of whether the right is committed to democracy only so long as its interests are not in danger, and whether it will revert to its pre-democratic traditions if it judges that the political climate has become threatening. In terms of international context, Grace Livingstone gives a historical account of US policy towards Latin America, stressing the continuity of Washington's objectives and its continued identification of the right – in and out of government – as being the best vehicle by which to further them. Geraldine Lievesley then considers the role of right-wing US think tanks in formulating those policy objectives and in providing financial and ideological support to those right-wing parties and institutions in Latin America that pursue the aims of the 'New American Century'.

The chapters by Alexander Dawson, Diana Raby and Francisco Durand examine the right in power in Mexico, Colombia and Peru, respectively. Dawson focuses on the 2006 presidential elections in Mexico. Despite the incumbent right-wing president's policy failures in areas such as immigration, insurgency and the eradication of drug trafficking, the candidate of the left was unable to win, partly as a result of his own errors, but also because of the pervasive institutional powers enjoyed by the executive branch of government. Dawson also draws attention to the general disillusionment among Mexicans and their lack of confidence in all politicians – characteristics not conducive to the political transformation that a left-wing victory would symbolize. In common with other chapters, he also highlights the resolute resistance of the right to what it regards as the moral depredation of 'modern' issues, such as feminism and gay rights. In her study of Colombia, Diana Raby identifies it as a client state chosen by the US to act as a bulwark against the spread of progressive politics. The country's repressive atmosphere inhibits normal political activity and offers scant opportunities for left-wing and popular organization. Its vaunted 'democratic security' has created a state that is neither democratic nor secure. Francisco Durand portrays a Peruvian right that is fragmented by personalist politics but that nevertheless manages to exercise considerable indirect political influence. The source of this lies in its support networks within business, religious and media circles, and its strong international connections. Despite this, the right has been unable to expand its support base and reach out to the middle and popular classes, and that is why it has not been able to win presidential elections.

The right in opposition occupies the attention of the rest of the book. Francisco Dominguez offers a chilling catalogue of the Venezuelan right's attempts to undermine the government of Hugo Chávez since his election in 1998. These have included economic sabotage, parliamentary obstruction, a media war, strikes, boycotts, an abortive coup and assassination plots. While undertaking these tactics, the right has consistently denounced the government as authoritarian and undemocratic! In his chapter, Andreas Tsolakis charts the secessionist activities of the Bolivian right, fuelled by its desire to control the country's hydrocarbon resources, as well as to prevent the creation of a 'plurinational' state based on repudiation of racism by the government of President Evo Morales. Tsolakis also contrasts the different approaches adopted by the US on the one hand, and by the European governments and multilateral development institutions on the other. While the former has pursued an explicitly anti-Morales policy, the latter have developed a far more sophisticated position, aimed at locking Bolivia into the structures of global capitalist production.

Steve Ludlam's chapter on the anti-Castro right living in exile in the US chronicles the history of that right's terrorist activities against the Cuban government and demonstrates the political influence it has exerted over Washington's Cuba policy – a policy that is devoted to promoting 'democratic transition' on the island and that reveals the violent instincts still close to the heart of US foreign policy. Marcos Costa Lima analyses the inability of the Brazilian right to constitute a critical mass capable of governing, but also describes how it was able to limit the speed and depth of President Lula's Workers' Party reform project after 2002. He also speculates on whether the government of Lula's successor, elected in 2010, will be able to forge ahead with that programme now that the right-wing parties have lost their congressional advantage. In his study of Paraguay, Peter Lambert assesses the political and personal weaknesses of left-leaning President Fernando Lugo as he faced a prolonged assault aimed at destabilizing his government, an attack that came from entrenched and conservative structures of power characterized by clientelism and corrupt practices and fuelled by incendiary media.

In their account of the relationship between the right and the government of Cristina Fernández de Kirchner in Argentina, Leonardo Díaz Echenique, Javier Ozollo and Ernesto Vivares describe a clash between two distinct models of economic development: one profoundly neoliberal and fuelled by the needs of large agribusiness, and the other state-led and committed to social redistribution. During the writing of this book, Chile moved from having a left-leaning government to a right-wing one led by Sebastián Piñera. Patricio Silva, who tracks the recent history and recovery of the right during the democratization process, suggests that there will not be a huge political rupture, given that the Concertación coalition of Christian Democrats and Socialists that had been in power for the previous twenty years had pursued neoliberal policies, albeit with programmes of poverty alleviation. In Chile, the policy differences between left-leaning and right-wing parties have appeared to be of degree, and all – bar the extreme right – seem to have agreed to pursue a politics based on compromise and consensus.

We hope that the chapters of this book will enlighten its readers, and especially assist those with an active interest in the role of the right in Latin America.

ONE | The continental right

1 | The South American right after 'the end of history'

GUY BURTON

The outlook for the right in South America in the early 1990s was optimistic.[1] The Sandinistas' 1990 election defeat had left Cuba the last socialist country in the hemisphere. Democracy was in vogue, following the end of military rule and more competitive elections. The region appeared to be on the economic road to recovery, following a traumatic decade of structural adjustment. At this time, Fukuyama presented his 'end of history' thesis: societies were now entering a period in which democracy and the market would become the dominant form of political and economic organization (Fukuyama 1992).

Nearly two decades later, the 'end of history' claim rings hollow in relation to South America. Since the mid-2000s, it has become almost commonplace to talk of a leftward shift across the region, from Brazil and Chile to Venezuela and Bolivia. Indeed, this has captured much scholarly and media attention (see Ellner 2004; Harnecker 2005; Panizza 2005; Petras 2005; Castañeda 2006; Castañeda and Morales 2008; Barrett, Chavez and Rodríguez-Garavite 2008; Lievesley and Ludlam 2009a). By contrast, the literature that has focused on the right in the region has been relatively sparse (Chalmers, Campello de Souza and Borón 1992; Middlebrook 2000a; 2000b). Furthermore, such material has largely focused on the right during the 1980s and 1990s, not on the period since 2000.

The impression the right gives in South America is one of 'winners'

---

1 I use the term 'South America' here to distinguish the countries studied in this chapter – the Spanish- and Portuguese-speaking countries on the continent of South America and Mexico – from the wider Latin America region of South America, Central America and the Spanish-speaking islands of the Caribbean. That I do so does not mean that the categorizations of the right laid out in the South American cases are not applicable to the wider region. However, given space constraints I am obliged to limit my comparative study of the right. I would like to thank Peader Kirby and Barry Cannon for comments on an earlier draft of this chapter, as well as the organizers of and participants in the 2009 Society of Latin American Studies panel, where an earlier version of the chapter was presented.

in the 1990s and 'losers' in the 2000s. But to what extent is that an accurate picture? If the left did indeed become the main political actor to watch in the current decade, how has the right reacted and responded to such developments, if at all? Such questions are deeply important, given scholarly observation that the inclusion of conservative forces, whether as political parties or social groups, is vital if democracy is to be sustained against the risk of military intervention (Gibson 1992; Middlebrook 2000a; 2000b). To address these questions, this chapter is structured as follows: first a definition of the South American right is provided; the role of the right in the political and economic changes of the 1980s and 1990s is discussed; and then the right's approach during the leftward shift of the 2000s is analysed.

Defining the right

The right can be understood in three main ways: ideologically, sociologically and organizationally. Its control of power (both economic and political) depends on its ability to exert sufficient influence, which may be achieved through formal or informal means, and may be conducted in a direct or indirect fashion.

Ideologically, the left–right distinction may be understood with regard to the values that underpin each pole. Although some Latin Americanists argue that the right cannot be defined in ideological terms (Middlebrook 2000a; Gibson 1992), Norberto Bobbio's distinction between a left that is committed to equality and a right that is committed to inequality seems applicable (Bobbio 1996). Indeed, the historical trajectory of the right in the region since independence demonstrates this: it has pursued the interests of the elite over those of others, ensuring an imbalance in terms of social, political and economic capital.

Sociologically, the interests associated with the left and right can be understood through their component constituencies, that is, the subordinate and dominant classes, respectively. The dominant class (or groups), on the right, is an elite that has the greatest material wealth, control of production and access to mechanisms of coercion. The subordinate class, on the left, consists of those without these things. The existence of these 'haves' and 'have-nots' has meant two groups that are structurally determined to struggle against each other (Miliband 1982; 1989), with the right seeking to maintain the status quo – and hence the unequal relationship between it and the left – while the left seeks to reduce differences, through redistribution. The distinction between these two classes may seem too neat and may overlook transfers of allegiance between them: for example, high-level bureaucrats who support redistribution; the poor who vote for the right; and social mobility from the subordinate to the dominant class. However, the total numbers who move between the two classes and their interests are few in number, making the distinction between the two both persistent and relevant.

Organizationally, the right is internally diverse. It can be separated into different actors that provide the social support for government, including specific interest groups, movements and political parties. Acknowledging these organizational factors is important, since it recognizes both intra-elite differences and preferences, and also the importance of building coalitions among social and political groups in order to aggregate their demands. Furthermore, while different actors within the right may make common cause with each other, for example, conservative parties and business organizations, they must also seek allies from among the poor and marginalized within the larger subordinate class. That the right is successful in this regard may be attributed both to its control of material and media resources and to the more heterogeneous nature of the left, which enables the dominant class to play off one section against another, especially through its powers of patronage and clientelism.

The rise of representative democracy and markets in South America

That the right has been skilful in exploiting its relative social, economic and political power over the left since independence is evident from the continent's recent history. From the 1960s to the 1980s, the main political form in South America was either military or was democratically 'thin'. In the wake of the Cuban revolution of 1959, many in the dominant class, including businessmen, industrialists, conservative politicians, reactionary sectors of the Church and the armed forces, became increasingly concerned at the socialist threat, opting for more repressive regimes while demobilizing and dividing the subordinate class by controlling and channelling political activity. Across the southern half of the continent, coalitions of armed forces and civilian politicians cooperated to seize power in military coups in Argentina, Brazil, Bolivia and Chile. Meanwhile, in the north, periodic elections continued in Colombia, Mexico and Venezuela, but led either to continued single-party rule as in Mexico or to an alternation within the elite as in Colombia and Venezuela.

For much of this period, both regime types pursued a similar economic model of import substitute industrialization (ISI), a state-led form of capitalist development that employed large state firms and protectionist barriers. However, the process was dependent on both the continued receipt of private loans and sufficient revenue to repay them. Rising input costs during the 1970s made loan repayments more difficult, and after 1982 resulted in successive Latin American countries defaulting. The crisis undermined ISI and obliged governments to undertake structural adjustment programmes that removed protectionism, to liberalize their economies and to privatize state industries. At the same time, governments began to cut back on public spending, including on redistributive measures. Greater austerity combined with the emergence of new social identities, issues and movements such as those that addressed post-materialist concerns like environmentalism and feminism and with public rejection including by some sections of the dominant class of the human rights abuses of repressive regimes.

In response to social and political pressure, the regimes undertook changes in this direction during the 1980s and 1990s. However, like the economic measures that preceded it, the move towards representative democracy was led 'from above' rather than by the grassroots (Kingstone 2001; O'Donnell and Schmitter 1986; Rueschmeyer, Stephens and Stevens 1992). The result of this right-directed political and economic change was a limited form of democracy, where political and civil rights were restored, where there was minimal change in social and economic conditions, where welfare spending continued to fall, and where job insecurity and vulnerability rose throughout the region (Petras 1999; Colburn 2004; Richards 2001; Grugel 1999; Oxhorn 2003).

The South American right and the post-2000 turn to the left

The political and economic changes of the 1980s and 1990s failed to meet the expectations of wider society. Consequently, economic insecurity and political disaffection prompted an electoral leftward shift across the continent during the 2000s. The right, it now seemed, was in retreat, especially following victories for the left or centre-left in Venezuela, Brazil, Chile, Peru, Bolivia and Ecuador (Lievesley and Ludlam 2009a: 4). But results in Mexico and Colombia, where the right was re-elected, showed that it was far from dead.

That the left's gains were only modest was apparent in its inability to offer an alternative to the prevailing economic model and to respond sufficiently to the demands of its electorates (Borón 2008: 246–7). The right has not only maintained economic power, but it continues to have significant political power despite the rise of the 'pink tide'. But how the right has achieved this has varied, being influenced by the rise of democracy and the impact made by the left across the continent. The right has had to change over the past decade and a half, and has consequently achieved varying degrees of influence over the political process and economic system. This has included influence through direct means (by having its own organizations and representatives in power, as in Colombia and Mexico) and indirect means (by participating within a governing coalition, as in Brazil). Other groups of the right may exercise influence informally, by providing the framework for a government's programme and objectives, regardless of whether they are in power (as in the case of Peru) or out of power (for example in Argentina and Chile until 2010). In some cases, though, the right does appear to be in flux. It may be argued that, while the right has lost political power in Venezuela, Bolivia and Paraguay, it still retains economic importance, even if it is more often organized as social movements than as political parties (though this is less true of Paraguay).

The right in power: Colombia and Mexico

The Colombian and Mexican cases provide the clearest examples of where the right maintains both political and economic power. Both countries have witnessed the consistent exercise of political power by the right, even as its organization has changed. Until the 1990s, both countries were dominated by old party systems: the Partido Revolucionario Institucional (PRI, Revolutionary Institutional Party) in Mexico and the intra-elite Conservative and Liberal parties in Colombia. Similarly, both countries saw control of the executive shift away from these parties to other actors on the right. But where the two countries differed was in the form the shift took: in Mexico it occurred within the party system, with a move from the PRI to the Partido Acción Nacional (PAN, National Action Party); in Colombia, however, the traditional parties' dominance was succeeded by personalism, under Alvaro Uribe.

These differences owed much to the political developments in the two countries, with the Mexican party system becoming democratic and the Colombian party system ossifying. In Mexico, prior to democratization, dominant-class interests were found both within and outside the party system. As well as business interest groups and socially conservative actors, the right could be found both in the state-oriented PRI and in the middle-class, 'liberal-democratic' and humanist PAN (Loaeza 1992; Shirk 2000). Following the 1982 debt crisis, private-sector actors began to abandon their previously exclusive influence with the PRI and to agitate more in civil society (Heredia 1992). Their activism coincided with increasingly competitive elections during the 1980s and 1990s, which the PAN capitalized upon by attracting wider social support.

By contrast, in Colombia the two traditional parties were dominant until the 1990s, mainly because they acted as 'machines' to collect votes in return for their politicians dispensing selective benefits to their supporters. Although this led to their support becoming depoliticized and fragmented, there was little incentive to reform the system, since it worked to the parties' advantage (Dugas 2000). Their fate was sealed in 2002, when Uribe was elected on a platform to address the issues that neither the Conservatives nor the Liberals had been able to resolve, by restoring public order and ending the guerrilla conflict. Uribe's support consisted of newly formed political parties, including some dissident Liberal politicians. Like the PAN in Mexico, his electoral support included voters drawn from across society and from different classes, including those who identified themselves as independents and others from within the economic and social elite (Gutierrez 2007). Despite the Constitutional Court's decision to bar Uribe from standing for a third presidential term, the general process has continued, with the realignment of Colombian politics around personalities rather than programmatic parties. This was evident in the 2010 presidential and legislative elections. In April 2010, Uribe's party gained the most votes and seats in the legislature, followed by its Conservative party supporters. In June, Uribe's defence minister, Juan Manuel Santos, won the presidential election with 69 per cent of the vote. Santos's victory was soon felt within the opposition: the majority of the congressional Liberal party declared its support for the president-elect, exposing its weakened and divided nature (Silva 2010).

While the Mexican and Colombian right differ in institutional and organizational terms, there is much overlapping regarding policy. Economically, both are committed to a greater role for the private sector. Because of Uribe's 'outsider' status in Colombia, he relied on a number of ministers who were appointed for their technical and professional background, and this led to an over-representation in government of the private sector and of its interests (Gutierrez 2007). Uribe's policies are likely to be pursued by his successor, even if the style differs: whereas Uribe revelled in his polarizing stance, Juan Manuel Santos has adopted a more conciliatory tone, calling for a coalition of national unity (Shifter 2010). In Mexico, the PAN government's economic liberalism is a continuation of the structural adjustment programmes undertaken by PRI administrations since the 1980s. Socially, the right faces similar challenges and difficulties, especially in relation to public security and drug crime. Moreover, governments in both countries have to deal with the influence of extra-legal actors within their political systems: paramilitaries in Colombia and organized crime syndicates in Mexico. But whereas Uribe and his successor have adopted a militaristic approach, including greater engagement with the US over drug-enforcement operations and agreeing the expansion of American military bases in the country, PAN presidents have maintained a less certain response and have sought to keep direct US involvement at arm's length.

The right with influence on government: Brazil and Peru

The right need not take straightforward control of the state for it to ensure that its interests are maintained. This can be done rather more informally, in one of two different ways: directly or indirectly. The case of Brazil demonstrates the direct way, through the right's entry into a coalition between its political parties/interest groups and the governing parties of the left. Peru, meanwhile, illustrates a more indirect approach, by which representatives of the right shape public discourse or provide personnel to participate within the executive. Initially, the right's economic priorities in the two countries were divergent, though they eventually ended up heading in the same liberal direction.

In Brazil, the right has enjoyed consistent access to power, as is clear from the defence of social conservatism and the role of the private sector since the military period 1964–85. Since 1985, all governments, including of the centre-left, have included politicians and parties associated with the free-market right, such as the Partido da Frente Liberal (PFL, Liberal Front Party, known as Democrats since 2007) in the Cardoso government or the Partido Liberal (Liberal Party) and its associates in the Lula administration (Baiocchi and Checa 2008). For the right, inclusion in government offsets its relative organizational weakness, and counteracts the leftward shift of the centre of political gravity in Brazil. For the centre-left, the inclusion in government of conservatives, with their views on law and order, abortion, family and public morality, is seen as a price worth paying for access to their clientelistic links. While weak at the national level, conservative parties have pockets of regional support among the well-educated and better-off in the more developed parts of the country, and among poorer, less-educated voters in the smaller counties of Brazil (Mainwaring, Meneguello and Power 2000a: 165).

In Peru, the dominant class has taken a more informal route to power. While this reflects the relative weakness of the party system and of political parties, it also shows the more extensive use of methods available to the right. Indeed, during the 1980s, New Right intellectuals advocated democracy and an end to corruption, while dominant-class interests gained expression in the emergence of vigilante groups in upper-class neighbourhoods and support for the business confederation against the first Alan García administration's attempted bank nationalization (Durand 1992; Conaghan 2000).

Economically, too, the Brazilian and Peruvian cases demonstrate differences. While the right in both countries now agrees on the need for more markets and for a leading role for the private sector, their starting points in the 1980s were noticeably different. In the first years following the return of democracy in 1985, much of Brazil's right retained a preference for state-led forms of development. Only at the end of that decade did it begin to adopt a more pro-market, modernization discourse (Mainwaring, Meneguello and Power 2000a; Campello de Souza 1992). But its actual implementation was to be effectively delayed until the Cardoso presidency of the mid-1990s, following the departure of President Fernando Collor de Mello and the subsequent interregnum. By contrast, in Peru the impact of the right's pro-market discourse was apparent when democracy was reinstated in 1980. The intellectuals' New Right discourse and opposition to bank nationalization demonstrated the dominant class's commitment to economic policy change. The right's ability to direct policy in a neoliberal direction was shown by the ease with which it abandoned its defeated presidential candidate, Mario Vargas Llosa, in favour of Alberto Fujimori in 1990. Its economic influence over government was further illustrated by the adoption of its policies by Fujimori, then by the Toledo and second García administrations in the 2000s, which appointed pro-business technocrats to key ministerial positions, and concentrated on generating economic growth through neoliberal means.

The right as 'loyal opposition': Chile, Uruguay and Argentina

The previous sections have dealt with the right in power, whether directly (Mexico and Colombia) or indirectly (Brazil and Peru). But the right's interests can also be sustained when in political opposition. The cases of Argentina, Chile until 2010, and Uruguay illustrate how dominant-class interests can be maintained without controlling the state, through the left's acceptance of structures previously imposed by the right. That the right is successful in this regard owes much to the repressive legacy of the military regimes in each country, even if democracy is the only option in all three cases. The effect of the left's self-restraint has been to fashion a right that has constituted a 'loyal opposition'.

That loyal opposition owes much to the acceptance of the political and economic model by the centre-left governments in the three cases. The reasons for this may vary: the model was willingly adopted in Chile, while in Uruguay and Argentina acceptance owed much to the constraints faced by leftist actors. In Chile, during the two decades that it was in government, the centre-left Concertación alliance maintained the various economic, social and political structures left by the military regime. This included some of the earliest structural adjustment programmes on the continent, which had followed the recommendations of the monetarist-inspired 'Chicago boys'. However, the process of economic liberalization in the 1980s had been unable to develop in a vacuum: increasingly, austerity led to social resentment and demands for political reform, and this culminated in rejection of Pinochet's continuation in power in a 1988 referendum.

By contrast, in Uruguay and Argentina the dominant interests of the right were assured less by government action than by the administrations' inability to implement change. In Uruguay, for example, although both the traditional centre-right Colorado (Coloured) and Blanco (White) parties introduced a series of neoliberal economic reforms after 1985, these were never implemented to the same degree or extent as in Chile. One of the main reasons for this was the constitutional provision that allowed certain measures to be struck down by civil society-generated plebiscites – for example the 1992 referendum vote against the privatization of all state-owned enterprises (Chávez 2008). Despite this opposition and the eventual victory of the centre-left Frente Amplio (Broad Front) coalition in 2004, the right could be assured that the 'pink tide' would not wipe out its economic measures: internal differences within the Frente Amplio, and its focus on social welfare and human rights, meant that it adopted a more pragmatic and ideologically moderate stance than its supporters further on the left would have liked (Panizza 2008).

In Argentina a centre-left president, the Peronist Néstor Kirchner, had come to power in the wake of the 2001–02 financial crisis. Although he sent out an early signal that he would reject IMF conditionality and would focus on greater redistribution, he was unable to challenge the structural power of the right. On the one hand, the right benefited economically through the government's reliance on economic growth to navigate out of the crisis. Instead of state control, it was dominant-class interests in the commodity sector that took advantage, through an export boom fuelled by the peso's devaluation. But whereas the previous beneficiaries had been large landowners who produced beef and wheat, it was now large landowners who produced soya beans (Richardson 2009; Wolff 2007; Boris and Malcher 2005). On the other hand, Kirchner was unable to weaken the right's political influence by the mid-point of his first term. Socially, the support he had from those sectors that had suffered in 2001–02 became progressively weaker. Politically, his efforts to build a 'transversal' coalition between the left within and outside the Peronist Partido Justicialista (PJ, Justice Party) floundered following opposition from within (Boris and Malcher 2005; Levitsky and Murillo 2008).

But while the right may form a 'loyal opposition' in all three cases, it differs in its organization. In Chile and Uruguay, both political parties and the party system are more consolidated than in Argentina. This ensures that voter choice for the left and the right is more discernible in the former two than in the latter. That Chile and Uruguay on the one side and Argentina on the other have such differences owes much to their respective experiences in the years prior to the military regimes that preceded the current democracies (Angell 1972; Chávez 2008; Altman 2008).

In Chile, a centre-left governing coalition was constructed between the Christian Democrats and the now moderate Socialists, while the right was divided between the more socially conservative Pinochet supporters in the Unión Demócrata Independiente (UDI, Independent Democratic Union) and the more Pinochet-sceptic market reformers in the Renovación Nacional (RN, National Renovation) (Angell and Pollack 2000). These two parties' support is sustained on several levels: by an electoral system that over-represents the right; by the appeal of the RN's commitment to economic liberalization among the better-off; and by the development of patron–client relations between the UDI and poorer urban neighbourhoods. The success of this coalition was felt in January 2010 with the election of the RN's Sebastián Piñera as Chile's first centre-right president since democracy's return and its employment of Concertación-era rhetoric and practices, including the use of subsidies and benefits to the poor, rejection of discrimination and the use of collective bargaining with trade unions (Funk 2010). Meanwhile in Uruguay the post-1985 system ensured that the left and centre-left Frente Amplio and Nuevo Espacio (New Space) were joined by the traditional centre-right Colorado and Blanco parties. Like the centre-right Chilean parties, the Colorados and Blancos rely on a cross-class coalition of the urban middle class and poor, the support of the latter achieved through clientelistic networks (Altman 2008; Panizza 2008).

By contrast, in Argentina party politics has been largely dominated by the Peronist PJ since the 1980s. The only challengers to its position, the middle-class Unión Cívica Radical (UCR, Radical Civic Union) and the centre-right Unión del Centro Democrático (Union of the Democratic Centre) saw their support drain away – in the case of the former after the 2001–02 financial crisis; in the case of the latter following its leaders' and cadres' desertion to the PJ in the wake of Carlos Menem's presidential election victory in 1989 (Borón 2000). The fact that the PJ is dominant reflects the incorporation of different political streams since the time of Juan Perón, and also its main aim of balancing the competing demands of left and right through the use of corporatist organizations for business and labour – although the former's concerns have tended to triumph over the latter's. That the PJ combines both the left and right within it illustrates why Kirchner had such difficulty in building a leftist coalition during his presidency.

The 'problematic' right in opposition: Paraguay, Venezuela, Bolivia and Ecuador

While Argentina, Chile and Uruguay present examples of a 'loyal' right, the same cannot be said of the right in Bolivia, Ecuador, Venezuela and Paraguay. In these countries, the right has lost political (if not economic) power to the left over the past decade. The lack of organized political power has arguably made it easier for the left in the first three countries to pursue constitutional reform in order to 'refound' the state. The first to do so was Venezuela in 1998–99, followed by Bolivia and Ecuador in the last decade. The effect of these measures has been to exacerbate tensions between left and right, including uncertainty over whether the latter remains committed to the changing structure of power in each.

That the Venezuelan, Bolivian and Ecuadorian left has reached this critical moment, while Paraguay has not, is due to the social and political changes in each country since the 1990s. While all four countries were subjected to structural adjustment and economic liberalization in the 1980s and 1990s, this occurred against a backdrop of steadily declining political parties, especially of the right, and of the growing strength of social movements. But whereas Bolivian and Ecuadorian parties have not played much of a role since the 1980s, it is the decline of the Venezuelan parties and party system that is the most significant. From the 1950s until 1998 two parties, Acción

Democrática (AD, Democratic Action) and Partido Social Cristiano de Venezuela (COPEI, more fully the Comité de Organización Política Electoral Independiente – Partido Social Cristiano de Venezuela or the Committee of Independent Political and Electoral Organization – Social Christian Party of Venezuela), dominated presidential elections. They were always pragmatic rather than ideological, and this reflected their factional nature and patron–client linkages with various interest groups, both inside and outside the state (Coppedge 2000). Their privileged position endured so long as they were able to buy support through their use of oil revenue. The decline in oil prices and the need for greater state efficiency and economic diversity coincided with government liberalization measures, which unleashed social protest and political instability, including several coup attempts during the 1990s. In 1998 the political outsider, Hugo Chávez, was elected. Though he drew support from across society, it was not until the mid-2000s that he began to institutionalize it by building a political party.

In Bolivia and Ecuador, political parties (and especially those on the right) had become largely redundant by the late 1990s. Instead much of the political pressure was exerted by social movements, and this saw successive presidents resigning before the end of their terms. In Bolivia, the most visible social movements of the period were associated with the left, including groups opposed to water privatization, the indigenous communities and the *cocalero* (coca producers) trade union, from which Evo Morales emerged as a leader and eventually successful presidential candidate in 2005 for the left-wing Movimiento al Socialismo (MAS, Movement towards Socialism) party. Meanwhile in Ecuador indigenous identity played less of a role in the emergence of the left, with the progressive deterioration of political stability in the late 1990s and 2000s due to various manoeuvrings across the left and right, including between different social movements, the military and politicians (Philip and Panizza 2011).

By contrast, in Paraguay the right remains a dominant political force through the Colorado party and sections of the Liberal party which joined Lugo in his election coalition. Indeed, Paraguay demonstrates the most consolidated of the four political and party systems: until 2008 the Colorado party enjoyed a monopoly on political power through both a personalist dictatorship under General Stroessner until 1989, and the use of corruption and patronage since (Lambert 2000). The large Colorado parliamentary presence in Paraguay effectively ended the prospects of any constitutional reform and deepening of democracy in that country. In the absence of any strong social movements and their support, the Lugo government has been unable to push through its programme, including the use of targeted social policies, agrarian, judicial and tax reforms (see Lambert below).

Given the constraints he has faced in Paraguay, Lugo has been unable to pursue the same kind of constitutional reform that has sought to challenge the right in Venezuela, Bolivia and Ecuador. But even in those countries there have been differences: whereas the left governments in Bolivia and Ecuador were able to dominate the reform process, and include important references to communitarian justice and indigenous rights, in Venezuela Chávez's 1999 constitution was more modest, including a reference to the right to private property. Despite the defeat of the traditional parties, they still retained significant support in the early years of the Chávez presidency (Sánchez 2008; Hedgecoe 2008; Crabtree 2009a).

The role that constitutional reform plays in wider structural change has not gone unnoticed by the right in each of these countries. Among the most visible of these elements of reform are efforts by the leftist presidents to weaken the material wealth of the dominant class and their clientelistic links through the state appropriation of revenues and the redistribution of these. But while this resulted in national conflict in Venezuela, in Bolivia and Ecuador it exposed regional and ethnic divisions in society. In Venezuela the Chávez government replaced the managers of the state oil company with its own supporters and built up a parallel welfare system through the *misiones* (missions, social provision programmes). These changes prompted an escalation in confrontation between Chávez and the right after 2001, which encouraged the president to adopt rule by decree and his right-wing opponents to explore avenues both constitutional (for example, the 2002–03 general strike and the 2004 recall election) and extra-constitutional (such as the 2002 coup attempt). Furthermore, it was over constitutional reform, when he presented his second package in a referendum in 2007, that Chávez suffered his first significant defeat in a national vote.

In Bolivia, the Morales government sought greater redistribution of tax revenues, which led to opposition from the wealthier, pro-market *criollo* (of Spanish descent) communities in the eastern lowlands. Already agitated by greater indigenous rights within the constitutional reform, they resented their declining political representation and the growing dominance of a non-white, anti-market left in government. The absence of strong national parties on the right meant that this opposition coalesced into conservative autonomy movements, which demanded greater regional representation for the eastern departments of Santa Cruz, Tarija, Beni and Pando (Eaton 2006, 2009; Crabtree 2009a). Their agitation was felt through growing support for a coup in August 2008, and rejection in those provinces of the proposed new constitution, which was passed in a January 2009 referendum by 61 per cent to 39 per cent. Similar regional pressures and differences have also emerged in Ecuador between demands for greater autonomy by the increasingly wealthy business sector in the port city of Guayaquil, which accounts for 26 per cent of GDP and 40.5 per cent of tax revenues, and the preference of the leftist government in Quito to redistribute state resources to the poorer, neighbouring highland communities. Like Chávez and Morales, President Rafael Correa has faced open revolt. In January 2010, he announced details of an alleged right-wing coup plot that, he asserted, was backed by the US government and right-wing US groups. In September of that year, an attempted coup failed. During the fighting, Correa was seized by rebel police, only to be rescued by loyal troops.

Conclusion

The end of the Cold War led to much discussion about an 'end of history', as socialist ideology withered away and liberal democratic forms of government and market economies replaced state-directed economies and repressive regimes in South America. A decade later, the talk was not of the success of the market and liberal democracy, but rather of their failure. Moreover, whereas in the 1980s and 1990s the right was viewed as the great beneficiary of the changes, by the mid-2000s the talk was of the left and what it would do to deal with the situation.

The answer, it seemed, depended on what the situation was. In the more consolidated and socially stable democracies such as Chile, Brazil and Uruguay, centre-left governments sought adjustments at the margin through targeted social spending, but avoided any actions that might undermine the right's power. By contrast, in places like Venezuela, Bolivia and Ecuador, where politics was in flux, the result was more confrontational and contributed to greater social and political polarization between left and right.

These different developments put pressure on the right. Just as the left had to change in the 1980s and 1990s, so the right is taking stock of a decade of rule by the left. Most notable in this respect is the growing role of the state in social (if not economic) policy. Few candidates of the right propose scrapping the targeted, conditional cash transfers paid to the poor in return for them sending their children to school, for example. That they do not see any need to drop such programmes reflects the modesty of the changes in Brazil, Chile and Uruguay. More challenging for the left must be how to ensure the right's participation in – or at least non-disruption of – change. Argentina provides an example of such efforts running into the ground; in Venezuela, Bolivia, Ecuador and Paraguay they remain both open and uncertain.

Indeed, the main challenge over the coming decade may be not for the right, but rather for the left in how best to engage the dominant class. Although the right has lost political power in some cases, it continues to hold material wealth – and this can be used against its opponents. Therefore, so long as the left does not challenge dominant-class interests, the right can be relied upon to support the political system. This reinforces the concern felt at the beginning of the 1990s: to what extent is the right a democratic actor? On the one hand, its associations with conservative social groups, such as the Church, its support for traditional family structures and its rejection of abortion and alternative sexualities place it diametrically opposite the growing liberalization in South American societies. On the other hand, its conditional support for democracy must be a source of concern, especially in relation to possible or actual coups, as illustrated by right-wing reactions across South America to the coup in Honduras in 2009.

2 | The United States of America and the Latin American right

GRACE LIVINGSTONE

'Somoza's a son of a bitch, but he's *our* son of a bitch.' The oft-quoted remark attributed to President Franklin D. Roosevelt highlights an enduring feature of US foreign policy: when choosing allies, it is not the form of government that most concerns US policymakers, but whether those governments support the economic and strategic interests of the United States. The Nicaraguan dictator Anastasio Somoza was, of course, just one of a number of Latin American dictators that Washington has backed.

But did President Roosevelt actually say it? The quotation is never sourced, and the historian who has combed the archives most thoroughly finds no written evidence. He notes that the printed phrase pre-dates Somoza's presidency and concludes: 'It seems quite plausible that one of the most recurrent quotations of inter-American historiography originated with Somoza rather than with Roosevelt. The language, certainly, was much more Somoza's style, and the notion conveyed would have served him well' (Crawley 2007: 153). The revisionism, however, need not go too far: Somoza may have hyped his 'friendship' with FDR, but the United States did fund and arm the Somoza dynasty. When Somoza came to Washington in 1939, Roosevelt personally met him at the railway station with full military honours, and he spent a night at the White House.

The remark has endured because it neatly sums up the practice of US policy in Latin America for almost two centuries. There are plenty of other sourced (although less pithy) quotations that reveal a similar tolerance of dictators. FDR's military attaché for Central America, Colonel Joseph Pate, wrote in 1939:

> As long as the present dictators of Central America do not swing in their aims and ambitions and policies in the direction of European totalitarianism, they undoubtedly represent the best, most secure, and most efficient system of government these small republics can have at their present state of political infancy. (cited in Crawley 2007: 154)

The influential State Department adviser George Kennan mused in the early 1950s: 'It is better to have a strong regime in power than a liberal one if it is indulgent and relaxed and penetrated by communists' (Livingstone 2009: 25). Ronald Reagan's adviser, Jeane Kirkpatrick, tortuously made the distinction between totalitarian (pro-Soviet) and authoritarian (pro-western) regimes, providing the most brazen intellectual defence of the 'our-son-of-a-bitch' argument anyone could wish to read:

> Only intellectual fashion ... [prevents] intelligent men of good will from perceiving the *facts* that traditional authoritarian governments are less repressive than revolutionary autocracies, that they are more susceptible of liberalization, and that they are more compatible with US interests. (Kirkpatrick 1982: 49, emphasis in the original)

More recently, George W. Bush showed that securing a pro-US regime was more important than defending democratic procedure, when his administration openly welcomed the 2002 coup against the elected president of Venezuela.

US interests in Latin America have remained fairly constant over the past century and a half: the promotion of stable capitalist governments, whether elected or not. US corporations want access to markets, commodities and sometimes cheap labour, while the US state needs to secure key strategic assets such as oil. It also seeks like-minded governments that will support the US diplomatically and that will cooperate militarily, ideally allowing US forces to use ports and airstrips and to construct radar and intelligence systems across the hemisphere, enabling the US to maintain its reach as both the regional hegemonic power and a global superpower.

Historically, right-wing governments have best suited US interests – if, by right-wing, we mean pro-business; in favour of private property rights and law and order; and suspicious of trade union activity. Washington has always regarded with deep suspicion any attempts to redistribute wealth or mobilize the poor, and keeping reformists and revolutionaries out of office has been a persistent theme – one might say obsession – of US policy since the turn of the twentieth century. Right-wing parties and the military have therefore been the beneficiaries of US funds, training and intelligence to halt the advance of the left. Except in a very few cases, it would not be accurate to say that the United States has determined who governs in Latin America; but it has acted as an obstacle to reform, by supporting the parties and institutions most likely to prevent radical redistribution or upheaval.

Conservatives in Latin America and the United States may also share certain social and religious values: anti-abortion, anti-homosexuality, a woman's place is in the home, the family as the bedrock of society. However, these values have not been the primary reason for forging international alliances. It is also worth noting that, although for the past two decades the US has been promoting neoliberal, free-market capitalism, in the past Washington was willing to work with protectionist, interventionist governments, such as the Southern Cone military regimes of the 1960s and 1970s, so long as US corporations were allowed to slip under tariff walls and into the protected markets. If the Latin American right moves back towards a more developmentalist attitude, the US could tolerate this as long as its corporations were given access. In short, it seeks governments that are not just pro-business, but pro-US-business.

New challenges to US hegemonic strategy

This is especially important today, as US hegemony has never been so contested. Within Latin America, the left-wing Alianza Bolivariana para los Pueblos de Nuestra América (ALBA, Bolivarian Alliance for the Peoples of Our America) is the most eye-catching challenge to US dominance, but just as important (and possibly more enduring) is the creation of new regional bodies: Unión de Naciones Suramericanas (UNASUR, Union of South American Nations) for South America (2008) and the Community of Latin American and Caribbean States (2010), which excludes the United States and Canada, but includes Cuba. These new bodies rival the Organization of American States (OAS), which, since its creation in 1948, has allowed the US to set the agenda for hemispheric affairs and, at its worst, has been little more than a tool of US interests. Perhaps even more worrying for Washington is the diversification of the region's economies and the growing diplomatic and economic links to Asia, Russia, Europe and Third World countries. Governments of all political persuasions have overcome any ideological aversions to seek investment from China, and Chinese penetration of Latin America is now one of the US's top security concerns. US economic influence in the Southern Cone, in particular, has been severely eroded: the United States is no longer the largest investor in Chile and Argentina. Trade shows the same picture: Brazil, Chile and Argentina sell less than 15 per cent of their exports to the United States; the markets of Asia, Europe and Latin America are just as important for these countries. Under President Luiz Inácio Lula da Silva, Brazil became a leading player in building alliances of developing countries, such as those of Brazil, Russia, India and China (BRIC); India, Brazil and South Africa (IBSA); and the G-20, which are chipping away at the US's dominant position in the United Nations and other international forums. Brazil is now a major challenger to become the hegemonic power of South America. The challenges to US hegemony were outlined by General Douglas Fraser, head of the US Southern Command, the US military command responsible for all of Latin America south of Mexico, when he testified to Congress in 2010:

> The US can no longer take for granted that our way of life is the sole ideology of choice in this region. We must now actively compete to ensure our message is accurately transmitted and received by the appropriate audience. Populism, socialism and democracy are *all* now prevalent ideas within the region. Money, trade, and other interaction from expanding players like China, Russia and Iran exist in Latin America and the Caribbean. We are also beginning to see a renewed polarization in the region. All of these factors combine to form a competitive marketplace of ideas, within which non-traditional actors have become very adept at operating. (US Southern Command 2010: 13)

In this shifting landscape, the United States has a number of strategic aims: to maintain its military hegemony in the region, pursue conditions favourable to US corporations, and build an alliance of countries ideologically and diplomatically opposed to the ALBA. Stemming the Chinese tide and maintaining the influence of the OAS and other US-dominated regional bodies are other key aims. Right-wing governments are crucial to the Pentagon because the US does not own any military bases in Latin America, and is reliant on friendly governments to lend or lease it facilities. Small, economically insignificant states can play a vital role in hosting US forces, for example Honduras, Aruba, Curaçao and El Salvador. Pro-market governments are also important to US corporations, which have two main strategies in the region: first, incorporating Mexico and Central America into the US production process. Secondly, by using cheap labour in *maquiladoras* (assembly plants in export zones), US manufacturers can compete with Chinese imports in the US domestic market. In South America, the United States has given up, for the moment, its pursuit of a Free Trade Area of the Americas, but is seeking access to markets and commodities on a state-by-state basis. This, incidentally, gives it greater leverage, because in each bilateral trade negotiation the US is by far the stronger partner. For now, the global financial crisis has also tempered the aggressive expansion of US companies into

Latin American services, such as banking, telecoms and basic utilities, such as water, that was so evident in the 1990s and early 2000s, and which in turn provoked the wave of left-wing movements opposed to privatization and the sale of natural resources to foreign corporations.

Obama, Venezuela and Honduras

Like all US presidents, Barack Obama will strive to maintain the US's pre-eminent position in the world, to secure the state's access to vital commodities such as oil, and to favour pro-US market-based states. US foreign policy is shaped by a number of agencies: the State Department, the White House, the Pentagon and intelligence agencies, Congress and, indirectly, corporations, the media and think tanks. But within these parameters, Obama does have room to carve out a different foreign policy from that of George W. Bush – one that places a greater emphasis on multilateralism, respect for human rights and negotiation. Nevertheless, to date, Barack Obama has allowed the Pentagon and right-wing republicans to dominate his foreign policy in Latin America. This is most clear in his response to the Honduran coup. Obama could have taken tougher action against the coup regime, which would have enhanced his standing in the eyes of moderate Latin America and arguably furthered US long-term interests.

Although Obama might have been expected to take a less aggressive stance towards Venezuela and the other ALBA countries, his policies are unchanged from those pursued in the second half of the George W. Bush administration, when the State Department, under the pragmatic leadership of diplomat Tom Shannon, eschewed overt confrontation in favour of quiet funding of opposition groups and subtle propaganda against Venezuela and its partners. This is because all branches of the US government regard the ALBA countries (Venezuela, Cuba, Ecuador, Bolivia, Nicaragua, Dominica, Saint Vincent and the Grenadines, Antigua and Barbuda) as incompatible with US interests, as this intelligence report makes clear:

> Venezuelan President Hugo Chávez has established himself as one of the US's foremost international detractors ... [Chávez] is likely to continue to support likeminded political allies and movements in neighboring countries and seek to undermine moderate, pro-US governments ... He and his allies are likely to oppose nearly every US policy initiative in the region, including the expansion of free trade, counter drug and counterterrorism cooperation, military training, and security initiatives, and even US assistance programs. (US Senate 2010a: 30–1)

Chávez's anti-US rhetoric, his links with Russia, Iran and China, and his promotion of new inter-American bodies corrode US hegemony in the region, while the nationalization of Venezuelan companies cuts out US investors. Most critically, there is growing concern about the security of US oil supplies. Some US analysts suggest that Venezuela could switch supplies to China as early as 2012. This rings alarm bells within the security services and indicates that the conflict with Chávez will become sharper in coming years (Ellis 2009: 110).

When left-wing President Manuel Zelaya was flown out of the country in his pyjamas by the Honduran air force in June 2009, Obama had the opportunity to make history by taking firm action to reverse the coup d'état. The United States wields enormous power over the small Honduran economy: it buys two-thirds of Honduran exports, and is by far the largest foreign investor. Obama condemned Zelaya's expulsion and cut off some aid, but he refused to define it as a 'military coup', which, under US law, would have forced his administration to cut all economic, military and diplomatic ties. The US ambassador was not withdrawn and, crucially, Honduras was not suspended from the Central American Free Trade Area. The Obama administration encouraged talks led by Costa Rica to discuss Zelaya's return, but the Honduran elite remained intransigent. As the months dragged on, right-wing Republicans led by Senator Jim DeMint began to openly support the coup, and blackmailed Obama by refusing to approve his nominations for diplomatic posts in Latin America unless his government agreed to recognize the results of fresh Honduran elections, regardless of whether Zelaya was reinstated. Right-winger Porfirio 'Pepe' Lobo won the highly controversial presidential elections in December 2010, while opponents of the coup continued to suffer arbitrary detentions, torture and sexual violations, according to the Inter-American Commission on Human Rights.

Obama was not prepared to expend political capital in Washington on reversing the Honduran coup, but this stance severely tarnished his image in Latin America. Only Colombia, Peru, Panama and Costa Rica recognized the elections: an indication of how fragile the right-wing alliance is in Latin America. All other major countries objected, including Brazil, which seized the moral ground from Obama by giving Zelaya sanctuary in its embassy in Tegucigalpa; and importantly Mexico, whose right-wing president, Felipe Calderón, expressed concern about the conduct and legitimacy of the poll.

Although it alienated many governments in Latin America, the outcome suited US interests: an ALBA government toppled; a pro-business president more pliant to US interests installed; and the protection of one of the US's most important military bases in Latin America. For right-wing Republicans, supporting the coup made perfect sense. Otto Reich, a controversial figure who held high-ranking posts in George W. Bush's administration and was a key player in the Iran–Contra affair under Reagan, spells out how neoconservatives viewed the stakes in Honduras and how they see the battle ahead in Latin America:

> The main threat to the peace, freedom, prosperity and security of the US and the hemisphere does not come from military coups, but from a form of creeping totalitarianism self-described as 21st Century Socialism and allied with some of the most virulent forms of tyranny and anti-western ideology in the world. Today in Latin America, democracy is being undermined by a new gang of autocrats who, counseled by the oldest dictator in history, gain power through elections and then dismantle democracy from within. Following Fidel Castro's direction, that has already happened in Venezuela and Bolivia; is happening in Nicaragua and Ecuador; almost happened in Honduras, and could happen in any other nation that falls into the grasp of something called ALBA, or the Bolivarian Alternative for the Americas ... In spite of its alliances with Russia, China, Belarus, Iran, Syria, FARC [Revolutionary Armed Forces of Colombia], Hezbollah and other criminal, terrorist or rogue governments and non-state actors, there are still policymakers in Washington, DC who maintain that the Castro-Chávez-Morales alliance is no more than a nuisance to US interests. It is time to care less about what others think of us and focus more on what they do to us. (US Congress 2010)

There are signs, although not conclusive evidence, that US neoconservatives played a role in fomenting the coup in Honduras. From the tangled web of names and groups involved in Honduras emerge many who had links to the Venezuelan coup in 2002. For many months before the Honduran coup, Otto Reich had been condemning corruption in Zelaya's government and the state-run telecoms company, Hondutel. A Washington-based think tank, the Arcadia Foundation, also lobbied intensively against supposed corruption in Hondutel. The Arcadia Foundation received a grant from the International Republican Institute (IRI). This body was the main tool of intervention under George W. Bush, funding opponents of Chávez in the run-up to the 2002 coup and inviting the leaders of the coup to Washington just weeks before. The head of the Arcadia Foundation is a Venezuelan lawyer, who wrote the decrees abolishing all of Venezuela's democratic institutions during the coup, and who fled soon after. During the weekend that Chávez was overthrown, Otto Reich, a former ambassador to Venezuela, was in touch several times with media magnate Gustavo Cisneros, whose Venevisión offices were the meeting place for the coup leaders on the afternoon of the coup.

The IRI receives grants from the United States Agency for International Development (USAID) and from the National Endowment for Democracy (NED), as well as from corporations such as Chevron and Halliburton. The IRI chairman is the 2009 presidential candidate John McCain. It was McCain's former legislative counsel, John Timmons, who invited a delegation of Honduran coup supporters to Washington a month after Zelaya's ousting 'to clarify any misunderstandings about Honduras's constitutional process and ... the preservation of the country's democratic institutions' (cited in O'Shaughnessy 2009a). The US ambassador to Honduras, Hugo Lorens, had previously been on the US National Security Council during the George W. Bush administration at the time of the anti-Chávez coup, along with Otto Reich and Elliot Abrams, another veteran of the Iran–Contra affair. Lorens had been in regular touch with the opposition and was well aware of its plans. He had warned Zelaya of one coup plot, but failed to tell him about the conspiracy that toppled him. His statements after the coup were opaque and ambiguous.

The last piece of the puzzle was John Negroponte, another notorious neoconservative who, as ambassador to Honduras during the Reagan years, had defended the repressive Honduran military. He visited the country a year before the coup, meeting both Roberto Micheletti, who became president of the interim coup regime, and the leader of the Supreme Court, another key figure in the coup. Negroponte expressed concern that Zelaya planned to open up the Soto Cano airbase to commercial flights. Soto Cano is one of the most important US bases in Latin America: the 500 troops of Joint Task Force Bravo are based there, as are 600 civilian contractors. The threat to the security and secrecy of US operations on this military base was one reason why neoconservatives were sympathetic to the coup. Whether or not US conservatives helped to plan it, they were vocal in their support for it once it had happened. These hard-liners want to roll back the tide of left-wing governments and turn back the clock to the days when coups were common practice. Honduras was the weakest link in the chain.

Conflict over US military bases

Since US forces left the Panama Canal Zone in 1999, the United States has been reliant on friendly governments to lend or lease it

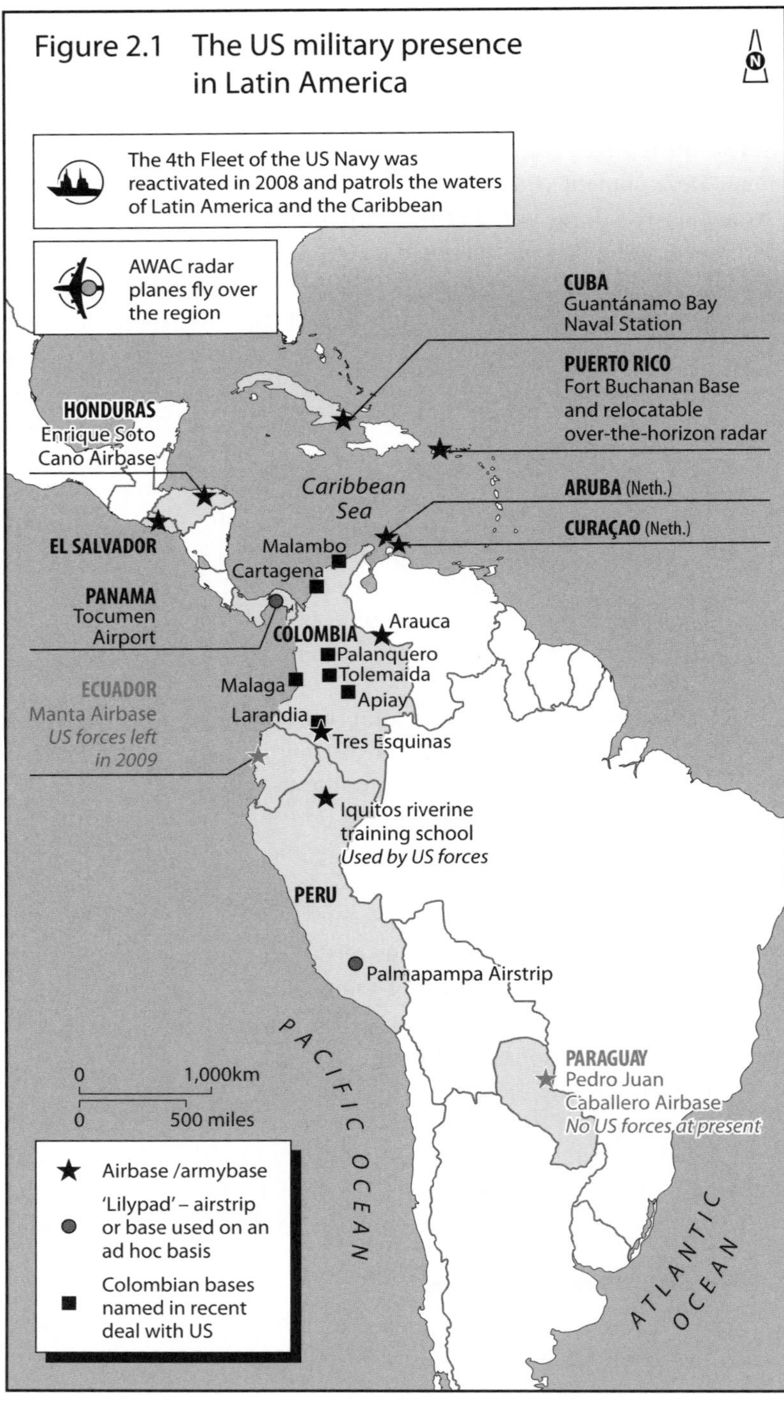

Figure 2.1 The US military presence in Latin America
N
The 4th Fleet of the US Navy was reactivated in 2008 and patrols the waters of Latin America and the Caribbean
AWAC radar planes fly over the region
CUBA
Guantánamo Bay Naval Station
PUERTO RICO
Fort Buchanan Base and relocatable over-the-horizon radar
HONDURAS
Enrique Soto Cano Airbase
Caribbean Sea
ARUBA (Neth.)
CURAÇAO (Neth.)
EL SALVADOR
Malambo
Cartagena
PANAMA
Tocumen Airport
Arauca
COLOMBIA
Palanquero
Tolemaida
Malaga
Apiay
ECUADOR
Manta Airbase
US forces left in 2009
Larandia
Tres Esquinas
Iquitos riverine training school
Used by US forces
PERU
Palmapampa Airstrip
PACIFIC OCEAN
PARAGUAY
Pedro Juan Caballero Airbase
No US forces at present
0 1,000km
0 500 miles
Airbase /armybase
'Lilypad' – airstrip or base used on an ad hoc basis
Colombian bases named in recent deal with US
ATLANTIC OCEAN

military facilities (see Figure 2.1). This has become increasingly difficult as left-wing governments have come to power in Latin America. The Pentagon signed ten-year leases in 1999 for the use of airbases in Aruba, Curaçao, Ecuador and El Salvador. The left-wing president of Ecuador, Rafael Correa, refused to extend the lease on Manta when it expired in 2009 and US forces have now left. The lease on Comalapa base in El Salvador was extended for a further five years just before left-winger Mauricio Funes was inaugurated as president, so he was not given the opportunity to expel US troops; but the Pentagon will be concerned that the long-term future of its Salvadoran base is in doubt. As we have seen, US officials had expressed fears about President Zelaya's plans to open up Soto Cano base. Down south, in Paraguay, in 2006, the US ambassador inaugurated a base complete with state-of-the-art radar systems funded entirely with US money, but there is no agreement for US forces to use this facility, and President Fernando Lugo is unlikely to sign any such deal.

In other ways, too, progressive governments are loosening the historically tight alliance with the US military. Latin American elites once gave US Green Berets free rein in their mountains and rainforests, and schooled their own officers in US academies. But today, Argentina, Venezuela, Bolivia and Uruguay have withdrawn from the School

> The extent of the US's official military presence, illustrated in Figure 2.1, is obscured by the use of US private military contractors. According to a declassified report, half of all US military aid to Colombia in 2006 was awarded through private contractors (US Department of State 2003). These included: DynCorp, Lockheed-Martin, ARINC, King Aerospace, ITT, Oakley Networks, ManTech, Northrop Grumman, Telford Aviation, PAE Government Services, Omnitempus, CACI, Tate, CCE and Chenega. ITT operates Colombia's military radar sites, including San Andres, Riohacha, Marandua, San Jose del Guaviare, Tres Esquinas and Bogotá. Many of these companies employ former military or intelligence personnel. On the board of ManTech, for example, which provides base operations support at the US Army South base in Apiay, Colombia, is Richard Armitage (the neoconservative former deputy secretary of state); Richard Kerr (former deputy director of the CIA); and Lt Gen. Minihan (the former director of the Defense Intelligence Agency).

of the Americas, the notorious institution which boasts eleven Latin American dictators among its graduates. Ecuador and Nicaragua are likely to withdraw their soldiers, and Costa Rica, which has no army, has pulled out its police cadets. The School of the Americas used to be based in the Panama Canal Zone, but has now moved to Fort Benning, Georgia and has a new, anodyne name: Western Hemisphere Institute for Security Cooperation.

US military hegemony is fraying in Latin America, and it relies heavily on right-wing administrations to maintain its ability to operate in the region. As the Southern Command's ten-year strategy makes clear, one of its main goals is to: 'Work through politico-military and diplomatic channels to enhance U.S. military freedom of movement throughout the Western Hemisphere' (US Southern Command 2008: 11). It is in this context that the Obama administration signed a deal with Colombia in 2009, allowing US forces to use seven named Colombian bases. The State Department said the deal related only to security matters within Colombia, but neighbouring countries feared its real purpose was to cement US military power in the region. The publication of a US Air Force budget justification, sent to Congress earlier that year, suggested that their suspicions were justified. The air force asked Congress for $46 million to expand one of the Colombian bases, Palanquero, and it stated, 'Palanquero provides an opportunity for conducting full spectrum operations *throughout South America* ...' (emphasis added). 'Full spectrum operations' is Pentagon jargon for dominating the battle space on land, at sea, in the air and in space. It can include nuclear weapons. The document continued:

> Development of this CSL [base] provides a unique opportunity for full spectrum operations in a critical sub region of our hemisphere where security and stability is under constant threat from narcotics funded terrorist insurgencies, *anti-US governments*, endemic poverty and recurring natural disasters. (US Congress 2009: 217, emphasis added)

The offending paragraphs were rapidly deleted, but it showed that Pentagon planners had considered the strategic value of the Colombian bases for their regional and global operations. This analysis was confirmed by another US Air Force think-paper, 'Global En Route Strategy', which showed how the Palanquero airbase slots into a worldwide network of 'en-route' airbases, giving US aircraft rapid 'global access' to areas of strategic interest. A base at Palanquero, it stated, would give the US Air Force the capacity to 'cover the entire continent, with the exception of the Cape Horn region' (US Department of Defense 2009: 22).

The deal with Colombia allows US forces to use two naval bases at Cartagena and Malaga, which give US forces strategic access to the Pacific and Atlantic; two army bases at Larandia and Tolemaida; and three airbases at Apiay, Malambo and Palanquero. Of these, Palanquero is the most important. It will have the capacity for large transport aircraft, such as C-17s, to land. These aircraft can carry tanks, helicopters or large numbers of troops, and have been used in Afghanistan and Iraq. US forces, however, are not limited to these bases. The US may use as many military bases or facilities as it likes, with the permission of the Colombian government. US forces have had an informal, irregular presence on many Colombian bases for some years, including Tres Esquinas in the south – a part of the country dominated by the FARC – and at Arauca on the Venezuelan border. The remit for US forces is extremely wide: the bases can be used 'in order to address common threats to peace, stability, freedom, and democracy'. The agreement does contain a non-intervention clause, but Latin American governments do not think the wording is watertight. Brazil and Argentina, for example, issued a strongly worded statement, saying that the bases were 'incompatible with the principles of respect for the sovereignty and the territorial integrity of states within the region' (Argentine Ministry of Foreign Relations 2009). Most of the text of the agreement focuses on which taxes the US will be exempt from. It will not have to pay road tolls, overflight or landing fees, harbour fees, entry or departure fees or import taxes. It does not need licences to construct satellite communication systems, and US vehicles and planes cannot be inspected by Colombian forces. US personnel will be immune from criminal prosecution (assuming that clause is ratified by the Colombian authorities). These threats to Colombia's own sovereignty have caused some unease within the country. A broad-based coalition, which includes the country's largest trade union federations, has been established to oppose the bases deal. Colombia's Constitutional Court has ordered a review of the agreement, saying it could violate the constitution.

In addition to leasing agreements in Latin America, the United States also uses a number of airstrips and airports on an informal, ad hoc basis for refuelling and minor repairs. These are known as 'lilypads' and, again, the Pentagon relies on like-minded governments for access. US Southern Command occasionally uses Tocumen airport in Panama for refuelling and US counter-drugs forces use a number of sites in Peru. The US Coast Guard (but not the military) has used Liberia in Costa Rica. To enhance its military reach across the region, the US reactivated the Fourth Fleet of the US Navy in 2008, despite protests from Brazil. The Fourth Fleet patrols the waters of Latin America and the Caribbean. Surveying the region from the air are the Southern Command's AWACS radar planes.

The United States now regards Colombia as the 'hub' of its military operations in Latin America, and it seeks like-minded right-wing governments that will allow its forces to remain. Within Colombia, the Pentagon has pursued for more than a decade a hawkish policy of encouraging the most hard-line sections of the Colombian elite to go for all-out victory against left-wing guerrillas, however elusive that victory may be and however much more bloodshed it causes.

ALBA and US subversion

Most ALBA states fall within the US's sphere of influence. Central America and the Caribbean are, of course, the United States' traditional 'backyard', but many of the Andean members, such as Venezuela, Ecuador (and Colombia), have also typically relied heavily on trade and investment from the United States. All the mainland ALBA countries were once firm military allies of the United States. US policymakers may view with a certain resigned acceptance the economic and diplomatic diversification of the Southern Cone, but they think there is still all to play for in the ALBA region. They do not regard the left-wing regimes in the ALBA countries as permanent, but as unstable and susceptible to pressure. For this reason, the United States is heavily funding opposition groups, right-wing NGOs and business organizations in all the ALBA states. Far from falling under the Obama administration, US funding for democracy promotion in Venezuela has actually risen, compared with the last two years of the Bush administration. The $5 million USAID funding allocated for Venezuela in 2009 was channelled entirely through the innocuous-sounding Economic Social Fund – a special fund for directing money 'to countries based on considerations of special economic, political or security needs and US interests'. The only other countries where opposition groups receive all their USAID grants through this account are Cuba, North Korea and Cyprus. The NED, which was found by the US Inspector General to have funded groups 'actively involved' in the anti-Chávez coup, gives generous sums to opposition groups in Venezuela (US Department of State 2002: 3).

Bolivia, as one of the poorest countries in the region, receives one of the largest USAID grants. Much of this aid goes to genuine poverty-relief programmes, albeit channelled through US-vetted NGOs that promote private enterprise. But some USAID funds in Bolivia have been used for overtly political purposes, as shown by documents obtained through a freedom of information request by journalist Jeremy Bigwood. 'Sensitive, but unclassified' USAID proposals for 2007 included plans to spend money on 'Public Diplomacy Programs' to 'counter attacks on the US Government (including USAID) from senior levels of the Government of Bolivia, including President Morales and key ministers'. USAID also proposed to 'build and consolidate a network of graduates who advocate for the US [Government] in key areas' and fund provincial governments in the various sub-national departments, some of which have spearheaded the opposition to President Morales (USAID 2007; 2008). As for NED funding in 2008, it is notable that by far the largest grant, $300,000, was given to the IRI, which played such a controversial role in the Venezuelan coup. Right-wing groups in Ecuador and Nicaragua also receive generous funding from USAID and NED.

The right in most ALBA countries remains a formidable force, backed by economic elites and large private media outlets. In some countries it controls regional or local governments. The United States is cultivating the right and centre-right opposition to undermine the ALBA governments and pave the way for their replacement with more amenable administrations. In one country – Cuba – Obama's policy is markedly different from that of George W. Bush, although fundamentally it is a difference of tactics. Both share the goal of ending one-party rule in Cuba, but Obama cautiously began to test the theory, long advocated by some Democrats, that engaging with Cuba was more likely to bring down the regime than were isolation policies. Obama lifted Bush's restrictions on travel and remittances, making it possible for Cuban Americans to visit and send money to relatives. He allowed US mobile phone operators to provide services to the island to improve communications, and started mid-level government talks with the Cubans. The Bush administration appointed a 'transition coordinator' and wrote a hugely ambitious plan for restructuring Cuba after the fall of communism. Obama froze $40 million that Bush had allocated for democracy promotion in Cuba, to examine where exactly the money was being spent. The death of hunger striker Orlando Zapata Tamayo in February 2010 prompted Obama to make his harshest criticism to date of Cuba and, while he welcomed the Cuban government's subsequent release of all the US-supported dissidents jailed on treason changes in 2003, he continued to insist that the embargo would not be lifted.

There is no question that Cuba lacks the basic freedoms of a liberal democracy, not least multiparty elections. The question for Latin Americans is whether the United States has the right to interfere in internal Cuban affairs to create a regime more to its liking. All the other ALBA governments are freely elected. Leaving aside the US media, which often grossly distort events in these countries, US officials regularly criticize democratic failings in the ALBA countries. In some cases, the criticisms are valid – Daniel Ortega's dubious suppression of an opposition party, for example, or Chávez's media restrictions, interference in the judiciary and prosecutions of political opponents. In other cases, the claims are unsubstantiated – such as the charges levelled at Venezuela of harbouring terrorists or drug traffickers – and can be seen as a diplomatic and propaganda attempt to discredit these governments. In all cases, there is a certain hypocrisy in the way the US portrays events in countries that are its allies, rather than its enemies. The State Department and the White House highlight human rights failings in Venezuela, but downplay abuses in Colombia, even though all independent bodies, such as the United Nations, say human rights violations are far worse in the latter.

Colombia, Mexico and the 'war on drugs'

If the US is pursuing regime change through civil society actors in Venezuela and Bolivia, it is the Pentagon that is most clearly driving policy in Colombia. The US military has long been concerned about Colombia: in 2000, the head of the Southern Command described it as the most threatened nation in the region. Plan Colombia, a counter-drugs strategy, but one with a clear counterinsurgency aim, was launched that same year. After 11 September 2001, President George W. Bush removed any pretence that the US was not involved in the war against left-wing guerrillas and lifted restrictions on military aid, so it was no longer limited to counter-narcotics but could also be used to combat 'terrorists'. This was a move that the Pentagon had long thought necessary but which, before the attacks on the Twin Towers, had been politically untenable. President Obama has not simply continued George W. Bush's policy, but has intensified it, disregarding many Democrats' concerns about human rights to sign the above-mentioned deal allowing the US to use seven military bases in Colombia. There is strong evidence that these bases are not only intended to support security policy within Colombia, but are also to maintain the US military's reach throughout Latin America. The victory of right-wing continuity candidate Juan Manuel Santos in the 2010 presidential election, after an unexpectedly close race with the Green Party, was a relief to US military planners, although a Colombian Supreme Court ruling that Uribe had short-circuited his legislature when signing the bases deal held up its implementation in 2010.

Mexico has always had a special place in US–Latin American relations, and now that the two countries are part of the North American Free Trade Agreement (NAFTA), their fortunes are even more entwined. Mexico is an integral part of the US production process, although not all US businesses and landowners are reconciled to NAFTA. Broadly speaking, free trade has benefited large corporations and landowners on both sides of the border, at the expense of small firms, peasants and the organized working class (a high proportion of those employed in the *maquiladoras* are young women who are banned by employers from joining trade unions). Cheap *maquiladora* labour is vital to US corporations seeking to drive down production costs and compete with China. Many Mexican businesses have also profited as export trade has soared. Large US corporations want a right-wing government in Mexico to ensure that this economic model continues. But Mexico is currently suffering a crisis of violence. In part, this stems from a change in the structure of the drugs trade, as Mexican traffickers have taken over the sale and distribution from Colombian cartels. In part, too, just as in Colombia, the economic model exacerbates the violence, as large numbers of landless, unemployed young men join armed drugs gangs. One of the injustices of NAFTA is that, while it has thrown many Mexicans off the land or out of work, they are forbidden from seeking employment or a better life over the border. The US response to the violence has been to pour in large amounts of US military aid, and Mexico has now overtaken Colombia as the largest recipient of US military aid in Latin America. One consequence is that the Mexican police and army, which for most of the twentieth century were wary of collaborating with the US military, are working more closely with their US counterparts than ever before. But even right-wing governments in Mexico share this historic wariness of the United States, whose high-handedness can still cause resentment. Business-friendly president Vicente Fox, for example, was insulted when the Bush administration decided to build a wall along the border without even consulting the Mexican government. For this reason, all Mexican governments try to maintain a certain level of independence in foreign policy; they have often refused to back the US's Cuba policy, and President Felipe Calderón's attitude to the Honduran coup is another recent example.

Prospects of sympathetic relations in the Southern Cone and Brazil

The victory of right-winger Sebastián Piñera in Chile's presidential elections of 2010 was an important political boost to Washington.

Piñera will be an ideological ally, supporting the propaganda offensive against ALBA and helping to shore up US diplomatic influence in the region. He has already echoed US criticisms of Chávez, spoken of the continued importance of the OAS, and may even defend the US military presence in Colombia. A glance at Chile's trading partners, however, shows that US economic influence has greatly receded in Chile. The country may have signed a free trade deal with the US, but it has similar agreements with Europe, China and other Asian countries. Chile has been the regional leader in developing links with China and, with well-equipped ports on the Pacific, will benefit if other Latin American countries trade more with Asia (although Ecuador is rapidly trying to upgrade its main port to gain a similar advantage). US companies operating in Chile will face competition and will not necessarily reap benefits from having a right-wing government in power; in any case, the centre-left Concertación governments implemented broadly neoliberal policies, with poverty-reduction plans as a mere palliative. Piñera will be important, diplomatically, for the United States, but will his government be able to negotiate from a position of relative independence? Argentina, which has had the loosest economic ties to the US, is in a similar position.

There is no doubt that José Serra of the Partido da Social Democracia Brasileira (Social Democratic Party of Brazil), the more right-wing candidate, would have been the US's preferred victor in Brazil's 2010 elections. As president, Luiz Inácio Lula da Silva had irked Washington by leading opposition to the coup in Honduras, criticizing US military expansion in Colombia and refusing to condemn Chávez. His Partido dos Trabalhadores (Workers' Party) successor, President Dilma Vana Rousseff, will not be changing Brazil's foreign policy. The sheer size of Lula's Brazil gave weight, muscle and gravitas to the new left in Latin America, and it was the real driving force behind regional integration. Perhaps for this reason the US has tried to strengthen the right in Brazil: recent freedom of information requests show that USAID funded efforts to promote political reforms that would stop party fragmentation, a problem that besets the right far more than the left (Dávila 2008). Nevertheless Serra, an economist who studied at Cornell and Princeton, would not have fundamentally changed Brazil's autonomous foreign policy, which the country pursued even under the military regimes of the 1960s and 1970s. Serra could have ended dialogue with Iran's President Ahmadinejad and might have distanced Brazil from Venezuela, but he would have been wary of joining a US-led anti-Chávez camp. He might not have been such a standard-bearer for Third World countries as Lula had been, but he would have continued to work with India, Russia, China and other developing countries internationally. As health minister in the Cardoso administration, Serra had stood up to the United States when it tried to stop Brazil manufacturing generic (non-patented) anti-AIDS drugs. Not only do Brazil and the United States compete to be the dominant geopolitical voice in South America, but they are also direct economic competitors, manufacturing many of the same products, and this gives rise to regular spats over trade.

Conclusion

US hegemony in Latin America, once a durable certainty, is waning. The rise of the left is part of the explanation, and the US will continue to promote market-friendly, pro-US parties in the region – and particularly in the ALBA bloc – not least to sustain its capacity to operate militarily across the region. But the economic strength of the emerging countries (Brazil, China, India), the diversification of the South American economies, the growing links between Latin America and Asia, Africa and Europe, and the inter-regional integration are all long-term challenges to US dominance that are unlikely to be reversed. The US will seek friends and allies in Latin America. That is uncontroversial. The question is whether it uses subterfuge and coercion, or negotiation and compromise.

3 | Unearthing the real subversives: the US state, right-wing think tanks and political intervention in contemporary Latin America

GERALDINE LIEVESLEY

Washington's efforts to subvert the 'pink tide' – both governments and popular movements – are the latest phase in a long history of intervention in Latin American affairs. The US state's policy positions have been informed by right-wing think tanks, which receive substantial federal financial support and which, through their membership of institutional networks, have been responsible for internationalizing the US's ideological ambitions. During the days of the George W. Bush administration, these centred upon neoliberalism, national security and the 'War on Terror'. The influence of conservative pseudo-intellectual lobbying is not a new phenomenon. One can trace its lineage back through the Cold War, with the creation of such institutions as Freedom House (1941), whose aim it was to supply the intellectual bullets in the war against communism. This was never, of course, just a war of words, but was put into practice in the US *mano duro* (strong hand) policy of supporting dictatorships and death squads under the aegis of the School of the Americas in Fort Benning, Georgia, where the Latin American military were taught counterinsurgency techniques; in Operation Condor, which was set up in 1975 by Latin American governments, in collaboration with Washington, to hunt down and assassinate left-wing politicians and activists; and through the endorsement of counter-revolutionary insurgency, such as the Nicaraguan Contras. In the 1990s, Washington adopted a more 'refined' approach towards facilitating the spread of 'militarized' or 'guardian' democracies, by which governments handed over non-military tasks involving domestic security and intelligence to the military, in such areas as drug trafficking, insurgency, immigration and counteracting anti-privatization movements (McSherry 1998).

The New American Century

In 1992, a draft 'Defense Planning Guidance' produced while Dick Cheney was secretary of defence and written by, among others, Paul

Wolfowitz and I. Lewis Libby (both stalwarts of the think tanks, particularly the National Endowment for Democracy (NED), and later Bush government appointees) was leaked to the press, causing the White House to issue a hasty repudiation, although Cheney agreed to its public release the following year. It can be seen as the precursor of the Bush doctrine, as it prioritized national security, economic neoliberalism and untrammelled access to resources for US corporations, and identified 'new threats' originating from poverty, inequality and corruption. The document made it clear that the war against guerrillas, *traficantes* (drug traffickers), social activists and terrorists was going to be militarized and that popular movements and governments critical of Washington's policies would be targeted. It was also explicit in its contention that popular opposition to neoliberal privatization of natural resources, such as water and gas, was unacceptable, since it slowed down the acquisition of such resources by transnational capital. As Spronk and Webber have argued: 'when social movements and the state negotiate over natural gas, they are effectively struggling over the future trajectory of the state' (Spronk and Webber 2007: 2). In 1991, Bolivia became one of the first countries to accept conditional aid and debt relief under George H. W. Bush's Enterprise for the Americas Initiative, which, in its desire to encourage trade, private investment and structural adjustment, was an early version of the free-trade area strategy. Implicit in this was the understanding that governments would act swiftly and savagely against sectors of the population that repudiated this economic model.

The broader ideological picture, particularly with respect to US national security, was encapsulated in the vision of the 'New American Century'. The Project for the New American Century was established in 1997 'to rally support for American global leadership' and was arguably the most influential advocate of neoconservatism until its demise in 2006. As with all the think tanks, it brought together a broad coalition of right-wing thinkers: veterans such as Elliott Abrams and Norman Podhoretz; a younger generation of individuals like Wolfowitz; business leaders; academics such as Francis Fukuyama, author of the triumphalist 'end of history' thesis; and politicians including Donald Rumsfeld, later George W. Bush's secretary of defence, and Cheney. The germ of its inception was an article published in *Foreign Affairs* in 1996. Written by William Kristol and Robert Kagan (later co-founders of the Project) and entitled 'Towards a Neo-Reaganite Foreign Policy', it called for a willingness to use force unilaterally and pre-emptively; the creation of a benevolent global hegemony; a recognition that internal enemies existed – 'an indifferent America and a confused America'; and a 'foreign policy of military supremacy and moral confidence' (Right Web 2008). As George W. Bush's vice-president, Dick Cheney clearly took on board the Project's 2000 'Rebuilding America's Defenses' report, written by Kristol, Wolfowitz, Kagan, Libby and Stephen Cambone, which argued that there were no necessary limits on US power in the world. It can be contended that Cheney used his political position in the Bush White House to institutionalize attitudes and strategies long in the making. Certainly the 'War on Terror' facilitated the consolidation of the Project for the New American Century's objectives at the very heart of government. It can be argued that while Bush was the figurehead for this war, Cheney was its architect. US hegemony would recognize no bounds and would respect no legal conventions. Speaking on the television programme *Meet the Press* shortly after the 11 September 2001 attacks, Cheney declared: 'We have to work the dark side ... A lot of what needs to be done ... will have to be done quietly ... using resources and methods that are available to our intelligence agencies' (Goodman 2008: 2). Guantánamo, Abu Ghraib, rendition, water boarding, the use of 'black states' (prisoners transferred to countries whose governments had no compunction about torturing them) – all would be employed in pursuit of this shining future (Bromwich 2009: 10).

Following 11 September, the US was in no mood to brook opposition to its consolidation of global dominance, to be accomplished by military means and by the formation of coalitions of its allies (such as the 2003 Coalition of the Willing, which included El Salvador, Honduras, Nicaragua and the Dominican Republic, although most Latin and Central American states demurred). Washington believed it had the right to intervene in any country that challenged its authority, that the argument of national sovereignty could not be used against such interventions, and that the distinction between external and internal threats no longer existed. One example was US support for Colombia's incursion into Ecuador in March 2008 in pursuit of guerrillas from the Fuerzas Armadas Revolucionarias Colombianas (FARC, Revolutionary Armed Forces of Colombia); Washington saw this as self-defence. In similar fashion, in July 2008 the US decided to resurrect its navy's Fourth Fleet and redeploy it to patrol the Caribbean and Latin American coastline (for the first time since 1950). This revival of Cold War military containment was also reflected in the existence of US military bases in El Salvador, Curaçao, Aruba and Ecuador (although the lease on the Manta base in Ecuador was not renewed after its expiry in 2009) and the announcement of seven bases in Colombia in October 2009 (see above). It was also evident in US Southern Command's decision that it would make its own judgement concerning 'ungoverned spaces' that threatened US interests, rather than seeking the adjudication of either the Organization of American States (OAS) or the UN (Tokatlion 2008: 8).

When Latin America's left-leaning governments appeared, there was intense US activity to destabilize them, exemplified by the approval given to the 2002 coup in Venezuela. In 2006, then Secretary of State Condoleezza Rice suggested that the OAS monitor the internal politics of member nations to ensure that they were adhering to 'the norms of democratic procedure'; if they were not, they should be subject to what she termed 'transformational diplomacy' – that is, the restructuring of their internal institutions (Grandin 2007: 22). The OAS rejected what was seen as a crude effort to isolate Venezuela. Ironically, US attempts to retain its hegemonic position with regard to other American states has led to growing assertiveness on the part of many of those states and a greater sense of regional identity and cohesion.

Ginden and Weld identify two forms of US interventionism. One is 'hard power' – that is, good old-fashioned military presence or its threat. The George W. Bush administration was not averse to using this, but it also 'expanded key civil and political mechanisms ("soft power") in order to safeguard US interests worldwide' (Ginden and Weld 2007: 1). Often hard and soft power worked hand in hand. When Ronald Reagan launched the NED in 1983, its brief was to intervene on behalf of democracy wherever it was under threat. Implicit in this was the notion that the only acceptable form of democracy was one embedded in free-market economics. Promoting such democracy has become a multibillion-dollar industry, with huge injections of federal money into institutions that are not open to public scrutiny or accountability. Much of the activity of the think tanks is ostensibly public and legitimate, but some is covert, particularly in terms of links to paramilitary organizations. They essay different levels of penetration, whether by encouraging subversion against elected governments (for example, the ongoing rebellion of the *Media Luna* – Half Moon – departments against Evo Morales' government in Bolivia); working to support US-oriented security networks (such as the National Academy for Public Security, founded in San Salvador in 2005); supporting the use of anti-terrorist legislation and strong-arm tactics against popular movements; or providing ammunition in the culture wars over abortion or indigenous citizenship rights.

Washington has used its wars on drugs and terrorism, as well as its homeland security and immigration agenda, 'to institutionalize a militarism in the region that risks returning us to the not so far off days of "dirty wars"' (Mychalejko 2009: 1). However, this latest form of imperial over-reach has been met with increasingly stiff resistance from both Latin American governments and peoples. Among a series of rebuffs that Washington experienced were the 2005 repudiation of the Free Trade Area of the Americas (the 'jewel in the crown' of Bush's Latin America policy), the expulsion of multinational companies and US ambassadors, popular protests against privatization of resources, and the creation of alternative institutional networks, such as the Alianza Bolivariana para los Pueblos de Nuestra América (ALBA, Bolivarian Alliance for the Peoples of Our America) and its Banco del Sur (an ALBA alternative to the World Bank), which repudiate the ideological underpinnings of the Washington Consensus and call for sustainable, equitable development. Furthermore, Brazil and Venezuela have spearheaded an initiative to create a South American Defence Council, from which the US would be excluded, and the region has enjoyed growing economic and political links with both China and Russia, which would have been unthinkable in the past. Additionally, the Cancún Summit in Mexico in February 2010 committed countries to the creation of a Community of Latin American and Caribbean States, which would include Cuba but exclude the US and Canada.

In the face of growing regional resistance, the US is no longer in a position to dominate Latin America; but that is not to say that Washington does not continue to try. Colombia was the testing ground for Washington's national security state strategy, which combines easily with its commitment to protect oil and trade interests. There has been intensive lobbying by the major oil companies to secure their investments in Colombia and safeguard future exploration of oil reserves. In 2007, Chiquita Brands International was forced by the US Justice Department to pay a $25 million fine for giving $1 million to the right-wing paramilitary Autodefensas Unidas de Colombia (United Self-Defence Units of Colombia) (Mychalejko 2009: 1). It was rumoured that the secretary of homeland security, Michael Chertoff, knew of this deal but did nothing to prevent it – not the first time that the actions of one branch of government were at odds with those of another. In 2005, the then Guatemalan president, Oscar Berger, asked for the creation of a Plan Guatemala along the lines of the Colombian model. The result has been, according to Amnesty International, a country full of 'clandestine groups', including private security firms, criminal gangs and retired and still serving military, which defend elite and business interests against anti-globalization activists. In this sense, the 'War on Terror' (as the previous war on 'communist subversion') has an elastic definition. As with the Weapons of Mass Destruction farrago in Iraq, the US is not adverse to exercises in imagination. The George W. Bush administration was adamant that Hamas and Hezbollah were active in the Tri-Border Area (where Brazil, Argentina and Paraguay meet) and were forming links with both guerrillas and drug cartels, although it was unable to provide any corroborating information.

Preaching counter-revolution: the role of the think tanks

The world of neoconservative think tanks is a labyrinthine network of connected organizations, with the same individuals featuring in several of them. People know each other and they know people in government who share their ideological visions and certainties. Some think tanks are very high profile, others more circumspect. It is often very difficult to trace a line of responsibility for a particular action, funding process or set of relationships. Since its very public support for the failed Venezuelan coup, the NED has taken to outsourcing some of its activities to lesser-known organizations, such as the Canadian Foundation for the Americas, which then disburse funds to anti-Chávez groups, while other institutions – including former Spanish Prime Minister José María Aznar's Fundación para el Análisis y los Estudios Sociales (FAES, Foundation for Analysis and Social Studies) – promote the policy objectives of the US Heritage Foundation. In an April 2007 Heritage Lecture entitled 'Latin America: an Agenda for Liberty', Aznar declared that FAES's major objective was to 'dramatically defeat the project of 21st-century socialism' and he identified 'the *altermundialistas*' (literally 'other worldists' – that is, activists associated with the World Social Forum), indigenous movements and populism as the new 'enemies of the West'. Latin America was faced with two roads leading in opposite directions, and it had to make a decision: 'One leads to ... democracy, respect for individual rights and freedoms ... This is the road travelled by successful countries' and is the way 'to attract investment ... and reduce poverty'; the other road follows 'outdated ideas that created suffering and misery in the twentieth century' (Aznar 2007: 3).

Let me shine a light on one major think tank. The NED has been described as 'the principal entity that promotes the economic and strategic interests of the US across the globe as part of counterinsurgency operations' (Golinger 2010a: 1). To accomplish this, it pursues a mixture of strategies. With respect to governments that are seen as enemies (Cuba under the Castros, Nicaragua under the Sandinistas,

Venezuela under Hugo Chávez, Bolivia under Evo Morales, Haiti under Jean-Bertrand Aristide), it works to promote 'democratic transitions' through political destabilization, media misinformation, the funding of opposition parties and electoral manipulation. Millions of dollars are spent on these activities, and even the most ostensibly 'legal' – the aim of 'democracy promotion' – can become highly provocative. In May 2009, the Center for the Dissemination of Economic Knowledge for Freedom (founded in the early 1990s in Venezuela with funding from the NED and USAID) hosted an international conference on 'Freedom and Democracy' in Caracas. Prominent speakers such as Mario Vargas Llosa (novelist and losing presidential contender in Peru in 1990), Jorge Quiroga (the ex-Bolivian president defeated by Evo Morales in 2005), Jorge Castañeda (the erstwhile Mexican foreign minister) and Francisco Flores (a former conservative president of El Salvador) joined members of the Venezuelan opposition in an open debate about how to oust Chávez from power. Imagine how such a gathering of people plotting against the incumbent president would have been received in Washington, DC! USAID established an Office of Transition Initiatives (OTI) in La Paz in 2004, a similar unit having been created in Caracas in 2002. The purpose of OTIs in Latin America and elsewhere in the world has been to function as 'rapid response teams to police crises in countries strategically important to US interests' (Golinger 2009a: 2). The Bolivian OTI has provided training workshops for political parties and has promoted the separatist projects that led to the regional referendums in the *Media Luna* departments of Beni, Pando, Tarija and Santa Cruz – referendums that were characterized by racism and a desire to expropriate the country's gas and water reserves (see Tsolakis below).

In countries where popular movements press for social justice and mobilize against neoliberal restructuring and privatization, the NED attempts to shore up 'weak democracies' – that is, it seeks to defend elite control (thus, in Bolivia, it regards indigenous activism as threatening the status quo). It also seeks to strengthen the grip on power of governments (such as those of Colombia, Peru and Mexico) which align themselves with US interests. In these pursuits, the NED and its sister organizations frequently circumvent both the laws of the countries in which they operate and international law. The NED is 90 per cent funded by federal government, despite the fact that it is a non-governmental organization. It liaises closely with the organs of the US government, particularly the White House, the State Department, the CIA and the Pentagon, and receives bipartisan support from Congress.

It enjoys a close relationship with USAID, which is allocated billions of dollars to disburse, directly or indirectly, to 'ostensibly private US organizations … which are in reality closely tied to the policymaking establishment and aligned with US foreign policy'. The NED then distributes funds to a wide spectrum of groups, including political parties, trades unions, business, the media, professional organizations and academics who are portrayed as 'independent and non-partisan but in reality … become integral agents of the transnational agenda' (Robinson 2007: 35). In essence, this is the universalization of the Track 2 ('people to people') agenda targeted at Cuba since the passing of the Cuban Democracy Act (the Torricelli Act) and the Cuban Liberty and Democratic Solidarity Act (Helms–Burton) in 1992 and 1996, respectively – that is, the ideological penetration of civil society (see Ludlam below). The NED's political agenda is orchestrated by its four core institutes: the International Republican Institute (IRI), the National Democratic Institute, the Center for International Private Enterprise and the American Center for International Labor Solidarity. Their personnel come from a variety of backgrounds, including transnational corporations, intelligence and ex-military networks, labour unions and private consultancy firms.

Looking a little more closely at just one of these bodies, the involvement of the IRI in the abortive 2002 coup in Venezuela and the successful 2004 coup in Haiti is well known. In April 2002, the then IRI president, George Folsom, celebrated helping 'Venezuelans forge a new democratic future'. The NED was furious with this public support for what was very soon a failed coup; it wanted US involvement to be covert rather than triumphalist. The IRI was formed in 1983 (and initially chaired by John McCain, the Republican senator from Arizona) as part of the Reaganite mandate to promote democracy. This remit led it to support the Nicaraguan Contras, as well as death squads and military dictatorships. In effect, it constituted a 'legal' way of continuing CIA operations, which had become increasingly constrained by congressional scrutiny. The IRI has also sought to influence the outcome of many elections with the remit of promoting 'good governance'. Thus, both it and USAID funded think tanks and pressure groups in the run-up to the November 2009 elections in Honduras. Under the guise of 'leadership training', it supported organizations such as the Archbishopric of Tegucigalpa, the Honduran Private Enterprise Council, the Confederation of Honduran Workers, the Chamber of Commerce, the Association of Private Media and the student group Generation XChange. Together these formed the Unión

Cívica Democrática de Honduras (Democratic Civic Union of Honduras) which publicly backed the 2009 coup against President Manuel Zelaya. Susan Zelaya-Fenner, assistant programme officer at the IRI, speaking just before the coup, described Honduras as a 'troubled state' racked by rampant corruption, crime and drug trafficking, which was 'being purposefully destabilized from within ... Coups are thought to be so three decades ago until now' (Golinger 2009b: 2). She was virtually calling for a pre-emptive strike by the right. The US government was aware of coup-mongering. Assistant Secretary of State Thomas Shannon was sent to Tegucigalpa the week before to try to broker a deal to prevent a coup, but the question remains: if Washington was so anxious to avoid violence, why had it continued to send in USAID and IRI money, which was helping to fuel the plotting?

The ideological origins of the NED itself can be located in that strange netherworld where extreme left can easily become extreme right. A number of its founding members, including Carl Gershman, moved from Trotskyism to neoconservatism in the 1970s. Following a split in the American Socialist Party in 1972, Gershman and others formed the Social Democrats/USA, a hawkish foreign policy lobby which exercised considerable influence over the AFL-CIO labour confederations and the Republican Party. It endorsed 'soft side' operations within trades unions and political parties (to oust radical left elements) and encouraged conservative publishing houses. Given that secret CIA funding of political and cultural organizations had been prohibited by Congress, it and similar groups were taking on that role. The NED has worked in close conjunction with a number of organizations, including Freedom House, which was founded by Wendell Willkie and Eleanor Roosevelt to support US involvement in World War II, before evolving into a leading anti-communist and now anti-Islamist lobby. In the 1980s, it channelled NED funds to the right-wing Alianza Republicana Nacionalista (ARENA, Nationalist Republican Alliance) in El Salvador during that country's civil war and to the Nicaraguan Contras. Other partners have been the Committee on the Present Danger, a Cold War group revived in 2004 to engage with the 'War on Terror', and the Project for Democracy in Central America. This last organization received covert support from the National Security Council's unofficial (and illegal) Project Democracy, operated by Oliver North and Elliott Abrams during the Iran–Contra scandal, as well as official USAID money (Right Web 2007). Bush's vice-president, Dick Cheney, had a close association with the NED during his time as chief executive of Halliburton between 1995 and 2000. He commissioned the think tank to conduct research into the effectiveness of employing private sub-contractors to fight in wars; the findings would be put to good use during the conflicts in Afghanistan and Iraq, where corporations such as Halliburton were employed in the privatization of state protection operations. A NED spin-off, Defense of Democracies, was created in 2008 to use the media to pressure the Democrat-led House of Representatives into passing controversial eavesdropping legislation.

In her book based on research from documents released under the US Freedom of Information Act, Golinger chronicled the NED's interventions in recent Venezuelan politics in terms of its support for the April 2002 coup, the management lockout and oil strike of late 2002 and early 2003, the 2007 media campaign around the withdrawal of a broadcasting licence from RCTV (Radio Caracas Televisión Internacional), and the 2004 and 2007 referendums. The Súmate organization orchestrated the 2004 campaign. When the legal system attempted to bring it to court for receiving foreign – i.e. NED and USAID – funding to manipulate a domestic political process, a state prosecutor was assassinated (Golinger 2007).

Since the passage of the Helms–Burton legislation in 1996 (which strengthened the Cuban blockade) and the creation of the US's Commission for Assistance to a Free Cuba in 2003 (which invested massive federal funding in plans to support dissident groups inside Cuba and to rebuild the island's social and economic structures in partnership with multinational corporations once the Castros depart government), USAID has spent millions of dollars on support for a 'transition to democracy'. Much of this expenditure has been mismanaged, according to a November 2006 report by the US Government Accountability Office, which criticized USAID for a lack of oversight. It also suggested that a great deal of the money had remained within Cuban émigré circles in Florida, while the cash that had been distributed to Cuban dissidents by the US Interests Section in Havana had been wasted on personal items such as clothing and food (US Government Accountability Office 2006). The contradiction between the need for a federal agency to show public accountability and its participation in corrupt and partisan practices was highlighted by the arrest on 4 December 2009 of an American citizen, Alan Gross, at José Martí International Airport in Havana on a charge of espionage. Gross, who had arrived on a tourist visa, worked for Development Alternatives Inc., which, in 2008, had won a government contract that was part of the USAID programme for Cuba. He had previously been linked to the 2002 coup in Venezuela, as well as to covert activities in Iraq and Afghanistan, and there was speculation that his organization was a CIA front (Collins 2010a). Certainly the Jewish group that he claimed to be supporting through the distribution of laptops and cell phones (which he must have picked up from the US Interests Section in Havana) denied all knowledge of him. Nevertheless, in July 2010, Secretary of State Hillary Clinton called on American Jews to rally behind Gross, who had been on a 'humanitarian mission'. In the wake of the Gross Affair, the Obama administration froze USAID funding, while the House Committee on Foreign Affairs began to investigate the Cuban programme (Collins 2010b; Landau 2010). Gross was sentenced to fifteen years' imprisonment in 2011.

Multiple forms of intervention

There was speculation that the Barack Obama administration, which took office in January 2009, might initiate a sea change in terms of the US state's relationship to both the think tanks and Latin America. During the election campaign, Obama released a somewhat ambiguous policy framework, 'A New Partnership for the Americas'. As president, he promised to pursue political freedom and democracy, including freedom from fear and freedom from want; but he also talked of extending the Mérida Initiative (see below) to all of Latin America. The Inter-American Dialogue (a think tank that numbers many former conservative government officials among its Latin American members) lobbied both presidential candidates to complete George W. Bush's policy agenda, and Obama certainly committed himself to Bush's Colombian strategy. Although Obama endorsed the role of the NED during the presidential campaign, the State Department's comment on the Venezuelan referendum of 15 February 2009 was that this was an 'internal matter' and that there should be no meddling from outside. It is, of course, impossible to verify whether the NED was involved in supporting the opposition (as it always had been in the past), but the new administration, indeed any new administration, might find it very difficult to rein in the subterranean activities of it and other think tanks, given that their architecture of power is so embedded in the US political system. It quickly became apparent that the Obama administration was preoccupied with other areas of domestic and foreign policymaking, and that a shift in approach towards Latin America was going to be put on the back burner. Campaign commitments and statements – including recognition that the US had failed in a number of areas, such as drug control and anti-arms trafficking; that there should be 'direct diplomacy' with Cuba; that his administration would rely on regional collaboration and a return to a

Good Neighbour strategy; and that there might be a renegotiation of the North American Free Trade Agreement (NAFTA) – were put to one side. As a consequence, many of the programmes and strategies promoted during the George W. Bush era (and often originating from the think tanks) have continued. The impression that many Latin Americans will gain from this is that US policy remains imperialistic and very much on the side of the right, the military, the political and the business elites.

Elements of this policy consistency include the maintenance and possible deepening of Plan Colombia (see Livingstone above, and Raby below) and replication of the model in the Mérida Initiative (often referred to as Plan Mexico). The creation of a Security and Prosperity Partnership was announced in March 2005 during a meeting between Bush, Vicente Fox and the Canadian premier, Paul Martin, in Waco, Texas. As one of the building blocks of NAFTA Plus, the Partnership's aim was 'to increase security and to enhance prosperity' (Carlsen 2008b). In April 2007, Thomas Shannon, the then US assistant secretary of state for western hemisphere affairs, boasted that 'we are re-armouring NAFTA', the implication being that US military power would continue to be deployed to protect neoliberalism. The Security and Prosperity Partnership's remit was incorporated into the Mérida Initiative in June 2008. This called for a draconian crackdown on so-called terrorism and on dissent (as represented by Zapatistas, social activists, women, indigenous communities and aspiring migrants) as well as the further militarization of the US–Mexican border (Carlsen 2008a). This three-year, $1 billion programme (with much of the money allocated to the Mexican military and police) suggested that nothing had been learned from the failure of the multibillion-dollar Plan Colombia. Moreover, it fed into racist discourse north of the border, which demonized illegal immigrants and was to reach its zenith in legislation passed by the state of Arizona in 2010 (although subsequently challenged by the judicial system, the federal government and the governments of Mexico, Ecuador and Argentina). It empowered police to check the immigration status of anyone they stopped, if they had reasonable suspicion that they were in the country illegally. Critics argued that this would lead to racial profiling and the targeting of Hispanics.

A similar example of the combination of social control and the defence of neoliberalism occurred in El Salvador. In September 2006, the right-wing ARENA government, led by Tony Saca, introduced anti-terror legislation based on the US Patriot Act, which was utilized to arrest anti-privatization protesters. In 2008, the US federal budget gave $16.5 million to fund the International Law Enforcement Academy in

San Salvador. This represented part of a shift in US strategy, in that the secretive training of Latin American military and police, previously conducted at the School of the Americas (now euphemistically known as the Western Hemisphere Institute for Security Cooperation) was being decentralized. The El Salvador facility enjoyed a large FBI and Drug Enforcement Agency presence, and training programmes were run by private US security contractors such as DynCorp International (Enzinna 2008: 2). Before agreeing to support the academy, the US insisted that its personnel should be immune from charges of crimes against humanity. This is chilling in light of the fact that the Salvadorean Human Rights Defence Office has reported links between the national civil police and death squads, with repression being directed against youth gangs as well as social activists. This latest development should not be surprising, given Washington's support for brutal counterinsurgency tactics during the civil war (during which some 75,000 people were killed). Following the 1992 Peace Accords, the Truth Commission report of 1993 detailed US complicity in these crimes, but the ARENA government immediately passed an amnesty to pardon those responsible for human rights abuses.

One area where the US right-wing lobby and the think tanks have tried vigorously to influence government policy in Latin America has been the field of women's rights and the contentious issues of family violence, divorce, contraception and abortion (on contraception, see Silva in this volume), and they have also organized to reject alternative concepts of citizenship based on diverse sexualities and ethnicities. They have coordinated their campaigns with conservative and religious voices from within the region. Think tanks such as Vida Humana International (which is based in Miami) and the World Congress of Families (located in Illinois) campaign against same-sex partnerships, for premarital celibacy, on the right to life and against the feminist agenda. The World Congress sponsors organizations such as the Red Familia (Family Network), which disseminates these ideas to civil society, while the Vida Humana television and radio programmes – working under the banner 'Defiende la Vida' ('Defend Life') – are broadcast throughout the Hispanic world. These groups adopt a missionary approach towards saving Latin Americans from the feminist and gay agendas, in a way reminiscent of the old Cold War stance. However, they appear unable to stem progress towards equal citizenship rights for women, gays and lesbians and indigenous communities. One such defeat for the right was the July 2010 legalization in Argentina of same-sex marriage and the right for same-sex couples to adopt children. Right-wing politicians and the Catholic Church condemned the new law – for Cardinal Jorge Bergoglio, the bill was 'the work of the devil' (Geen 2010: 2) – but they were in the minority in an increasingly secular (and, one would like to say, more humane) society.

The explosion in the number of anti-immigration groups in the US was stimulated both by a xenophobic reaction to the opening of the US–Mexico border, which NAFTA appeared to presage, and by the fallout following 11 September 2001. The Department of Homeland Security was created in November 2002; in March 2003 the Immigration and Naturalization Service was replaced by the Immigration and Customs Enforcement Agency (ICE). Its detractors have argued that the ICE launched 'a war on immigrants', which intensified after the agency's 2006 decision to begin workplace and home raids to find and deport undocumented immigrants. It is estimated that many hundreds of thousands have been detained, and many families have been broken up as a result. Lovato has described it as the 'militarization of migration policy' (2008: 15). Thousands of additional National Guards have been posted to police the border, and corporations such as Halliburton and Boeing have received multibillion-dollar contracts to provide real and virtual border walls, surveillance drones and sensors, and migrant detention centres. This initiative – which has brought violence and death to the borderlands, territories already beset by the escalation of the drug cartel wars – has been closely identified with the anti-terrorism agenda. This has allowed many far-right groups to jump on the bandwagon – such as the Minuteman Civil Defense Corps (armed volunteers who patrol the border and have been implicated in hundreds of cases of human rights violations), white supremacists, the Ku Klux Klan, anti-Semites and others. They, in turn, belong to various networks that also include smaller think tanks, such as the Federation for American Immigration Reform, English First and Numbers USA, which themselves are often in larger contact circles that encompass state and federal lobbyists, radio and television pundits and the right-wing press, as well as more prominent think tanks. While the more virulent make little or no attempt to moderate their language, the more sophisticated couch their protests in the form of rational arguments about how immigration will harm the economy or the environment. This enables them to have a far greater impact on policymaking processes (Larsen 2007). It is a constituency that would also feed into growing support for the Tea Party in its attempts to divide the Republican party and refashion it as an anti-intellectual, homophobic, racist organization in the run-up to the 2012 US presidential elections (Lilla 2010).

Concluding thoughts

At the Summit of the Americas, held in April 2009 in Trinidad and Tobago, Barack Obama promised to bring 'an attitude of mutual respect and a genuine desire for engagement', and said his administration would condemn any violent overthrow of a democratically elected government. However, when the military coup against President Manuel Zelaya of Honduras took place on 28 June 2009, the White House's response (as discussed in the introduction to this book) was extremely disappointing. Complicity with the *mano duro* approach to politics in the hemisphere had reared its ugly head again. Zelaya was demonized by the US media as a friend of Hugo Chávez, and thus a threat to regional security. In the period between the coup and the US-legitimized elections in November of that year, think tanks such as the Inter-American Dialogue, the New America Foundation, the Wilson Center and the Hudson Institute attempted to appropriate what one observer has called 'the debate over who owns the concept of democracy' (Pine 2010: 18). One of the main lobbyists representing the *golpistas* (coup plotters) in Washington was Roger Noriega. His is a name well known in Latin America as the man responsible for organizing aid to the Nicaraguan Contras in the 1980s (via USAID) and for being the senior staff member of arch-conservative Jesse Helms on the Senate Committee on Foreign Relations. In this capacity he helped draft the 1996 Helms–Burton legislation, which strengthened the US trade embargo on Cuba. He is also generally recognized as the architect of the 2004 coup against President Aristide in Haiti. As a visiting fellow of the American Enterprise Institute for Public Policy Research, he wrote an article just days before the Honduran coup, in which he spoke of the need to act against 'weak political institutions, authoritarian populism and the illicit drug trade in Latin America' and the *caudillismo* (strong or charismatic leadership) represented by Chávez and his 'acolytes' (Noriega 2009). Among other pro-military lobbyists were Otto Reich, one of the creators of the Reagan Doctrine in Central America in the 1980s; Diana Villiers Negroponte, a Brookings Institute analyst and wife of John D. Negroponte, who was the US ambassador to Honduras in the 1980s, when the country was used as a launching pad for intervention in the Central American wars in Nicaragua, El Salvador and Guatemala; and Jorge Castañeda, former Mexican foreign minister and academic scourge of 'twenty-first-century socialism'.

If the US wants to normalize its relations with Latin America, it must stop the illegitimate activities of organizations such as USAID and its allies, which seek to destabilize elected governments in the name of 'democracy', 'good governance' and 'national security'. It also needs to stop regarding Venezuela, Bolivia and diverse social movements as problems. The influence of the radical right (or the new populism or whatever other label it goes under) needs to be excised from foreign policymaking. The same anti-intellectual, ahistorical mindset that has moulded generations of right-wing Republicans and beyond – for example, Barry Goldwater, the neo-Nazi fringes, pundits such as Rush Limbaugh, the Religious Right, Sarah Palin and the Tea Party – occupies a parallel universe alongside the policy positions the US right and its think tanks have taken towards Latin America. Lesley Gill makes the connection between domestic attitudes and attitudes towards Latin America:

> the same fear and xenophobia ... not only feed justifications for the loss of domestic civil liberties, the deportation of immigrants, the militarization of the border, and the 'tough on terror' logic, but also undergird support for, or at least indifference to, a hyper-militarized foreign policy and the trampling of human rights abroad. (Gill, Grandin, Poole and Weisbrot 2009: 17)

The US needs to recognize that its influence over Latin American politics has waned because of the leftward tide, because of the IMF's loss of economic control, because of greater regional assertiveness and because of civil resistance to the effects of its policies. This perception would require a massive change in mindset on the part of US politicians and citizens. Unfortunately, if we take the historical long view and reflect on the relationship between the US and Latin America, this may prove to be wishful thinking.

TWO | The right in office

4 | PAN Para Todos: elections, democracy and the right in contemporary Mexico[1]

ALEXANDER DAWSON

By most accounts, Vicente Fox Quesada was an ineffectual president. Although hailed as an economic whiz, during his time in office (2000–06) Mexico's GDP grew at a lethargic pace, and unemployment and rural poverty increased. In spite of record global oil prices, by the end of his administration Petróleos Mexicanos (PEMEX), the national oil company, was losing money. Fox's major legislative promises – immigration reform in the US, a public accounting of Mexico's Dirty War, and a quick end to the Chiapas rebellion – went unfulfilled.[2] Mexico's Congress spent much of this time deadlocked. What is more, his squeaky-clean image took several hits when the public learned of the sweet deals his family members received during bidding for government contracts (Hernández and Quintero 2005). Towards the end of his term, he even lost control of his own political party, the Partido de Acción Nacional (PAN, National Action Party).

One would think, then, that the country would have been ready for a change in 2006; that having just endured an ineffectual right-wing president, Mexicans might join the citizens of several other Latin American nations in rejecting neoliberal orthodoxies and embracing some version of 'twenty-first-century socialism'. Given the widespread poverty and inequality in the country, social conditions seemed favourable. Mexicans had their own left-wing icon, Andrés Manuel López Obrador, who, in the lead-up to the 2006 election, was an enormously popular figure nationally. Indeed, six months in advance of the July presidential elections, López Obrador had a decisive lead over his

1 PAN Para Todos means 'PAN for All', referring to the Partido de Acción Nacional (National Action Party).

2 During the 1970s, the Mexican government murdered several hundred radical activists, some of whom were attempting to foment rebellion in the countryside. No one has ever been held accountable. The Chiapas rebellion was launched by the Zapatista Army of National Liberation in 1994. It first demanded land reform and later the implementation of a new indigenous-rights regime. This conflict remained unresolved in mid-2011, despite repeated attempts at negotiated solutions.

rivals in the polls. And then he lost to Felipe Calderón Hinojosa, who would succeed Fox as the second president ever elected from the right-wing PAN.

The lessons we choose to take from this election tell us much about how we narrate the general trajectories of left and right in contemporary Mexico. Today the country has the misfortune of being both one that is deeply divided but closely balanced electorally, and one where relatively few people have any great faith in the political system and its processes. Added to this, Mexico has recently been confronted by a number of crises, which serve to up the stakes at every election. Its three dominant political parties have tried to play these crises to maximum benefit, though at least since the late 1990s the party that has done this most effectively has been the PAN.

This leaves us with a series of questions. Was the PAN (which, for most of its history, was a small, northern, conservative, Catholic party) merely well placed to take advantage of recent trends, or does the ascendance of a conservative political agenda signify something more for the country? Is Mexico better described as a deeply divided country in which dirty political tricks sway elections, or a place where the new right can legitimately claim to enjoy a significant plurality (if not a majority) of support at the national level? In an era when so many countries in the region have trended to the left, what does it mean that Mexico has gone in the opposite direction?

Democratization and the right

The Mexican right is distinct from most of its Latin American cousins. In the first place, for most of the twentieth century it represented the democratic opposition to Mexico's 'Perfect Dictatorship' (1929–2000) under the Partido Revolucionario Institucional (PRI, the Revolutionary Institutional Party). When it was founded in 1939, the PAN's early leaders imagined the party as a humanistic political alternative to the state-centred corporatism of the PRI. Inasmuch as the PRI situated itself as a secular party, and was linked to a long and often violent history of conflicts with the Church, the PAN identified itself with Catholic values. Whereas the PRI insisted that, as the de facto state, it could be entrusted with the welfare of Mexicans, with alleviating poverty, illness and unemployment, *panistas* (the party's supporters) believed that faith-based organizations were the most appropriate mechanisms for curing society's ills.

Although it spent most of its history as a loyal opposition – as a pragmatic party that cooperated with the PRI to give the illusion of democratic processes in the Congress, while using its limited purchase in the political sphere to address fairly doctrinaire conservative issues, in the late 1970s the PAN increasingly became a genuine opposition party. Amid a growing public distaste for the corrupt excesses of the PRI, members of a series of ultra-rightist groups, such as El Yunque (the Anvil) and the Legionnaires of Christ, increasingly penetrated the PAN, pushing the party towards ultra-right ideologies that were intended to cure what they believed to be the ills of an increasingly degenerate society. Against youth rebellion, teenage sex, growing drug use, radical political activists, and a state beset by allegations of widespread graft, they favoured the strict rule of law, devout religiosity, intolerance and hostility to feminism and gay rights. Many came into politics after having participated in a web of secret societies that, for the most part, originated on the campuses of Catholic universities during the 1950s. Apart from El Yunque, these included Los Tecos (a neo-Nazi network), the Movimiento Universitario de Renovadora Orientación (Renewal Orientation University Movement), the Frente Universitario Anticomunista (University Anti-Communist Front) and Antorcha (Torch). Their associations linked businessmen, opposition politicians, priests and others in networks that were personally and politically useful.

The PAN expanded further during the economic crises of the early 1980s, especially after the PRI government nationalized the banks in 1982. Some joined the PAN out of a sense of betrayal, but the market-based economic reforms that a new generation of technocrats in the PRI pursued in order to deal with the crisis also allowed many businesses to abandon the national economy and the old systems of patronage. As global markets became increasingly important, some Mexican businessmen found that they could reduce their ties to the Mexican state without suffering severe adverse consequences. In turn, these businessmen increasingly favoured the PAN as a party of open markets and transparent government, over what they viewed as a necrotic PRI.

The new segment of the party (called *neopanistas*) was well represented in the largest businessmen's group in the country, the Confederación Patronal de la República Mexicana (Employers' Confederation of the Republic of Mexico). The party that emerged from these accretions was, in turn, a series of fragmentary alliances between businessmen, social conservatives (including the Comité Nacional Pro-vida (National Pro-Life Committee), Desarrollo Humano Integral y Acción Ciudadana (Comprehensive Human Development and Citizen Action) and the Asociación Nacional Cívica Femenina (National Women's Civic

Association)) and shadowy figures from the extreme right. Always relying on a shared sense that Mexico's crises were the product of a combination of political, economic and moral decay, the coalition held together in part because it posited a moral alternative to the disasters that Mexicans saw all around them.

These networks left the PAN well situated to push for national political openings during the late 1980s, when the PRI found itself under increasing scrutiny for its electoral shenanigans. After clearly fraudulent state elections in 1986 and a fraudulent presidential election in 1988, Carlos Salinas de Gortari (who claimed the presidency with an alleged 50.4 per cent of the vote) decided that the regime needed to bolster its democratic credentials. In July 1989, Salinas conceded the gubernatorial elections in Baja California Norte to the PAN, the first time an opposition party had held an office this high since the 1920s. He then set to work with PAN leaders on a series of reforms to national election laws, which helped the PAN win gubernatorial elections in Guanajuato in 1991, Chihuahua in 1992 and Jalisco in 1995, along with later elections in Nuevo Leon, Querétaro and Aguascalientes, and Nayarit. The PAN held only thirty-eight seats in the national Chamber of Deputies in 1985 (to the PRI's 292), but after 1988 it steadily gained seats in the 500-member chamber.

Not coincidentally, Salinas froze the left-wing opposition out of this process. He likely believed that the most serious threats faced by the PRI came from the left, especially since most critics believed that the true victor in the 1988 presidential election had been the leftist Cuauthémoc Cárdenas Solórzano. Salinas fought a war of no quarter against Cárdenas's new party, the Partido Democrático de la Revolución (PRD, Party of the Democratic Revolution). PRD activists were systematically harassed, jailed and sometimes killed. In spite of the popularity of the PRD in parts of the central and southern regions of Mexico, the PRI claimed victory in every major election held in these regions during Salinas's term.

The PRI's hostility towards the emergent left was, in some ways, understandable. The new PRD party was made up almost entirely of former *priistas* (supporters of the PRI – Cárdenas was both the son of one of the party's iconic presidents and a former PRI governor of the state of Michoacán) who called for a return to the populist values the PRI had embraced before the economic crisis of the early 1980s. Old-style *priistas* viewed them as turncoats, and the now-dominant neoliberal wing of the PRI abhorred their leftist rhetoric, finding in general that it could work more easily with the PAN. Though they might lose some power to the right-wing opposition, their larger project of neoliberal reform was only strengthened by PAN victories. Still, the PRD kept coming. Cárdenas won the first free elections held for mayor of the Federal District (Mexico City and its environs) in 1997. In the same elections the PRD won 125 seats in the Chamber of Deputies, while the PAN won 121.

With the Chiapas rebellion, the December 1994 economic meltdown and a series of lurid stories of corruption, intrigue and murder emanating from the PRI, the party found itself haemorrhaging voters; yet it was unclear which opposition party would benefit. The anti-globalization and social justice rhetoric of the PRD played well among the millions of Mexicans who felt left behind by the neoliberal Washington Consensus; but by the late 1990s the PRD was forced to compete with a PRI that was returning to its populist roots. *Panistas*, by contrast, promised economic growth based on open markets and more investment, along with a culturally reactionary, sectarian agenda based on moral renovation, family values and honesty in government (Méndez and Luis 2008), a strategy that set them apart from the other parties (Reyes García 2005).

These competing visions played out in the 2000 presidential elections, which featured Cárdenas (in his third tilt at the presidency) against Francisco Labastida Ochoa of the PRI and Vicente Fox Quesada of the PAN. Fox was, in many ways, the most compelling candidate. A wealthy businessman from Guanajuato, he joined the PAN after the 1982 bank nationalizations, and held elected office in the Chamber of Deputies and as governor of Guanajuato. Aside from the matters of his divorce and his relationship with Marta Sahagún, whom he would later marry, he was a family man and devout Catholic. Nonetheless, because he came from the far right, Fox was not exactly a favourite of traditional *panistas*, and instead of advancing his candidacy through traditional means, he took his campaign direct to the Mexican people through the 'Friends of Fox', which used a national media campaign to successfully demand the party's nomination. His 'friends' were, of course, mostly ultra-right businessmen from the Bajío, whose ascendance within the party had been marked by the election of Luis Felipe Bravo Mena as party leader in 1999.

Fox caught both the PRI and the PRD relatively flat-footed. Cárdenas (who had finished with only 16.59 per cent in 1994) made a number of serious gaffes during the campaign, which played into Fox's efforts to argue that a vote for the PRD was ultimately a vote for the PRI (de Bell and Pansters 2001). Labastida, in turn, ran a campaign that promised many different things to many different communities, but faced an electorate that was deeply fatigued of his party and hopeful that, for the first time in seventy years, they might elect an opposition candidate. In the end, Fox won 45.52 per cent of the vote, an unprecedented figure for the PAN. Labastida won 36.11 per cent and Cárdenas 16.64 per cent. The PAN also obtained 206 seats in the Chamber of Deputies, coming a close second to the PRI (Alarcón Olguín and Freidenberg 2007).

The right in power

The PAN faced new opportunities and challenges in shifting from the opposition to the ruling party. It could take on some of the patronage roles traditionally reserved for the PRI, and use those roles to bolster its networks. The PRI's family benefit programme, *Progreso* (Progress) became PAN's *Oportunidades* (Opportunities), a system of government handouts thinly veiled as a social programme (Rocha Menocal 2001). The national teachers' union, long a bulwark of PRI domination, shifted allegiance to the PAN. PEMEX, the national oil company, which Fox had proposed privatizing, became the principal source of funding for a *panista* presidency (PEMEX would provide upwards of 40 per cent of annual government revenue during the 2000s).

Inside the right, however, 2000–06 saw considerable turmoil. After initially naming a fairly heterogeneous cabinet, Fox whittled his advisers down to a cohort commonly known as the Grupo Guanajuato (Guanajuato Group), drawn from the extreme right of the party. Bravo Mena was re-elected to run the party between 2002 and 2005, further consolidating the far right's hold on the party (Hernández Vicencio 2005). Manuel Espino took the campaign against the traditionalists further when he took over the party in 2005, increasingly identifying the party with a form of right-wing politics that was closely associated with anti-statist forms of savage capitalism.

Still, while the far right dominated the party and national executive, traditional *panistas* remained powerful in the 128-member Senate, and ultimately prevailed against Espino, Fox and his clique in the battle for the party's presidential nomination for the 2006 elections. While the ultra-right pushed hard for Santiago Creel Miranda, the traditionalists managed to change party rules so that his candidacy was not automatic. Insisting that only party members (and not the general public) vote in the primaries, the traditionalists gave the edge to their choice for the nomination, Felipe de Jesús Calderón Hinojosa (Hernández Vicencio 2005).

Calderón's victory in the nomination fight was testament to the internal dynamism of the party. Unlike the PRI or the PRD, where backroom deals determined the nominees, party members in the PAN actually chose a candidate against the wishes of the party leadership – a candidate who seemed more akin to the more moderate right and who was clearly linked to the tradition of Catholic humanism in the PAN (Alarcón Olguín and Freidenberg 2007; Ling Sanz Cerrada 2008). That said, Calderón would not have an easy path to victory in 2006. Though the PAN continued to make inroads in several states, in the 2003 state elections its national vote fell to 31 per cent, while the PRI (in alliance with the Green Party) won 41 per cent. The PRD also made a small gain, winning 18 per cent of the vote nationally.

Between 2003 and early 2006, many believed the upcoming presidential elections would be won by Andrés Manuel López Obrador of the PRD, a charismatic leftist who had assumed the party leadership in the aftermath of the 2000 elections. López Obrador was a popular mayor of Mexico City (2000–05), was widely admired for his public rhetoric in defence of the poor, and during this time led all potential candidates in the polls. In May 2005 he had the support of 43 per cent of potential voters in the Mitofksi poll, while the potential PAN candidate, Santiago Creel, had the support of only 20 per cent. So threatened were the other parties that in 2005 the PAN and PRI cooperated in an effort to have López Obrador arrested for supposed abuse of power as mayor of Mexico City. Their transparently cynical efforts to make him ineligible to run in 2006 backfired spectacularly, and López Obrador now became a martyr as well as an advocate for the poor.

López Obrador's numbers held up through early 2006. Polls in January indicated that he had the support of 35–40 per cent of the electorate, compared to 30–35 per cent for Calderón (only one poll had them level-pegging). In March, with some polls still showing López Obrador with a nine-point lead, the PAN and PRI (represented in the election by the old-style populist Roberto Madrazo Pintado, who consistently ran a distant third in the polls) flooded the radio and television airwaves with attack ads. Noting that unemployment was higher in Mexico City than anywhere else in the country, one mocked López Obrador for calling himself 'the employment president'. Vicente Fox began attacking the PRD candidate in his speeches – a course of action that was unprecedented for a sitting Mexican head of state. Carlos Salinas took a similar tone, calling López Obrador a populist *caudillo* and a threat to democracy (*El Universal*, 12 March 2006).

Fox's attacks in particular stung López Obrador, who, at a rally in Oaxaca in late March, insisted that the president should '*cállate, chachalaca*' ('shut up, turkey'). This utterance became a defining moment of the campaign, and spread virally through the media. Seizing on the image of López Obrador as an angry demagogue, the PAN wasted no time in reminding voters that they did not want another Hugo Chávez or Fidel Castro running their country. By the end of March, Mexicans were inundated with the slogan 'López Obrador, un peligro para Mexico' ('López Obrador, a danger to Mexico'), despite these attacks being categorically false: as mayor of Mexico City, he had governed as a relatively pro-business moderate.

Mexico has fairly strict election laws, and the PRD lodged numerous complaints with the Instituto Federal Electoral (IFE, the Federal Electoral Institute) about the misleading nature of media commentary. In May, the IFE ordered some of the PAN attack ads to be pulled from the airwaves. Around this time the López Obrador campaign also released ads intended to counter the PAN and PRI's 'dirty war'. Still, by this time Obrador's numbers had fallen, and he was polling between 31 and 37 per cent, with Calderón at between 35 and 41 per cent. His figures never recovered (Sánchez Murillo and Aceves González 2008).

On 2 July, the polls suggested that the election was too close to call. That evening the IFE announced that it would need several days to amass the final tallies and declare a winner. Calderón, who believed he was winning by a fraction of a percentage point, elected to wait; but López Obrador, stung by the campaign and perhaps fearing a repeat of 1988, declared himself the winner that very night. In the following days, as the IFE moved to certify the victory for Calderón, López Obrador mobilized his supporters to challenge the vote. The challenge came on several levels. López Obrador demanded a complete recount because of alleged irregularities at 50,000 polling stations. Beyond challenging the count, however, he also claimed that the election itself was invalid both because of President Fox's intervention and because of a series of illegal ads comparing the PRD candidate to Chávez. These legal strategies were supplemented by a campaign of civil disobedience, in which his supporters created 300 camps in Mexico City.

It was a risky strategy. Polls taken in July by the Proyecto de Elecciones Nacionales Comparadas (National Comparative Elections Project) suggested that 50 per cent of voters had faith in the election results, while 45 per cent doubted them. Similarly, 40 per cent thought there should be another vote, but 56 per cent did not. This suggested that a significant number of Mexicans distrusted both the process and the results, but also indicated that a majority of Mexicans were satisfied with the elections – even apparently a significant number of Mexicans who had not voted for the PAN. Even many of the PRD's leaders in the Congress opposed López Obrador's strategy, some evidently believing that the significant gains the PRD had made in the elections were a sign that the electoral system was in fact working. Their confidence was reinforced by the fact that the PAN did even better in voting for the Congress than it did in the presidential poll.

In the end the IFE did not validate López Obrador's claims, concluding that, while there had been irregularities and illegal ads in the election, the irregularities they found would not have changed the election results (Becerra Chávez 2007); and since the impact of the illegal ads could not be demonstrated, the IFE concluded that they did not merit invalidation of the results. (It was not even entirely clear that the IFE had the power to annul the election based on the attack ads and other dirty tricks.) When the election was ratified in September, Calderón was declared the winner with 15,000,284 votes (35.89 per cent). López Obrador was credited with 14,756,350 votes (35.31 per cent) and Madrazo with 9,301,441 votes (22.3 per cent). The Chamber of Deputies remained deadlocked, with 206 seats in the hands of the PAN, 127 held by the PRD, 106 for the PRI, and the rest going to a collection of other parties.

Breaking down the election

The 2006 elections once again revealed a country deeply divided along regional lines. The PAN did best in two regions, the north and the centre-west. Outside of these regions Calderón won only two states, Puebla and Yucatán. López Obrador dominated the central-south and southeast of the country. Outside of these regions the PRD coalition (with a number of small left parties in the Coalición Por el Bien de Todos, Coalition for the Good of All) won only Baja California Sur, Nayarit and Zacatecas. The PRI did not win a single state, though it came second in many. However, it remained dominant at the level of the sub-national states, controlling more than half of the governorships in the country after 2006.

Other regional trends were also noteworthy. While the PRD made considerable gains in the south, the PRI remained strong in most areas won by the PRD. By contrast, the PAN completely dominated Guanajuato, Jalisco, Nuevo Leon, Sonora and Tamaulipas. The PRD won 58.13 per cent of the votes in the Federal District, but had almost no presence in the north or in the Bajío – for instance, it won just

15.37 per cent of the votes in Guanajuato. Nonetheless, the PRD vote grew across much of the country, while the other two parties both lost votes. Compared to 2000, López Obrador's coalition gained 12 per cent nationally, whereas the PRI lost 12 per cent and the PAN lost 6 per cent. In voting for the Chamber of Deputies, the PRD gained 10 per cent, the PRI lost 16 per cent and the PAN lost 2 per cent.

Exit polls also revealed some fascinating demographic tendencies. Men voted more for Calderón and women for López Obrador, although, as a sub-group of all women, housewives favoured Madrazo. Among poorly educated, rural voters, those earning less than the minimum wage tended to vote for Madrazo, as did older voters and indigenous Mexicans (naturally, there was a great deal of overlap in these categories). Students, teachers, intellectuals and the unemployed tended to vote for López Obrador. On the other hand, business owners, employees, workers earning several times the minimum wage and urban dwellers more generally favoured Calderón. Calderón drew most support from people aged thirty-five to forty-nine, followed by people aged between twenty and thirty-four. Madrazo did best among fifty- to sixty-four-year-olds, while López Obrador drew support fairly evenly from the young (those aged nineteen and younger) and from voters over fifty (Zavala Echavarría 2008).

Opinion polls in the aftermath of the election also revealed that views on the voting process aligned closely with voting preferences. PRI and PAN supporters overwhelmingly believed that the elections had been fair, while PRD supporters overwhelmingly believed that the 2006 elections had been stolen. These numbers remained consistent well into 2007, when a poll conducted by the newspaper *Reforma* in March indicated that 54 per cent of the electorate believed the election had been legitimate, while 34 per cent believed it to have been fraudulent. Breaking down these numbers further, Alejandro Moreno (2008) found that, in the months following the election, 40 per cent were completely confident in the results; 30 per cent believed they were generally good, with only minor irregularities; and 27 per cent did not have faith in the results at all. Some 75 per cent had faith in the IFE's findings.

It is hard to make perfect sense of these numbers. Winners almost invariably have faith in the system, and we can expect a certain percentage of the electorate to tell pollsters that they believe in the system for reasons that are not entirely transparent (nationalism, distrust of the pollster, conservatism, respect for authority, etc.). It is clear, on the other hand, that those who voted for López Obrador overwhelmingly questioned the legitimacy of the results. This reminds us that, even after more than a decade of concerted efforts to produce transparent democratic processes, millions of Mexicans remained convinced that the system was plagued by fraud.

There is still more to this claim. PRD supporters questioned both the vote itself and the nature of the campaign, arguing that each served as a basis on which the results should be annulled. The second claim is somewhat more complex than the first, and deserves some consideration. All three parties relied on aggressive public relations campaigns leading up to the election, spending staggering sums of money to sway voters. The PAN spent 257,837,990 Mexican pesos (MXN; at the time the rate was around MXN 10 to the US dollar) on 11,904 TV ads and 106,960 radio ads. López Obrador's coalition spent even more – MXN 383,612,118 on 16,316 TV ads and 60,410 radio announcements. They were both topped by the PRI, which spent MXN 444,844,809 on 10,425 TV and 59,414 radio ads (Emmerich 2007). Media critics were harshly critical of the ads, which were often misleading, simplistic and largely designed to appeal to a limited array of anxieties and hopes. Because of the ads, Hugo Sánchez Gudiño (2008) suggests that Mexico is an 'esoteric democracy' – simulated and largely controlled through media images.

López Obrador seems to share this sentiment. Did he not claim that voters were misled into voting against their interests through a smear campaign? Did he not insist that Fox's utterances were illegal because, as president, he was in a position to sway voters unduly? This makes sense if one imagines voters as naïve and easily influenced by people in a position of authority, but it is a sorry commentary on López Obrador's views of the electorate. It is reminiscent of an era when the PRI positioned itself as a paternalistic authority that could protect Mexicans from a variety of threats, in return for their complete loyalty. By contrast, in most contemporary democracies voters understand that elected officials come from specific political parties and are interested in keeping those parties in power. Fox's partisanship thus tells us something about the competitiveness of Mexican politics. That it was unprecedented really only tells us how recent this phenomenon is.

In effect, both the suggestion that Mexico is an esoteric democracy and the larger sense (shared by all three parties) that the Mexican electorate can easily be manipulated may represent a tendency on the part of elite Mexicans to discount the sophistication of Mexican voters. I believe, however, that an alternative reading of the impact of the ads on the voter is in order. We must begin by acknowledging that the images used in the PAN/PRI's dirty war against López Obrador – Hugo Chávez, the Kalashnikov, the constant replaying of '*cállate, chachalaca*' – were metonymic devices, powerful signifiers of a series of hopes and anxieties that are shared by millions of Mexicans. Mexicans on the left easily ignored them, knowing that they were misleading (and perhaps even admiring figures like Chávez and Castro). For others, the ads reminded voters of the real danger of political and social unrest that poor and marginalized groups posed – of ongoing uprisings in Chiapas and Oaxaca that might spread to other parts of the country if left unchecked. More fundamentally, the very fact that poor voters (who easily represented a majority of the country) had a candidate who openly advocated on their behalf threatened significant social transformations, should López Obrador be elected.

Also unspoken were the ways that race was reflected in these sentiments. As the party of the north, the PAN is also most clearly the party of whiteness in Mexico, of progress, prosperity and a foot in the modern world. The PRD, by contrast, is more clearly a party of the south, of regions that are more heavily indigenous and desperately poor. Though the PRI won more of the indigenous vote, this was a function of old-style politicking. The PRD's ideology is more openly identified with indigenous Mexicans, but it is a version of indigeneity that does not have much appeal among a significant segment of the urban working class – voters who are perhaps only a few generations removed from their indigenous heritage, but who have distinguished themselves from their origins, have improved their circumstances and who opted for the PAN's vision of the future because it was more closely aligned with their aspirations.

Or perhaps rather both aspirations *and* fears. Possibly the issue that, more than any other, pushed voters towards the PAN in 2006 was personal security, driven by both an escalating drug war on the northern border and an epidemic of violent crime in cities across the country. It does not seem intuitive that the right should have a better claim to be defenders of law and order than the left, but this appears to have been the case in 2006. Mexicans believed they needed not only to fight crime, but to dramatically reform the country's security agencies and judiciary, both of which were deeply tainted with corruption and strongly identified with decades of PRI rule. The PRD did not have this taint, but many party loyalists were either concerned with other social questions, or were deeply uneasy with the militarization of policing and periodic abuses of civil rights, both of which have characterized most efforts to curb the violence. Calderón, by contrast, promised to make the personal security of Mexicans paramount, even if it meant calling in the army to govern the most troubled regions. It seems unlikely that Mexicans believed that the army would respect civil rights, but many were willing to accept that prospect if Calderón could improve their safety.

In the end, in spite of all the ads and other attacks, public support for Calderón and López Obrador did not shift very much from January to July 2006. Even when the PRD candidate was in the lead, most polls showed Calderón within the statistical margin of error, and it is just as likely that factors other than the ads (escalating violence, unrest in Oaxaca, or some other factor) closed the gap between the candidates. Moreover, given the significant ideological divisions between the parties, it seems unlikely that many voters shifted from the PRD to PAN (or vice versa) during these months. It is more likely that voters moved into and out of the PRI camp, as a result of a complex array of personal calculations. Poor Mexicans in particular had to weigh up their future under a pro-growth, pro-trade and investment president, who would focus heavily on law and order, against their prospects under a candidate who promised to enlarge the role of the state and move the country away from the trajectories that had characterized the past thirty years. Both of these options were fraught with risks, which is perhaps one reason why voters kept the PRI relevant in these calculations, as a buffer to both the PRD and the PAN. This ultimately reveals an electorate that is, in some ways, more sophisticated than its elected officials.

Conclusion: a PAN for All?

One could fairly conclude that, had a few things gone differently, we might be talking today about the ascendance of the Mexican left. But the facts are what they are, and since 2006 the collapse of the PRD has been a dominant narrative. Much of the blame for that collapse lies with the party and its erstwhile leader. Leftists were already abandoning the PRD in the lead-up to the election, accusing it of being little more than a vehicle for the personal aspirations of its leaders, and since then it has fractured further. López Obrador is today widely mocked as a demagogue whose maximalist desires weakened the institutions of democracy and marginalized his party (Palma and Balderas 2007).

The PRD was punished heavily. In the July 2009 state elections, when the PRI won 36.6 per cent of the vote, the PAN gained 28 per cent and the PRD just 12 per cent. The PRI gained 2 million voters between 2006 and 2009, taking many of those voters from the PRD and winning five of the six contested governorships (two in PAN strongholds). The PRI is once again the largest party in the Chamber of Deputies (the PAN dominates the Senate). Most believe that the PRI is well positioned to reclaim the presidency in 2012. That said, predicting the outcome of Mexican elections is a fool's game. Mexicans have relatively little faith in their political parties, and are more willing than electorates in other parts of the region to switch party loyalties for a variety of reasons: the PAN went from winning 26.69 per cent of the overall popular vote in 1994 to 43.43 per cent in 2000 and 35.89 per cent in 2006; meanwhile the PRI polled 50.18 per cent, 36.87 per cent and 22.26 per cent in those same elections, and the PRD 17.06 per cent, 17.0 per cent and 35.31 per cent (Ramírez Mercado 2007).

Felipe Calderón has been a popular president, though he has confronted a series of intractable problems. His militaristic approach to dealing with the escalating drug-related violence on Mexico's northern border had cost 35,000 lives by spring 2011. More than 40 per cent of Mexicans believe that the government is not winning the drug war (*La Reforma*, 14 April 2010). The deep economic crisis that began in 2008 has likewise damaged national support for the PAN. In 2008 Calderón's plans to allow some privatization of PEMEX met with enormous public opposition: 70 per cent of Mexicans oppose privatizing the company, in spite of its problems.

The PAN now also faces a challenge from the extreme right. With the traditional *panistas* once again in control of the party, in 2007 several prominent leaders abandoned it for the newly formed Movimiento de Participación Solidaria (Solidarity Participation Movement). The new party counts on support from both the Union Nacional Sinarquista (National Synarchist Union, a fascist group) and El Yunque, along with thousands of supporters organized under the slogan 'Vida, Familia, Justicia Social' ('Life, Family, Social Justice'). It is in some ways a throwback to nineteenth-century socialist romanticism, tinged with twentieth-century fascism. Members long for a return to traditional corporate identities, are deeply nationalist and are critical of liberal capitalism, relativism and postmodernity (Uribe 2008). Continuing violence, crime and social crises are likely to swell its numbers.

If we want to understand right-wing phenomena in Latin America today, we ought to try and understand these supporters, who vote for such parties in spite of the fact that these right-wing movements do not represent their material interests. These voters constitute a values-based right, which relies on forms of nationalist Catholicism that imagine family and Church as bulwarks against the depredations of the modern world, and that endeavour to build national solidarity around these foundations. The Legionnaires of Christ – for all the recent scandal surrounding the revelations that its founder, Father Marcial Maciel, sexually abused a number of children and fathered others – is a movement that is constructed on a deeply Catholic foundation of doing good works. Synarchism, along with any number of right-wing Catholic traditions in Mexico, can also be understood thus.

Since its founding, the PAN has been integral to these visions of national solidarity. This, in turn, is why the PAN can imagine itself as the party of all Mexicans, and not exclusively of the privileged business elites of the north. In the face of a Mexican state that has so spectacularly failed to meet the needs of its citizens, and global capitalist forces that take their labour and offer little in return, the PAN advocates new forms of faith and nation based upon mutual obligation, order and moral government. Of course, this does not appeal to all Mexicans, but it has helped the PAN dominate national politics since 2000. Whether or not it will translate into an ongoing ability to dominate Mexican politics is anyone's guess.

5 | Colombia as the linchpin of US hegemony in Latin America

DIANA RABY

The right in Colombia, or the Colombian oligarchy, occupies a strategic position, engaging as it does in activities to counter democratic and popular movements across the continent. The establishment parties, conservative and liberal, have conspired to monopolize politics in a tightly controlled two-party system that has remained virtually unchanged since the mid-nineteenth century, and, apart from limited ideological differences regarding the Catholic Church and civil liberties, are almost indistinguishable. This political stasis is almost unique in Latin America: with the possible exceptions of Paraguay and Honduras, every other country has at some point undergone fundamental regime change in which oligarchic parties have been replaced by mass populist, democratic or revolutionary parties and/or movements – revolution in Mexico, Cuba and Nicaragua; the rise of the Radical Party and later Peronism in Argentina; the emergence of socialist and communist parties in Chile; and so on. This exceptional political longevity of the oligarchic system is crucial to understanding Colombia's reactionary role in the region.

Another Colombian peculiarity, closely linked to its closed party system, is the virtual absence of military regimes in the country's history. Apart from one or two brief episodes in the nineteenth century, the only overt military dictatorship was that of General Gustavo Rojas Pinilla from 1953 to 1957. Otherwise, regular elections with a four-year presidential term have enabled the Colombian regime to present itself internationally as one of the most stable democracies in Latin America. But closer examination reveals that the political presence of the military is all-pervasive, and that the country's democratic credentials are limited to highly circumscribed liberal formalities.

Ever since independence, political differences in Colombia have tended to lead to violence. This has affected all social classes, but has always been resolved in favour of the dominant elites. After the final defeat of the Spanish, liberal–conservative conflicts began, with civil wars in 1839–41, 1851, 1860–62, 1876, 1885, 1895, 1899–1902 (the 'War of the Thousand Days'), *La Violencia* of 1948–58, and the ongoing armed conflict from 1964 to the present, involving Colombia's guerrilla groups, the state and right-wing paramilitary groups.

In many ways, the Colombian experience down to the early twentieth century was unexceptional: it was, after all, common across the region to have oligarchic rule with liberal constitutional conventions, parties that borrowed the European labels of 'conservative' and 'liberal', and frequent armed conflict. The country's real exceptionality began to emerge in the mid-twentieth century, when the socio-economic changes of incipient urbanization and industrialization produced radical upheaval and the emergence of new political forces in most Latin American countries: the populist regimes of Vargas in Brazil, Perón in Argentina and Cárdenas in Mexico, for example. In Colombia the Liberal government of Alfonso López Pumarejo (1934–38) attempted to embark on a similar path, with limited measures of labour and agrarian reform; but in the next few years its timid reforms were neutralized or reversed, giving rise to a tense stalemate.

It was this situation that led to the meteoric rise of the crucial figure in modern Colombian politics, Jorge Eliécer Gaitán. With intense charismatic appeal and a powerful anti-oligarchic discourse, Gaitán was a classic populist leader: 'populist' not in the pejorative sense of 'opportunistic' or 'manipulative', but in the more analytical meaning proposed by Ernesto Laclau of an 'emblematic' leader, a tribune of the people intimately linked to a powerful mass movement that bypassed established parties and institutions (Laclau 2005; Raby 2006: chapter 7). Gaitán thus both expressed and further galvanized the mass working-class and peasant movement that was demanding fundamental political change of a radically democratic nature – a movement that had been growing steadily for two decades and that was not adequately represented by either the Liberals or the Communists. His assassination on 9 April 1948 precipitated the insurrection in the capital Bogotá known as the *Bogotazo* and the fratricidal, decade-long conflict labelled *La Violencia*, in which 200,000 to 300,000 people were killed, often in very sadistic fashion (Palacios 2006: 135–6).

Although, as has been demonstrated by Gaitán's daughter Gloria, targeted violence by the state and the landlords against the popular movement began more than two years before Gaitán's assassination (Gaitán 1985), and despite the varied and complex interpretations of *La Violencia*, there can be no doubt that the fundamental issue in this catastrophic breakdown of the political order was a brutal oligarchic reaction against Gaitán and the popular *gaitanista* movement. Although Gaitán worked through the Liberal Party, he had made it crystal clear that his aim was to defeat the oligarchic forces in both the Conservative and the Liberal parties and to 'turn the Liberal Party into the People's Party' (Gaitán 1985: 330). His movement was a direct challenge to oligarchic domination and had evident revolutionary potential, and its violent suppression was the fundamental cause of the ongoing internal conflict that has plagued Colombia ever since. It was from this time onwards that the exclusion of any alternative political movement – certainly of any alternative representing the popular classes – became systematic.

For the better part of two decades, this exclusion was made explicit by the bipartisan regime known as the Frente Nacional (National Front), from 1958 to 1974. To put an end to the chaos of *La Violencia*, and also to leave behind the embarrassment of military dictatorship, the elite leaders of the Liberal and Conservative parties agreed for sixteen years to share power, alternating in the presidency and sharing out the spoils of office. Not surprisingly, this cosy arrangement had only limited success, whether in excluding alternative forces or in putting an end to the violence. Left-wing organizations such as the communists participated, sometimes with the open complicity of certain establishment politicians, in factional tendencies of the Liberal Party, like the Movimiento Revolucionario Liberal (Liberal Revolutionary Movement) of Alfonso López Michelsen (Pearce 1990: 62–3). Other dissidents found a home in a surprising new formation, the Alianza Nacional Popular (ANAPO, National Popular Alliance), a populist tendency within the Conservative Party led by the former dictator, Gustavo Rojas Pinilla. But when ANAPO became too successful, leading to Rojas Pinilla's possible victory in the 1970 presidential election, the authorities declared the official Frente Nacional candidate Misael Pastrana to be the victor in what Rojas's followers (and many others) regarded as a fraudulent decision (Pearce 1990: 170–1).

In the early years of the Frente Nacional violent conflict was indeed reduced, but it was never eliminated and it soon began to increase again with the emergence of new, explicitly revolutionary guerrilla organizations – the Fuerzas Armadas Revolucionarios de Colombia (FARC, Revolutionary Armed Forces of Colombia) and the Ejército de Liberación Nacional (ELN, National Liberation Army), both founded in 1964. Within a few years they were joined by other armed movements, such as the Ejército Popular de Liberación (Popular Liberation Army) and the Movimiento Revolucionario M-19 (M-19, 19 April Revolutionary Movement), founded in protest at the perceived electoral fraud of 1970 and intended to promote urban insurgency.

In the 1960s and 1970s these armed movements were part of a general Latin American trend inspired by the Cuban revolution and Third World insurgencies, but the persistence of some of them (mainly the FARC and ELN) to the present day is a peculiarly Colombian phenomenon that can only be explained by the ongoing regime of political exclusion. After the formal end of the Frente Nacional in 1974, the Liberal–Conservative duopoly continued on a less formal basis, and while other parties (including the communists) have been legal for most of the time, de facto repression of them by state agencies (the military and police) and by informal paramilitaries has been constant.

Political exclusion has been maintained by systematic violence, but also by legal devices. States of siege or exception have been used repeatedly, occasionally at national level but much more frequently on a regional basis, to suspend constitutional guarantees and impose de facto military rule. Parties of the left have also been systematically tarred with the brush of subversion, labelled as guerrilla agents on the basis of flimsy or often blatantly fabricated evidence, using paid informants, guerrilla deserters or unsubstantiated military intelligence. These techniques have also been used to criminalize social protest, with trade unions, peasant organizations, indigenous and other popular movements being targeted in the same way.

The result of all this has been the consolidation of a profoundly conservative social and political formation, in which the legal left is reduced to a small minority under constant suspicion of subversive and unpatriotic connections. A Cold War-style siege mentality prevails, in which neighbouring countries are viewed with distrust and can easily be labelled as supporters of terrorism. Colombia is thus the perfect regional ally (or client state) for the US, in a relationship that has reached a new level of intensity in the past two decades but that has roots going back more than half a century.

Colombia and the US: a history of complicity

The history of Colombian subordination to Washington can be traced back to the 1903 Panama affair, in which this former Colombian province became independent, with direct and blatant US assistance, in order to facilitate control of the Canal Zone. But this was at the height of 'Big Stick' interventionism, when the marines were intervening all around the Caribbean basin in the first flush of Washington's emergence as a world power. More significant for our analysis is what happened in the early 1950s under ultra-conservative President Laureano Gómez.

Gómez came to power in 1950 at the height of *La Violencia*, through an election that was boycotted by the Liberal Party because of arbitrary measures implemented by the previous government. An overt sympathizer of Franco in Spain and of the Axis powers in World War II, Gómez was initially distrusted by the US. Partly in order to ingratiate himself with Washington, and also to obtain state-of-the-art US arms to combat the liberal guerrillas in the Colombian *llanos* (the eastern plains region), in 1951 Gómez agreed to send a battalion of Colombian troops to fight alongside US and UN troops in Korea (Ortiz 2010); Colombia was the only Latin American country to do so. As a result, the US signed a Military Assistance Treaty with Colombia in 1952, and US advisers began to operate in the country.

In the context of the Cuban revolution, the continued unrest in Colombia was a cause of heightened concern in Washington, and in October 1959 a US Special Survey Team of counterinsurgency experts arrived in the country (Stokes 2005: 69–70). Their recommendations were reinforced in 1962 by a second mission, a US Army Special Warfare Team led by General William Yarborough. It urged that internal counterinsurgency should be the Colombian military's prime concern, with US Special Forces training Colombian military and civilian personnel to 'execute paramilitary, sabotage and/or terrorist activities against known communist proponents' and to permit 'clandestine execution of plans developed by the United States Government ... rather than depending on the Colombians to find their own solution' (Stokes 2005: 70).

This strategy found swift practical application with Plan Lazo from 1962 to 1965, a major military offensive against independent peasant resistance groups in southern Tolima and Cundinamarca. Although the offensive succeeded in reclaiming control over the territory of what had been described as 'independent republics' in Marquetalia and neighbouring areas, it further radicalized the armed peasants, who escaped to form the FARC shortly afterwards. From 1961 to 1967, total US military assistance to Colombia reached $160 million, the largest amount for any Latin American country prior to the 1980s (Pearce 1990: 63; Stokes 2005: 73–4).

One of the most significant aspects of US aid in this period was its deliberate promotion of paramilitarism as a key component of state policy. The sinister and cynical terminology used by the Yarborough report found legal expression in Decree 3398 of 1965, issued by President Guillermo León Valencia, later confirmed by Law 48, passed by the Colombian Congress in 1968. These laws authorized the executive to create civil patrols by decree and to provide them with weapons normally restricted to the armed forces. In the words of Human Rights Watch, they 'laid the legal foundation for the active involvement of civilians in the war from 1965 until 1989' (quoted in Stokes 2005: 72). The brutal tactics of the Colombian oligarchy in *La Violencia* were thus systematized and legitimized by imperial counterinsurgency strategy.

In the turbulent regional context from the 1960s to the 1980s, with armed insurgencies and/or military regimes in most countries, the Colombian situation was, in some respects, not so unusual. US intervention, whether in supporting or sponsoring military coups in the Southern Cone or in participating actively in the Central American conflicts, was extensive and was rationalized by Cold War rhetoric. But after the fall of the Berlin Wall and the Soviet Union, and with the peaceful resolution of the Central American confrontations, it soon became apparent that Colombia was an anomaly in a region increasingly characterized by peaceful and democratic political processes.

A very significant feature of this period was the repeated failure of peace initiatives in Colombia. From the 'political opening' of the Conservative President Belisario Betancourt (1982–86), through the demobilization of the M-19 and other small insurgent groups in 1989–91 and the talks with the FARC and ELN under President Andrés Pastrana (1998–2002), all attempts to resolve the conflict have failed, or at least have achieved only very limited results. It is easy to identify failures of political tact or goodwill on both sides, but two crucial factors have remained constant: the state has refused to make substantive concessions on social and economic issues, such as agrarian reform; and those guerrilla activists who have demobilized have consistently been harassed, threatened and, in many cases, assassinated by paramilitaries. Although some responsibility must attach to the insurgent movements, there is much to suggest that the Colombian establishment was never seriously interested in peace. This became much clearer under Alvaro Uribe (2002–10), with his stated policy of eliminating the guerrillas through military action. Indeed, when even limited moves towards détente (such as an *acuerdo humanitario* or humanitarian agreement on prisoner exchange between the state and the insurgents) seemed to be making progress, Uribe repeatedly resorted to actions that seemed deliberately designed to sabotage the progress, first accepting and then suddenly abandoning mediation by Venezuelan President Hugo Chávez or Colombian Senator Piedad Córdoba.

Here, yet again, Colombian establishment intransigence seemed to dovetail perfectly with US policy. Just when peace seemed to be breaking out with the end of the Cold War in the early 1990s, the 'War on Drugs' acquired greater prominence as Washington's number one priority in Latin America, providing a convenient pretext for continued intervention, with Colombia taking pride of place in US strategy. There was, of course, no doubt that illegal narcotics production and trafficking had already become a serious problem in Colombia: it was quite significant from the 1970s onwards and had a dramatic impact on the country's politics in the 1980s, with a series of targeted assassinations of politicians and members of the judiciary associated with efforts to combat the drug mafias. Beginning in 1984 with Minister of Justice Rodrigo Lara, the list of victims continued with a series of judges, the editor of *El Espectador* newspaper (Guillermo Cano) and culminated with Liberal Party presidential candidate Luis Carlos Galán in August 1989. Mafia bombs extended the terror to the general population in Bogotá and other cities (Livingstone 2003: 82–4).

To impartial observers it soon became apparent that repressive anti-narcotics policies were counterproductive for as long as demand in the consumer markets of North America and Europe continued to grow. But more significant for our purposes was evidence that mafia interests had penetrated the highest ranks of the state. In the mid-1990s, Colombia was twice 'decertified' by the US Congress for non-compliance with drug interdiction policy. And when President Ernesto Samper suffered the humiliation of being denied a US visa because his election campaign had received narcotics funding, there was widespread sympathy with him on the grounds that his main mistake had been to get caught out; for politicians across the political spectrum were believed to be tainted with similar connections.

Under Samper's successor, the conservative Andrés Pastrana Borrero, it looked briefly as if there might be a breakthrough on the two crucial issues: the internal conflict and the narcotics problem. In his election campaign Pastrana made much of his willingness to engage in dialogue, and as president-elect he arranged a dramatic personal meeting with the legendary FARC leader Manuel Marulanda in early July 1998, a month before his inauguration. This would lead within a few months to formal talks in a demilitarized zone, famously described by the media as 'the size of Switzerland', and also to discussions with the second-largest insurgent organization, the ELN. Pastrana likewise launched an ambitious counter-narcotics strategy with a strong rural-development component, Plan Colombia; but as eventually formalized it was essentially financed and controlled by the Clinton administration in the US and almost 80 per cent of the funding was for military purposes.

The peace talks in the demilitarized zone of San Vicente del Caguán would drag on for more than two years, together with intermittent contacts with the ELN in Cuba, Europe and Colombia itself, with no real progress. Plan Colombia became the main pretext for continued US intervention, having little discernible impact on the narcotics trade but further consolidating a pattern of military and police repression, human rights abuses and environmental damage through coca fumigation. With the 'War on Terror' strategy of George W. Bush, the pretext for intervention and militarism would become what many suspected had all along been the real purpose of Plan Colombia, namely counterinsurgency. But the most damaging effect of all has been the continued repression and marginalization of the Colombian poor, criminalized as narcotics producers when coca leaf or opium poppies are their sole means of survival, or as subversives when they try to organize in unions or social movements to defend their land and their rights.

In this tragic history, it is hard to overemphasize the role of the United States – a role that almost always encounters the willing complicity of the Colombian oligarchy. In the words of the respected journalist Antonio Caballero:

> Ever since our so-called independence, Colombia has been the United States' whipping-boy down here: since Santander invited them to participate in Bolívar's Panama Congress [1826]; since Mariano Ospina Rodríguez [president 1857–61] proposed that Colombia should be sold to become a US state; since Marco Fidel Suárez pointed to the north with his Latin phrase, 'respice polum' [follow the North Star]; since Laureano Gómez sent Colombian troops to fight in Korea ... since Julio César Turbay took the side of Great Britain and the United States in the war for the Argentinian Malvinas [Falkland] islands, gaining for Colombia the nickname of 'the Cain of Latin America'. (Caballero 2010: 1)

This tradition continued with Uribe's support for the US wars in Iraq and Afghanistan, and the decision to grant the US facilities at seven military bases, a decision that was declared unconstitutional by the Colombian Supreme Court in August 2010.

Paramilitarism and mafia control of politics

The Colombian oligarchy has always been exceptionally resistant to change and remarkably astute in maintaining control, despite the social changes and upheavals of the mid-twentieth century. But the contemporary situation cannot be understood without analysing a more recent and profoundly disturbing development: the penetration of the oligarchy by, and its partial fusion with, a new and even more ruthless bourgeoisie based on mafia interests and paramilitarism. As we have seen, the US Yarborough mission in 1962 recommended military training of civilian collaborators in the counterinsurgency effort, and this was formalized in Colombian law from 1965 onwards. In the following two decades, popular discontent with entrenched economic and social inequality and political immobility grew steadily and found expression both in ever more powerful social movements and in guerrilla insurgency. The state's repressive response reached its overt peak under President Julio César Turbay Ayala (1978–82), who used a state of siege to permit de facto military rule, with widespread arbitrary arrests and torture and large-scale counterinsurgency campaigns.

Turbay's heavy-handed approach soon proved counterproductive, increasing popular sympathy with the guerrillas and earning the armed forces international opprobrium for human rights abuses. At the same time, the rise of the drugs mafias was changing the social and political landscape in unanticipated ways. Pre-existing political and judicial corruption was greatly intensified, while both narcotics production and money-laundering through agrarian enterprises brought the mafias into conflict with the guerrilla movements. The first clear manifestation of this was Muerte a Secuestradores (MAS, Death to Kidnappers), formed in 1981 in response to the M-19's abduction of Marta Nieves, the daughter of a prominent drug baron; it swiftly became an instrument of terror in the Magdalena Medio and then in Antioquia, Urabá and other regions. The mafia competed with established elites in buying up land and business enterprises, but identified with their conservative and anti-communist politics:

> This formed the basis of the 'functional alliance', the so-called 'dirty war', that emerged in the 1980s between the drug barons, sectors of the army, businessmen, landowners and political bosses to eliminate suspected guerrillas and left-wing civilian activists ... In their hands, MAS grew into one of the most powerful paramilitary groups, operating out of Puerto Boyacá in Magdalena Medio. In the mid-1980s the mafia began to invest huge sums into turning MAS and other groups into private right-wing armies which, when not murdering peasant and worker leaders, could help to defend the drug industry. (Pearce 1990: 155–6)

Right-wing paramilitarism proved so effective at suppressing dissent and destroying social movements, while also undermining the insurgent organizations (less by open armed conflict than by destroying their social base of support), that it was more and more widely adopted – sometimes officially, but more often covertly – by military and police commanders, politicians, landowners and business interests of all kinds. By the 1990s it was clear that the main paramilitary organizations were becoming political actors in their own right, a kind of Frankenstein's monster which threatened to escape from the control of its masters.

Before examining this development more closely, it is necessary to insist that Colombian paramilitarism was originally sponsored by the state, and in particular the military, with a strategy clearly derived from Pentagon counterinsurgency doctrines. In the Magdalena Medio, increased FARC activity in the late 1970s was met by the establishment of a new infantry battalion in Puerto Boyacá in 1982 and the 14th Brigade in Puerto Berrío in 1983. The 14th Brigade's commander, General Faruk Yanine Díaz, was particularly active in recruiting peasants into 'self-defence groups' and working with MAS to target guerrilla suspects. MAS was promoted not only by drug mafias but also by traditional landlords, business interests and the military; in 1983, a report by the Colombian attorney general named fifty-nine active military officers among 163 members of MAS (Stokes 2005: 76). Most of these officers had been trained in the US School of the Americas (see Livingstone, and Lievesley, above).

Recent studies have suggested there is a need to view the rise of the drug mafias and their political insertion within the context of multiple regional and sectoral power struggles. Thus, for Romero:

> The explanations which identify drug trafficking alone as the main factor in the increased violence in Colombia fail to take into account the important connections between the armed conflict and drug trafficking; between the armed conflict and organized crime; between drug trafficking and legal politics; and between formal politics and transgressive politics. (Romero 2003: 34)

Initially the paramilitary were a counterinsurgency instrument subordinated to the armed forces, the landlords and the traditional political class, with the drug mafias playing a secondary role. But from the mid-1980s to the early 1990s the narcotics interests became powerful autonomous actors, and then fused with the armed 'self-defence' forces of new and emerging regional economic groups to form ruthless paramilitary armies under warlord control, challenging the state's monopoly of force while simultaneously claiming to protect the established order.

Certainly there continued to be close ties between the paramilitary forces and the state; Gearóid Ó Loingsigh has made a powerful case for the intimate relationship between state agencies, transnational capital and the Autodefensas Unidas de Colombia (AUC, United Self-Defence Units of Colombia), the main paramilitary organization for a decade or so from the mid-1990s onwards (Ó Loingsigh 2002). But the fact that the state had to rely so much on irregular and criminal forces had profound implications for the political process:

> The clientelist foundations of political power in Colombia continued to be the source of the state's overall governability. However, the new equilibrium implied that the central State, faced with the overwhelming force of the regional self-defence groups, had to delegate social control to organizations distinct from its own bureaucracy and institutions. (Duncan 2006: 314)

The full implications of this became apparent during the presidency of Alvaro Uribe, an upstart from the traditionally restless region of Antioquia. Uribe was himself tainted with narcotics connections in his early years: a document from the US Defense Intelligence Agency, declassified in May 2004, included his name as number eighty-two on a 1991 list of Colombians wanted for drug trafficking (Calvo Ospina 2008: 318). Also, as governor of Antioquia in the mid-1990s, Uribe actively promoted paramilitarism in the form of the then-legal *Convivir* ('to live together') Rural Vigilance Associations; although designated by the national government as a means of recruiting civilians to improve security and provide intelligence, they were almost universally condemned by human rights organizations as providing legal cover for larceny, extortion and assassination, frequently being composed of notorious criminal paramilitaries (Contreras 2002: 130–47). By such means, Uribe developed an extensive network of support among the most reactionary sectors of the military and the landlord class. Having begun his political career in the Liberal Party, he carved out an autonomous position for himself within the establishment, successfully presenting himself in 2002 as a right-wing, populist alternative to the two main parties, with a hard-line counterinsurgency platform.

Uribe's populism was so successful that he came closer than anyone else in forty years to breaking the two-party electoral hegemony: both the Conservative and the Liberal parties suffered serious defections by pro-Uribe sectors, and the upstart *paisa* (Antioquian) created his own electoral vehicle, the Partido Social de Unidad Nacional (Social Party of National Unity) generally referred to, suggestively, as simply the Partido de la U ('U' Party). He also came to be supported by several more new parties with misleading or bizarre names, like Cambio Radical (Radical Change), Movimiento Mira (Mira Movement), Alas Equipo Colombia (Wings Colombia Team) or Por el País que Soñamos (For the Country of Our Dreams), essentially clientelist structures known to be linked to paramilitary or narcotics interests (or both). Indeed even in the most recent legislative elections, in March 2010, a new grouping called the Partido de Integración Nacional (National Integration Party) elected nine senators and eleven representatives, despite apparently having been created by an agreement drawn up in La Picota gaol by former congressmen condemned for paramilitary connections (*Semana*, 2 August 2010).

Uribe acquired genuine popularity through his tough counter-insurgency line, but also by promoting carefully targeted welfare programmes and *consejos comunales* (community councils), in which he conversed with the common people and attended to individual grievances. This even led to superficial comparisons with Hugo Chávez, but the differences were fundamental. Uribe's community councils were not autonomous and permanent popular organizations, as in Venezuela, but staged events tightly controlled by the presidential staff; the welfare programmes were strictly limited and there was no large-scale redistribution of resources to the poor (in fact the reverse); and power was further concentrated in the hands of a violent and kleptocratic elite, not devolved to popular movements. It is by no means fanciful to suggest that the combination of the terms 'National' and 'Social' in the name of Uribe's party was an authentic indication of its ideological inclinations, as a fascist project in the true sense.

Uribe was remarkably successful in gaining the support of western governments and the media, tarring all opponents with the brush of 'subversion' or 'terrorism' and proclaiming the virtues of his 'democratic security' policy, which dovetailed conveniently with George W. Bush's 'War on Terror'. But an article by the respected political scientist Arlene Tickner puts matters in perspective, for she argues that 'there was nothing "democratic" about it' (Tickner 2010). In his second term, Uribe's problems accumulated, with ninety-seven members of Congress – the great majority of them *uribistas* – implicated in the *parapolítica* scandal, that is under investigation for alleged links to the right-wing paramilitary; of these twenty-five have been condemned, ten are currently on trial and the rest are under investigation. They represented 55 per cent of Uribe's supporters in the Senate, and his government had to rely on *suplentes* (substitutes) to keep control (*Aporrea* 2010). Another major scandal was that of the 'false positives', innocent people (especially peasants and young men from poor neighbourhoods) killed in extrajudicial executions by the military, who would present them as guerrillas 'killed in combat' and therefore 'positives' in the lists of enemy casualties for which they could claim rewards. Finally, there was the scandal of the *chuzadas*, illegal telephone intercepts by the state security service, which were shown to include leading opposition politicians, members of the judiciary and cultural figures.

As such evidence accumulated and pointed more and more directly towards the president himself and his immediate circle, Uribe's reaction was to accuse all and sundry – even the justices of the Supreme Court – of being 'soft' on the guerrillas, if not actually linked to them. In the end he clearly over-reached himself, and his project of standing for a second re-election in 2010 was rejected by the Constitutional Court, forcing him to step down and make way for a more conventional establishment politician, Juan Manuel Santos. This appeared to mark a return to more legal and constitutional norms, but it remains to be seen how far Santos intends (or is able) to overcome the entrenched power of the narco-paramilitary mafia at the highest levels of the Colombian state. The Uribe phenomenon merely marked the culmination of a long process by which a new bourgeoisie of criminal origin rose to claim a major share in political power.

The process began in the late 1970s and early 1980s with the so-called 'dodgy window' (*ventanilla siniestra*) of the Banco de la República, which allowed foreign currency transactions with no questions asked, and a series of tax amnesties which facilitated money-laundering. In the next few years, the most blatant attempts at political intervention by the narcotics mafias, such as that of Pablo Escobar, would fail, but a more covert process of infiltration into, and co-optation by, the political parties continued without interruption. Subsequently, in the words of Medófilo Medina: 'The combined power of the mafia and the paramilitary made *parapolítica* a privileged means of ascent to the political leadership of society and the state.' Although some of the paramilitary are now in gaol (with very light sentences), they are merely the scapegoats who 'are paying the price of domestication so that the new class as a whole can take its place in the establishment without constant upheavals' (Medina 2010: 7). The process is neatly summed up in the title of a new book edited by the Colombian political scientist Claudia López, *Y refundaron la patria*: literally, 'they (the narco-paramilitary in collaboration with the politicians) refounded the fatherland' (López 2010).

The political and human cost of the Colombian model

Although formally very little has changed from the 1991 constitution (which on paper is quite advanced), the foundations of political power in Colombia have thus undergone a profound, and negative, process of restructuring. It should also be noted that the rise of the new mafia-paramilitary class has further reinforced the undemocratic nature of the Colombian system, contributing powerfully to the marginalization of any political alternative by corruption, intimidation and assassination. The most notorious case was that of the Unión Patriótica (Patriotic Union), a political party formed following the demobilization of a large sector of the FARC in the 1984–85 peace process; in the next few years it began to achieve significant success in local and congressional elections, but over a period of twenty years some 4,000 of its members were assassinated or disappeared. Other parties and movements formed subsequently by various groups that laid down their arms, such as the Alianza Democrática M-19 (M-19 Democratic Alliance) from 1990 onwards and the Corriente de Renovación Socialista (Socialist Renewal Current), which left the ELN in 1991, also lost hundreds of members in this way (Celis Méndez 2005: 208–9). This pattern has continued up to the present, although since 2004 the rather more successful unified left party known as the Polo Democrático Alternativo (PDA, Democratic Alternative Pole) has gained sufficient national and international recognition to give its leaders somewhat greater security. But provincial PDA activists continue to be attacked and even murdered, and even its national leaders periodically receive anonymous death threats.

Colombia's 'democratic security' is thus neither democratic nor secure for those who take seriously the right to organize a real political alternative. Moreover, this insecurity is by no means confined to those engaged in explicitly political activities. People involved in social movements of any kind – trade unions, peasant organizations, indigenous and black movements, student activists, women – are equally under threat. The Colombian Commission of Jurists estimates that between 2002 and 2008 more than 14,000 civilians were killed or disappeared through violent acts connected with the armed conflict. The cumulative total of forced disappearances is estimated at approximately 50,000 by the Colombian attorney general's office (*Fiscalía*) – more than the number of people who disappeared during the Chilean, Argentinian and Uruguayan dictatorships combined – and an even more unimpeachable source, the Consejo Nacional de la Política Económica y Social (National Council of Economic and Social Policy), which is directly answerable to the president's office, recently recognized 27,000 cases. As many as 2,177 civilians were killed by the armed forces, most of them during Uribe's 'democratic security'. From 2002 to 2009, on average 300,000 Colombians were forcibly displaced each year, and the country is second only to Sudan in this respect (Tickner 2010; Uprimny 2010).

Despite all this, Colombia is generally regarded internationally as a democracy, and international observers tend to give the country's elections a relatively clean bill of health. But there are grounds for very considerable scepticism in this regard: abstention rates are very high, even with a very incomplete electoral register. Thus, in the May–June 2010 presidential elections, abstention was approximately 50 per cent in the first round and nearly 56 per cent in the second (Peñaloza Díaz 2010; *Universal*, 20 June 2010). In the March 2010 congressional elections, abstention was almost 60 per cent. In many rural areas, there were reports of overt intimidation or even outright coercion of voters, in some areas by guerrillas but more frequently by the paramilitary. Thus, in Magdalena Department, the AUC's candidate won the governorship unopposed in 2003 after all other candidates resigned under threat, and even though more voters cast blank ballots than voted for the winner, making a complete mockery of the elections (Hylton 2006: 111).

Colombia is frequently presented as an economic success story, with a vigorous manufacturing sector and diverse resource industries. Overall GDP growth was quite strong in the mid-1990s, but this was followed by severe recession from 1999 to 2002, before a spell of renewed growth that reached 6 per cent in 2006 (Reid 2007: 259, 262, 302). But in comparative perspective and in the long term the country's economic performance has been at best mediocre. Growth has been based on cheap labour (due in part to the virtual elimination of trade unions, Colombia accounting for most of the world's assassinated labour activists) and the giveaway of the country's natural resources. In social terms its record is appalling: in 1997 it was second only to Brazil among Latin American countries in economic inequality; in 1991 the richest 10 per cent of the population had fifty-two times the income of the poorest 10 per cent – a difference that had increased to seventy-eight times in 2000 (Avilés 2006: 91). The concentration of landed property is also extreme, in large part because of the seizure of huge tracts of land by the narco-paramilitaries, who were estimated to have taken over some 5 million hectares between 1997 and 2003 alone. In the past thirty years, Colombia has undergone what amounts to a massive agrarian counter-reform (if one can use such a term when very little real agrarian reform, in the sense of distribution of land to the peasantry, had occurred in the first place). In 1984, holdings larger than 500 hectares accounted for 32.7 per cent of the land, and in 2001 this had risen to 61.2 per cent; by 2004, 0.4 per cent of landowners possessed 61 per cent of all titled land (Hylton 2006: 118).

Although the internal conflict has always been considered 'low intensity' and has been decreasing in recent years, Colombian military spending is far and away the greatest in Latin America, at 5.47 per cent of GDP in 2008 (followed by Chile with 3.5 per cent; Brazil, Venezuela, Peru, Uruguay and Bolivia with between 1.0 and 1.5 per cent; and the rest with less than 1 per cent). As regards military manpower, with 285,000 men under arms Colombia was seventeenth in the world, and in Latin America was second only to Brazil (which has four times its population). In the eight years of Uribe's presidency Colombia's total military expenditure came to approximately $100 billion – an extraordinary amount which, if invested in infrastructure and productive enterprises, would surely have raised the country to first-world status (Otero Prada 2010).

The Colombian right and Latin America

The singular configuration of power in Colombia and the exceptional strength of the oligarchy over the past half-century (and especially with its new characteristics of the last two decades) have given the country particular significance for right-wing politics and US policy in Latin America as a whole. In the post-Cold War context, its availability as a reliable client state, with a strategic location linking Atlantic and Pacific, Central and South America, is of inestimable value to Washington. This significance has only increased with the rise of anti-imperialist and/or independent-minded governments in neighbouring countries. Venezuela in particular, and with it the countries of the Alianza Bolivariana para los Pueblos de Nuestra América (Bolivarian Alliance for the Peoples of Our America), are viewed as a strategic threat by the Pentagon and the State Department. But the new assertiveness of Brazil and Argentina and the spread of leftist or autonomist politics to several other countries (Uruguay, Paraguay, El Salvador, Guatemala) also cause the Washington establishment concern.

Colombia has thus become more important than ever as a centre for the assertion of hegemonic power and the containment of the 'Bolivarian' virus. Its role is manifested sometimes in explicit threats or acts of aggression against its neighbours, as with the military raid on Ecuadorian territory in March 2009 or Uribe's decision in July 2010 (only a couple of weeks before leaving office) to take legal action against

Venezuela at the Organization of American States and the International Criminal Court. But it is also expressed through implied military intimidation, as with the 2009 decision to grant the US use of seven military bases with apparently hostile intent towards Venezuela (and potentially towards other neighbours). On the diplomatic scene, Colombia has been a reliable ally of Washington in seeking to push the free-trade agenda (even when it was clearly rejected by most countries in the region, as at the 2005 Mar del Plata summit in Argentina) and undermining or limiting the scope of independent regional initiatives, such as Unión de Naciones Suramericanas (UNASUR, Union of South American Nations). Bogotá has also acted as a centre for the ideological coordination of counter-revolutionary forces in the region, privileging ties with conservative governments in Mexico, Peru and Chile and hosting gatherings of right-wing intellectuals and politicians, such as Mario Vargas Llosa of Peru, José María Aznar of Spain and Jorge Castañeda of Mexico.

Such diplomatic and cultural activity could be regarded as normal and unexceptional; but there are other and much more problematic forms of Colombian intervention. The most important is the export of paramilitarism, which may not be official policy, but has been well documented by many observers. In Venezuela, the presence of Colombian paramilitaries is notorious, in particular in the border states of Táchira, Zulia and Mérida, but also in Caracas and other areas. There was a notorious incident in May 2004, when some 130 Colombian paramilitaries were arrested just outside Caracas, apparently intent on undertaking armed assaults and assassinations (Calvo Ospina 2008: 304–5), and Venezuelan ministers and parliamentarians have repeatedly denounced the presence of Colombian paramilitaries and their involvement in narcotics trafficking, violent crime and political destabilization. Colombian paramilitaries have also been reported in Ecuador and Bolivia, which may imply that they are training locals in their sinister techniques. Moreover, their presence has been noted in Honduras since the coup there – a logical development, given the military regime's need to suppress popular resistance. The disturbing implication is that the Colombian model of mafia-paramilitarism as a means of undermining popular democratic movements is being promoted across Latin America. On the positive side, moves by President Juan Manuel Santos to normalize relations with neighbouring countries may contribute to a reduction in such activities, but so long as mafia-paramilitary networks retain their iron grip on crucial regions and economic sectors in Colombia itself, their international connections are unlikely to disappear. Furthermore, their proven efficacy as an instrument of counter-revolution means that the most conservative interests across the continent, and in particular in Washington, are unlikely to abandon them as a tactical option.

6 | A right for all seasons? Right-wing politics in contemporary Peru

FRANCISCO DURAND

Conservatives in Peru have proven highly influential in national politics since the late 1980s, despite the fact that their parties have lost five consecutive elections. In spite of its limitations, the right has been effective in defining its country's policies, an achievement that is quite distinctive for conservatives in Latin America. To date, Peru has not rejected neoliberalism and nor has it shifted to the left, as did many countries in the wake of the electoral victories of Hugo Chávez in Venezuela in 1998 and Luis Ignácio Lula da Silva in Brazil in 2002.

It has been argued that weak conservative parties may diminish the chances of democratic consolidation (Middlebrook 2000c), but there is also a larger issue of how, and under what circumstances, conservative forces (traditionally attached to political and economic elites) have managed to exercise power so effectively and for so long. The issue of the relationship between the right and democracy cannot be overlooked. Democracy, as political developments in Latin America have demonstrated, is a regime better suited to the right's historical rivals. Populists and socialists can more easily appeal to the mass vote, get elected and then reorient the trajectory of the state, thus cancelling or weakening conservative influence. The challenge the right faces is how to adapt to democratic conditions. To understand this dilemma, it is necessary to consider the right's strengths as a political force (its material advantages and powerful constituents, and its ability to both accommodate and achieve positive economic performance), as well as its weaknesses (internal divisions between democratic and authoritarian factions, an inability to attract multiclass support and vulnerability to populist and left-wing electoral competition). The fact that its strengths have thus far prevailed over its weaknesses suggests that Peruvian conservatism has been able to exercise influence and control over the state in indirect ways. This chapter assesses the evolution of the Peruvian right since 1985 by looking at the internal and external circumstances that shaped its political options, and by analysing the factors that enabled it to limit the impact of its electoral weaknesses.

This study is pertinent in light of the fact that there has been relatively little scholarly discussion concerning the Peruvian right, and what there is needs updating. What initially attracted national and international attention was the emergence of the New Right in 1987 (Lauer 1988; López 1989). Since missing out on victory in the 1990 election and failing to reorganize after that setback, the right, as one author argued, became 'irrelevant' (Conaghan 2000). When conservative party performance declined in the 1990s and 2000s, scholarly interest also waned; academics were more interested in the authoritarianism of the government of Alberto Fujimori (1990–2000) and its negative impact on democracy, as well as in the emergence of political outsiders and independents (Roberts 1996; Cameron 1997; Cotler and Grompone 2000; Weyland 2001). As suggested above, this chapter takes a realist perspective, focusing on the role of power holders and the means used to achieve their goals, while de-emphasizing the issue of whether the right can operate in the context of democracy in order to consolidate an ideal (or idealized) regime type.

Peru in comparative perspective

Many Latin American countries were deeply affected by the spreading left-wing tide in the early twenty-first century, and by 2010 only Peru and Colombia remained attached to conservative rule (though Chile returned to it, see Silva below). However, despite the similarity in political outcomes, the means employed to achieve conservative goals have been quite different. In contrast to the case of Colombia, the strategy adopted by Peruvian conservatism is not based on electoral victories won by strong, highly organized parties; rather in Peru, as in other countries (such as Argentina), the aim is indirect or informal rule. The fact that the Peruvian right continued to exercise such power during both Fujimori's authoritarian regime and the period of democratization that followed may seem surprising, but is explicable. A number of writers have warned of the difficulty of comparing countries politically because of the influence of many different variables. For Middlebrook, who focuses on conservative parties as the key vehicles for the representation of elite interests within democracies, part of the problem is that variations are to be expected in analysing socio-political identities and political roles, because those factors 'are strongly shaped by national circumstances' (Middlebrook 2000c: 2). Zibechi goes further in his analysis of conservative influence in Latin America in the twenty-first century, stating that 'there has not been a single, unitary new right in Latin America, since the political processes in every country are markedly different' (Zibechi 2008: 19).

Yet a focus on political outcomes, means of influence, and governmental and economic performance provides a basic comparative foundation on which to analyse the Peruvian case. To see how variables work, it is necessary to take a long view of trends in regime change. Together with Colombia, Peru clearly belongs to the category of countries where right-wing parties and conservative policies have prevailed over the long term. But Peru also seems similar to Argentina, a country where indirect rule is typical. For Borón, Argentina (and, by inference, Peru) lacks strong conservative parties, but elites use political accommodation and influence over civil society to form ruling coalitions and to exert policy control (Borón 2000: 162). This would, however, only explain developments in the 1990s, the decade when 'neopopulists' such as Carlos Menem and Fujimori governed (for the application of the concept of neopopulism – otherwise known as *populismo de derecha*, right-wing populism – to Peru, see Roberts 1996 and Weyland 2001). It would not help in understanding the subsequent decade, when political circumstances in the two countries were very different. The changes can be attributed in part to variations in economic and political governmental performance. Macroeconomic stability is, in great part, generated by governmental policies that emphasize fiscal conservatism, strong monetary reserves, growing private investment and low inflation, and as such are strongly supported by conservative and business interests. Yet, the social shortcomings of neoliberal economics help explain why it lacks legitimacy, since it offers benefits and opportunities to the elite and the middle class, but not to the working class and the poor (Reinhardt and Peres 2000). After the 2002 financial meltdown in Argentina, the crisis triggered criticism of neoliberal policies and capitalist globalization and Argentina moved leftwards, to the radical *peronismo* of the governments of Néstor Kirchner and Cristina Fernández de Kirchner (*peronismo* is the political movement inspired by Juan Domingo Perón). In Argentina, the economic disaster eroded neoliberal legitimacy and placed conservatives and *menemistas* (supporters of Menem) in a weak position, while in Peru the export bonanza (which began at the time Argentina was falling apart) helped the right both to defend neoliberal policy continuity and to retain its influence and continue to be part of governing coalitions. The export bonanza (2002–08), in particular, gave elite forces ample room to manoeuvre, even if conservative parties did not perform well in elections. The outcome of the 2006 election was particularly significant, in that it was the first one in which voters had to choose between pro- and anti-system candidates. The right supported Alan García of the Alianza Popular Revolucionaria Americana (APRA, American Popular Revolutionary Alliance, an anti-imperialist, populist party when founded in 1924, but which has moved steadily rightwards since), who won a hotly contested clash with Ollanta Humala, the nationalist, vaguely left-wing candidate.

The New Right emerges (and fails)

The Peruvian New Right came to life in 1987, during the first García administration, in response to the president's announcement that he wished to nationalize the banking system. This move created a rift between the government and the country's business community, undermined the attractiveness of interventionist policies and triggered a decision by upper- and middle-class groups to become involved in electoral politics. It thus brought together all conservative forces. Mario Vargas Llosa, the eminent novelist (and once a man of the left), emerged as the leader of this conservative revolt; he called for an end to statism and populism and for the pursuit of economic modernization through market reforms, which he also believed would help in the fight against the Sendero Luminoso (Shining Path) guerrilla movement, which had launched an insurrection in 1980. Social conservatives and neoliberal economists, as well as business organizations, converged around Vargas Llosa, demanding change before it was too late to prevent what they saw as a descent into economic and political chaos, fuelled by the presidential decision and rising political violence (Paredes and Sachs 1991: 11). Right-wing forces mobilized to prevent the bank nationalizations and began a media blitz against President García, sensing that they had an opportunity to defeat populism once and for all. The president was forced to back down over nationalization, but continued to exacerbate the political climate with policies that aggravated the impact of the recession and caused inflation to escalate. The elite was not appeased by the concession over nationalization; rather the climb-down reinforced its conviction that the time was right for action to overcome the economic crisis and re-establish political order.

The right-wing coalition was well organized both in Peru and abroad. Initially, old and new conservatives looked to Vargas Llosa and his Movimiento Libertad (ML, Liberty Movement) for leadership. ML was allied to the Frente Democrático (FREDEMO, Democratic Front) and to older, more traditional parties, Acción Popular (AP, Popular Action) and the Partido Popular Cristiano (PPC, Popular Christian Party). Vargas Llosa also received the enthusiastic support of conservative religious groups, as well as of intellectuals, neoliberal economists, business leaders and upper-class professionals, many of whom were new to party politics (Vargas Llosa 1993: 174–6). Vargas Llosa was joined at the head of this coalition by Hernando de Soto, the author of the bestselling book, *The Other Path*, published in 1986, in which he expounded an anti-statist discourse (for a systematic critique of developmental economics and the need to embrace a neoliberal paradigm, see also Paredes and Sachs 1991). Together, Vargas Llosa and de Soto were able to create a network of domestic and external forces, based on their strong connections with other intellectuals, European conservatives, economists and US Republicans, as well as multinational corporations, neoliberal think tanks, the global mass media and multilateral organizations (Bromley 1990). All these entities supported drastic policy change in Peru and promised financial and political support once adjustment policies were implemented; they also provided institutional and material resources to the conservative lobby within Peru.

Despite this momentum and the fact that Vargas Llosa won the first round of voting, FREDEMO failed to win popular support in the May 1990 run-off election. Conservative forces quickly switched their allegiance away from Vargas Llosa and to Alberto Fujimori, a political unknown. This proved to be a successful strategy: as president, Fujimori, guided by de Soto, forcefully implemented the conservative agenda. Peru entered a period of economic and political stability, and the right managed to set and maintain a course consistent with its ideas and aspirations – despite internal divisions between democratic and authoritarian factions, particularly over Fujimori's *auto-golpe* on 5 April 1992 (literally his 'self-made coup', when the president, with the support of the army and the security services, closed down all the institutions of representative government and concentrated power in the executive). It was clear that García's disastrous economic performance and misguided, erratic policies had facilitated this outcome. Although poor voters did not massively support Vargas Llosa, they did embrace a conservative agenda of order and progress. Fujimori rapidly concentrated power and proved to be a leader capable of effectively addressing the nation's most pressing problems (Durand 1996). Thus, although Vargas Llosa, the candidate of the right, lost the election, the right actually won it by switching its support to Fujimori. The real catalyst for change had been de Soto. Breaking from Vargas Llosa the day after the election, he contacted Fujimori and orchestrated his contact with both Washington Consensus institutions and international investors (Vargas Llosa 1993: 177–8; Boloña 1993: 21–2). Once the new neoliberal policy course was set, Peruvian conservatism followed de Soto's lead, abandoning Vargas Llosa and pledging itself to Fujimori.

The gradual growth of conservative power

No matter how important the events of 1987–90 were in terms of stimulating a political response from Peruvian conservatives and setting their policy goals, this progress was only possible because of a broader trend of empowerment, which had been initiated years earlier. What the 1987 'battle of the banks' did was to tilt the balance of forces in an immediate and decisive fashion. In earlier decades, the right had lost its influence over key institutions: the military and the Catholic Church (two traditionally powerful actors), the educational system, the mass media (crucial for the dissemination of conservative values) and the business community (a vital constituent, but one weakened by nationalizations under the military regime of 1968–80). But by the mid-1980s, it had begun to rebuild these close relationships. Thus the business sector was worried by what it saw as creeping state intervention in the economy, and was considering the efficacy of embracing neoliberalism. In 1984, a new generation of business leaders created the Confederación Nacional de Instituciones Empresariales Privadas (CONFIEP, National Confederation of Private Business), a group that aimed to resolve internal divisions by focusing on specific issues, such as opposition to increased taxation and the need to establish management authority in the workplace. Although many businesses were dependent on government subsidies, and although there were clashes of interest between the domestic market and the export sector, all were gradually moving towards an anti-statist agenda and thus converging ideologically with the right. Business was positioning itself to ignite the conservative rebellion, support electoral strategies aimed at destroying populism and embrace neoliberalism. Following Fujimori's victory, the president-elect held meetings with Peruvian business leaders, many of whom agreed to take key cabinet posts. Business support proved decisive when Fujimori launched the *autogolpe* in 1992, when CONFIEP was the only civil society organization to support him. Many prominent businessmen, such as Juan Antonio Aguirre Roca, CONFIEP's president in 1992, and the leading family conglomerates (Benavides, Brescia and Romero) became enthusiastic defenders of free-market economics (Durand 2003: 367).

The 1987 crisis also helped conservatives develop links with the media, and New Right politicians increasingly appeared as pundits on television and radio programmes. This connection strengthened during the Fujimori era, when many of the media developed a cosy relationship with the government. When Peru returned to holding free and fair elections in the 2000s, the mass media, now more dependent on corporate advertising, played a critical role in shaping public opinion, paving the way for candidates who favoured the conservative agenda and demonizing those who opposed it. A similar move rightwards took place within the military. During the government of General Velasco (1968–75), the institution was seen by many as having shifted to the left, but the counterinsurgency war against Sendero Luminoso and the smaller guerrilla group, the Movimiento Revolucionario Túpac Amaru (Túpac Amaru Revolutionary Movement), in the 1980s and 1990s saw the emergence of conservative officers who favoured a 'get tough' approach. As the guerrillas escalated their attacks, ever-increasing areas of the country were placed under a state of emergency, where extrajudicial executions, massacres and torture became the norm. The military's conservative trajectory was fuelled by a belief that neoliberal economics seemed to offer the best way out of the recession and, as both business and the military were the targets of guerrilla attacks, it appeared sensible to adopt a common front. Thus, in 1990, CONFIEP created a secret committee to support the military's counterinsurgency campaign.

The Catholic Church also became an important pillar of support for the Fujimori government. Two conservative Catholic organizations, Opus Dei and Sodalitium Christianae Vitae, openly supported both Vargas Llosa and the anti-bank nationalization lobby. Founded in 1971, Sodalitium is an umbrella organization representing seven groups. In 2001, its leader, Luis Figari, was named Consultor to the Pontifical Council for Laity and, in 2005, auditor to the Synod of Bishops on the Eucharist. Sodalitium runs elite schools in Peru and Chile, and a university in Arequipa, Peru. Through their educational activities, both religious groups were able to develop close links with upper- and middle-class families, while also establishing ties with Catholic business elites. Dionisio Romero, arguably the most powerful business leader, identified with Opus Dei and worked to propagate its views on family values and discipline in the workplace (Alvarez Rodrích 1986). Since the 1990s, a generation of managerial and professional individuals have graduated from these elite private schools and universities and have embraced neoliberal economics and conservative Catholic values, reconciling in this way religious piety with material well-being.

John Paul II's pastoral visit to Peru in 1985 helped to reinforce the influence of religious conservatism. He did this by publicly condemning liberation theology – the doctrine, originating in the 1960s, which argued that the Church should advocate socio-economic reform in order to promote 'the preferential option for the poor' – and by appointing young, conservative bishops at the same time as the Jesuits, the leaders of social progressivism in the 1960s and 1970s, were experiencing internal splits and waning influence (Klaiber 1996: 495, 511). Conservative influence was finally consolidated when Juan Luis Cipriani, the leader of Opus Dei, was appointed bishop of Ayacucho in 1988 (Moncada 2006). Ayacucho was the region where Sendero Luminoso began its armed rebellion in 1980, and the new bishop vigorously defended the military's repressive tactics and harshly criticized human rights groups that condemned them. Cipriani was appointed archbishop of Lima in 1999, and soon after became cardinal of Peru, thus becoming the first Opus Dei cardinal in the world. As of 2010, of forty Peruvian bishops, ten came from Opus Dei and two from Sodalitium (for Opus Dei, see Moncada 2006; information on the number of bishops is from the author's interview with Jeffrey Klaiber, March 2010).

Last but not least, think tanks and consultancy firms became the epicentre of policy renovation, helping to disseminate market values and demolish populist and interventionist ideologies. Many advisers, ministers, vice-ministers and directors of state institutions since the 1990s have come from organizations such as the Instituto Peruano de Economía, Libertad y Democracia (Peruvian Institute for the Economy, Freedom and Democracy, founded by de Soto) and Apoyo (Support), both of which receive generous support from international institutions and corporations. This new generation of experts were regarded as opinion leaders. Using the modern media of the internet and television, as well as more traditional portals such as radio and the press, they defended the new economic orthodoxy and praised the benefits of macroeconomic stability and private investment, while declaiming the failure of populism.

Self-doubt on the right

Despite these impressive gains, several commentators noted that the New Right in particular, and conservatives in general, appeared uncertain of the strength of their political renaissance both during the period 1987–90 (Lauer 1988; López 1989) and then under *fujimorismo*. As mentioned before, Catherine Conaghan (2000), in her assessment of the electoral results of the 1990s, described it as an 'irrelevant Right', while other scholars talked of the collapse of the party system, a process affecting all parts of the ideological spectrum (Planas 1996; Tanaka

1999; Lynch 1999). However, after Fujimori fled to Japan in 2000 (in an attempt – ultimately unsuccessful – to escape a corruption scandal and charges of human rights abuses) and the democratic restoration began, traditional parties came back to life, although they perhaps never quite regained their earlier political weight. This recovery was aided by the introduction of US-style elections, which focused more on candidates than on parties and relied more on polling and advertising than political discourse (Planas 1996: 185).

There were two obvious constraints on the right's revival. One was Vargas Llosa's 1990 defeat and the other was its continuing inability to create a strong party capable of winning elections. Vargas Llosa left Peru after the debacle; he became a Spanish citizen but remained a powerful voice in the international media, making his opinions known about Peruvian current affairs. *Fujimorismo* weakened the democratic process throughout the 1990s, thus limiting the right's prospects of becoming a legitimate political force. Fujimori's personalist and authoritarian style of government attracted enthusiastic support from the Church, business and the military, and all defended the *auto-golpe*; but Vargas Llosa and his small band of supporters condemned the president as a dictator. The right was thus split in its approach to Fujimori, and this debilitated it. Conaghan argues that Fujimori had effectively robbed the right of its political identity (Conaghan 2000: 257–8). He exploited the economic recovery over which he presided and became the darling of the authoritarian right. With the end of his regime, the political opportunities for the right appeared brighter, but its organizational weakness hampered its progress. This is demonstrated by looking at its electoral performance between 1990 and 2006. In 1990, FREDEMO obtained only 32.6 per cent in the first round of voting and only 37.4 per cent in the run-off vote. Fujimori, whose election promise was a vague 'Honesty, Technology and Work', attracted the support of APRA and independent voters, and won with 62.4 per cent (source: Oficina Nacional de Procesos Electorales, at www.onpe.gob.pe/index.html). In succeeding elections, Fujimori created ad hoc, neopopulist parties which gained support across the classes. In 1995, he won with 64 per cent of the vote, and in the controversial 2000 election, when the democratic right joined forces to oppose him, he failed to win in the first round but obtained 74.3 per cent in the second. The democratic right and its candidate, Alejandro Toledo (who received the support of Vargas Llosa, the PPC, APRA and even the left), did not contest the final vote, arguing that the result would be fraudulent (Cotler and Grompone 2000: 152).

During the Fujimori decade, Renovación Nacional (RN, National Renovation) took up the banner of the right. Led by Opus Dei member Rafael Rey, the party supported Fujimori until the very end. However, it fared poorly in elections, as did de Soto's Capital Popular (Popular Capital) which failed to register as a party to contest the 2000 and 2001 elections. In the wake of Fujimori's departure, many Peruvians were disgusted by revelations about the corrupt regime presided over by him and by his right-hand man, Vladimiro Montesinos, head of the Sistema de Inteligencia Nacional (National Intelligence System) (Bowen and Holligan 2003). Fujimori was replaced by a provisional president, Valentín Paniagua from AP, who governed for eight months until elections were held in 2001 (Cotler and Grompone 2000). For that election, Unidad Nacional (UN, National Unity – a front formed by RN, the PPC and other smaller groups) chose a new presidential candidate. Lourdes Flores was a young lawyer committed to conservative values and an advocate of honest government. She received only 24.3 per cent of the vote in the first round, while APRA's Alan García (who had been in exile since Fujimori's *auto-golpe*), obtained 25.77 per cent, allowing him to progress into the second round. This was a remarkable result, given the reputation he had acquired during his first administration as a corrupt and incompetent president. Toledo, the outsider who had taken on Fujimori in the first round in 2000 and who now led the Peru Posible (literally, Possible Peru) party, became the frontrunner, obtaining 36.51 per cent in the first round and 53.10 per cent in the second. The right and part of the left voted for Toledo to ensure that García did not win. Vargas Llosa gave him his endorsement, too, in order to reinforce the democratic wing of conservatism.

Although Toledo could be considered an economic conservative, who was supported by the New Right and the business sector, his political agenda was also influenced by progressive and left-wing ideas. He led a multiparty, multiclass challenge to the authoritarian right. He possessed mass appeal because of his poor, indigenous origins and he capitalized on this by presenting himself as an Inca; he was also admired for the fact that he had succeeded thanks to his own educational and work efforts. Toledo's appeal was, thus, a quality which hardcore, Opus Dei-believing conservatives would never possess. Toledo, like Fujimori, could be placed in an intermediate category, as a political outsider with a populist style but also a defender of conservative economics. Both were leaders who attracted mass support with clientelistic promises as a means of overcoming the electoral limitations of the right. As Barr has argued, Toledo followed a 'two-tiered policy approach of distributing benefits to the poor while maintaining a neoliberal economic orientation' (Barr 2003: 1169). In the 2006 elections, Flores and UN continued to represent the conservative agenda, but this was at a time when neoliberalism and privatization policies had become the targets of intense criticism. In 2002, for example, the people of the southern city of Arequipa mobilized against the privatization of a local energy company and Toledo was forced to stop the bidding process; many similar demonstrations followed. In 2006, García advocated 'responsible change' from the centre-right of politics, while newcomer Ollanta Humala (warmly endorsed by Hugo Chávez – a fact that the right-wing media made much of) occupied the left of the political stage. Flores received 19.98 per cent, Humala 25.7 per cent and García 20.41 per cent. In the second round, Humala increased his support to 47.38 per cent, but García, supported by all conservative forces, obtained 52.64 per cent. The right would unite if there was a possibility of a nationalist, populist, pro-Chávez left-winger being elected president.[1]

In sum, then, from 1990 to 2006, no conservative party – either new (ML, RN) or old (PPC, AP) or in coalition (FREDEMO, UN) won a national election. Conservative parties constituted a minority political force, incapable of getting more than 25 per cent of the vote in six consecutive presidential elections. As a consequence, they were compelled to support the lesser of two evils: Fujimori in 1995, Toledo in 2001 and García in 2006. Their only option appeared to be to play the politics of accommodation.

Final thoughts

In order to complete this assessment of the Peruvian right as a political force, some critical issues need to be addressed. As mentioned before, Peru is distinctive in the Latin American context, in that the political influence of conservative forces is exercised in an indirect manner but continues to produce positive political outcomes. Several interrelated questions come into play here. First, how can the disappointing electoral results of conservative parties be explained? Secondly, were those disappointing results the consequence of particular conservative failings or were they systemic? Thirdly, given this electoral record, how is it that the various conservative constituencies (the Church, business, the military, the media) have remained the

1 In June 2011, as this book was in the production process, Ollanta Humala defeated Keiko Fujimori, Alberto Fujimori's daughter, in the second round of the presidential elections, by 51 per cent to 49 per cent.

most influential political forces since 1990? Fourthly, what specific mechanisms of indirect domination have they employed to constitute this influential lobby? Besides the right's tactical mistakes during the 1990 election (poor management of its media image; tensions between old and new factions; Vargas Llosa's lack of political experience; and an underestimation of its populist and socialist opponents), the results revealed a deeper problem – one that had affected traditional conservative parties before the advent of populism. Conservative forces in general, and the New Right in particular, have advanced horizontally but not vertically: that is, they have been unable to extend their support base beyond the elite and the upper middle class. The 1990 election appeared to present a golden opportunity for progress. The right's political opponents were weak and on the defensive, and the ability of either the populists or the socialists to address Peru's pressing problems was questioned by many. Sinesio López, who analysed the emergence of the New Right before 1990, has argued that negative populist performance enhanced conservatism's chances to change the balance of power in its favour (López 1989: 58). This did not mean that populist and left-wing influence was insignificant. The reason Vargas Llosa lost the election was that APRA and the left (which polled 22 per cent and 13 per cent, respectively, in the first round of voting) then decided to support Fujimori in the final round explicitly in order to block FREDEMO.

Voting behaviour along class lines appears to be the main factor in explaining the inability of conservative parties to attract majority support. Several studies of electoral behaviour in the 1990s indicated that, while right-wing parties were able to attract strong elite support, as socio-economic status declined so did their appeal (Cameron 1997: 43; Durand 1996: 105–6; Dietz and Dugan 1997). Although Peruvian conservatism experienced ideological renovation, saw the emergence of new leaders and parties, recovered its influence over key institutions, enjoyed a special connection to de facto powers and could count on solid international support, it failed to obtain broad popular support (Lauer 1988: 134–6; López 1989: 59). What happened to Vargas Llosa and FREDEMO in 1990 was repeated in succeeding elections, as voters identified conservative candidates with elite interests. In the 2006 election, one of the factors which prevented Flores from obtaining more than 20 per cent of the vote was the perception that she was the candidate of the rich, an image that García cleverly exploited. Thus, one important conclusion is that the existence of a well-established class hierarchy inhibits conservative parties from moving beyond their core elite constituents and diminishes their electoral chances. As Gibson has noted, 'the social power of the economically privileged cannot be translated into political power democratically without multi-class support' (1992: 21). Multiclass support, and in particular popular support, is an essential requirement to win elections. Latin America is a continent traditionally divided along class lines, and this is expressly manifested in the way the Peruvian party system has evolved. The political game is shaped by the fact that elites have more money than votes and the poor have more votes than money. Given this divide, the right's inability to transform discourse into political action comes as no surprise (López 1989: 60). Poor leadership (more intelligent than street smart) and the absence of sustained organizational effort have contributed to making this weakness more acute. Given these limitations, the right was compelled to accommodate itself to supporting 'second-best' options in 1990, 2001 and 2006.

To fully answer the second question, it is important to look at the party system during the 1990s and 2000s. The right's inability to create a strong competitive political party in 1990, despite the high expectations Vargas Llosa's candidacy generated, should come as no surprise. All political parties, including the traditional conservative ones, were weak at this time. The political void was filled by independents and outsiders, or else party insiders who saw better opportunities for advancement outside the party system (Cameron 1997: 47; Lynch 1999; Cotler and Grompone 2000: 141–52). These new political developments also created possibilities. As Middlebrook has noted in reference to the 1990s, a weaker party system gave the right 'a whole area of maneuver with potential allies found across a range of independent, pragmatically uncommitted and ambitious *presidenciables*' (Middlebrook 2000c: 281–3). Connections with powerful socio-economic institutions at home and abroad and Fujimori's positive economic performance also contributed to the right's chances of success. In the 2000s, traditional parties recovered, but they had to compete with this new generation of independent politicians and new party organizations, making the political system far more fluid.

With reference to the final two questions, the right has managed to become a driving force behind the scenes, making Peru an example of 'conservatives ruling without a party' (Borón 2000: 149). In her analysis of the Fujimori era, Conaghan correctly acknowledges the importance of inside lobbying, but does not sufficiently appreciate it (Conaghan 2000: 256). Political accommodation is facilitated by the existence of resources and networks, by the creation of pacts, by the co-optation of traditional parties and organizations, and by negotiations which precede the election of governments. The elite has the capacity to fund and pursue such strategies, whereas social groups that do not must have recourse to other tactics, such as collective action. In this manner, the Peruvian right is able to continue to shape the political arena. In 1990, de Soto's grooming of Fujimori led to the latter's embrace of neoliberalism and his acceptance by the Washington Consensus institutions (Boloña 1993). De Soto has continued to act in the capacity of facilitator to all governments since 1990. In a similar vein, Alan García would not have been elected president in 2006 had he not committed himself to neoliberalism and aligned himself with the forces of the right. Peru has enjoyed economic growth and sustained private and international investment since 1990, and the export bonanza that began in 2002 has consolidated the country's reputation for positive macroeconomic performance. Had Peru suffered serious economic problems, the electorate and APRA could have moved to more populist positions. At the same time, conservatives and independents willing to support the continued dominance of the neoliberal model would have had a harder time defending it.

THREE | The right in opposition

7 | Venezuela's opposition: desperately seeking to overthrow Chávez

FRANCISCO DOMINGUEZ

Venezuela's elite has been out of political power since 1998, and since then it has concentrated all its energies on seeking to create the conditions for the overthrow of the government of Hugo Chávez. This elite is composed of a powerful coalition of political parties, economic groups, sections of the labour aristocracy, business bodies, university students, state cadres from the old regime and intellectuals, and thus constitutes a formidable force. It nearly succeeded in toppling Chávez in April 2002; had another try with an oil lockout in 2002–03; again in 2004 with a recall referendum; and in 2005 with a boycott of parliamentary elections. And although it grudgingly accepted electoral defeat in the 2006 presidential elections (interpreted by commentators with a superficial understanding of the situation as a rejection of subversion and an acceptance of democracy), during the 2007 constitutional referendum it waged a campaign of street violence, billboard and media scaremongering that was highly reminiscent of the events leading up to the overthrow of the government of Salvador Allende in Chile in 1973. Indeed revelations in 2008 of a plot by retired and serving military officers to assassinate President Chávez signalled that a coup strategy had not been abandoned. This was made evident by the orgy of violence that followed opposition electoral victories in several key urban centres in the 2008 regional elections and that targeted anything smacking of Bolivarian development (including Cuban doctors). The Venezuelan right's objective throughout has not been to defeat the government in order to govern itself, in normal democratic fashion, but to destroy the Bolivarian Revolution. In pursuit of this aim, it has relied on the privately owned media (which depict the opposition as waging a desperate battle for liberty against an increasingly authoritarian regime) and the political and financial support of US state agencies. This chapter seeks to examine the reasons that underlie the intensely undemocratic nature of Venezuela's opposition.

The Fourth Republic: a rotten regime

The election of Hugo Chávez to the presidency of Venezuela in 1998 was a critical turning point in the fate of the discredited Fourth Republic (on the rise of Chávez, see Gott 2006; Kozloff 2007; B. Jones 2008; Wilpert 2007). The most recalcitrant members of the elite, such as the ex-president, Carlos Andrés Pérez, and the traditional right-wing parties, Acción Democrática (AD, Democratic Action) and the Comité de Organización Política Electoral Independiente (COPEI, Committee of Independent Political and Electoral Organization), opposed him from the start, but others, such as the media tycoon Gustavo Cisneros, who 'was among those of the country's financial oligarchs who hoped the untested officer could be bent to their will' (Gott 2006: 155), thought they could co-opt him. This latter strategy was rapidly abandoned on inauguration day when, to general astonishment, Chávez altered the wording of the presidential oath, declaring: 'I swear in front of my people that over the moribund constitution I will push forward the democratic transformations that are necessary so that the new republic will have an adequate magna carta for the times.' Gott reports that 'his supporters ... erupted into cheers [but] his opponents gasped. Chávez's message was unmistakable' (ibid.: 155).

Chávez had declared war on an oligarchy that was accustomed to run the affairs of the state with very little democratic accountability, as though endowed with the divine right to rule, and that did not expect to be questioned by the country's darker-skinned majority (for a discussion of how race and class have permeated Venezuela's political discourse, see Gottberg 2004: 115–35). Represented by AD and COPEI (parties which had rotated in government since the Punto Fijo Pact of 1958, which followed the overthrow of the Pérez Jiménez dictatorship), the oligarchy had a reputation for economic and political promiscuity with few parallels in the region. In forty years it had developed a culture of speculation, parasitism and corruption, which was both fuelled and funded by the country's oil revenues (Coronil 1997). Thus, for example, under the government of Jaime Lusinchi (1984–89), a small but very influential group appropriated around $5 billion through manipulation of differential exchange rates (Lander 1996: 70). The title of a bestseller at the time is telling: the *Diccionario de la Corrupción en Venezuela* catalogued 300 cases of graft and corruption by the high and mighty between 1958 and 1989, and this was by no means the total (on corruption, see Navarro 2004). President Carlos Andrés Pérez (1989–93) was impeached for embezzlement and misuse of state funds, forced to resign and condemned to two years' house arrest. By 1993, the Fourth Republic was clearly moribund and the legitimacy of the AD–COPEI power axis was in tatters. Rafael Caldera, the frontrunner in the election caused by Pérez's departure, was compelled to set up a new party as the only way to be elected (B. Jones 2008). To add to the elite's woes, Aristóbulo Isturiz, a left-winger and the first Afro-Venezuelan to be elected to the office, became mayor of Caracas.

These political upheavals within the elite took place in the wake of growing popular discontent. Venezuela's external debt rose from $1,709 million in 1980 to $35,842 million in 1994 (Cooker 1999: 78). In February 1989, Pérez had introduced an IMF-dictated austerity package (known as the *paquetazo*), which provoked the largest riots in the country's history (the events became known as the *Caracazo*), during which between 600 and 3,000 people were killed by the military on the president's orders. Most of the deaths took place after the riots had ended, when hundreds of soldiers, led by tanks, raided the shanty towns around Caracas and shot indiscriminately at the population (Sonntag 1992: 66). These tactics exacerbated an ongoing radicalization within the armed forces that would lead to two armed rebellions by young officers, the first led by one Hugo Chávez in 1992. The *Caracazo* demonstrated that the *puntofijista* regime had the trappings of democracy (elections and formal constitutional rights), but was in reality deeply undemocratic and was not prepared to countenance the democratic aspirations of the Venezuelan people protesting against policies whose main function was to prop up the rich and their foreign partners, mostly US companies (for the *Caracazo*, see the 1992 documentary *Venezuela Febrero 27*, directed by Liliane Blaiser).

The Fourth Republic's disastrous economic performance was compounded by high levels of inequality: in the fifty years before Chávez's election, income per head in Venezuela rose by just a quarter of the average rate of the other large Latin American economies, a situation that was exacerbated by almost total neglect of the country's infrastructure. Between 1990 and 1997, income per capita dropped from $5,192 to $2,858; Venezuela's human development index declined from 0.821 to 0.746; and poverty rose from 17.65 per cent (9.06 per cent in extreme poverty) to 48.33 per cent (with 27.66 per cent in extreme poverty). In 1997 the richest 5 per cent of the population earned 41.58 times more than the poorest 5 per cent. In 1983, 41.3 per cent of working Venezuelans were in the informal sector, while by 1998 the figure was 48.2 per cent; meanwhile public sector employment declined from 22.67 per cent of total employment in 1983 to 16.33 per cent in 1998 (Cannon 2009: 35–6).

If Chávez's inauguration speech had put the fear of God into Venezuela's oligarchy, once in government his actions worried it even more. He swept away the old political structures, including the parliament, sacked a large number of judges closely associated with the *ancien régime* and established a Constituent Assembly, whose function it was to draft a new, Bolivarian constitution. Once this was approved by referendum he was able to initiate a thoroughgoing process of transformation of Venezuela's economy, politics and society. A critical moment came when he moved decisively to assert state control over Petróleos de Venezuela SA (PDVSA, Venezuelan Oil), a company that had previously acted as a state within the state; Gott has described this as a 'vast conglomerate dispensing favours and bribes' (2009: 170). In future, oil revenues would be used for social and economic development with the aim of lifting people out of poverty. The elite had supported the creeping privatization of the oil industry, but this process was stopped in its tracks by the appointment of a new PDVSA management; by the new constitution, which made privatization unconstitutional; and by Venezuela's adoption of a newly assertive position within the Organization of the Petroleum Exporting Countries (OPEC), which ensured that production quotas would lead to increasing oil prices and thus higher revenues. With the loss of PDVSA, the oligarchy lost the foundation on which much of its privilege and parasitism had rested.

Another hard blow for the right was the knowledge that Chávez inspired millions of Venezuelans, particularly the poor, which made it very difficult to defeat him in elections. He was also clearly not going to be bought. As early as 1999–2000, the elite drew the conclusion that only force could address its predicament. This perception would lead to the 'insurrection of the bourgeoisie', the most dramatic episode of which was the brief ousting of Chávez in April 2002.

The insurrection of the bourgeoisie

There are uncanny parallels between the experiences of Venezuela under Chávez and Chile under Allende. Chile's right-wing opposition formed a coalition called the Confederación de la Democracia (Confederation of Democracy) while its Venezuelan counterpart was known as the Coordinadora Democrática (Democratic Coordinating Committee). Both relied heavily on support from the US and from the domestic private media (*El Mercurio* and Channel 13 in Chile and *El Universal*, *El Nacional* and most television channels in Venezuela). The media in both countries waged scare campaigns based on the same themes (defence of the family, private property, tradition, democracy, freedom and anti-communism) and both received the political endorsement of the Inter-American Press Association (which, under US leadership, represents media corporations in the region) in the form of regular denunciations of government 'attacks' on the freedoms of expression and the press. Both used violent extra-parliamentary demonstrations to create a sense of panic and chaos, so as to scare the population, and both used billboard posters and economic strikes to disrupt the economy and demoralize government supporters. Both whipped up anti-communist sentiment, charging the government with intending to subject the nation to the dictates of *castrocomunismo* and the creation of a totalitarian dictatorship. Both mobilized women to stage demonstrations (they were dressed in black to symbolize a state of mourning for the imminent death of democracy). Both combined extra-parliamentary struggle with participation in elections, and both aimed to overthrow the elected government and destroy its ideology. Both staged coups – one successful, one unsuccessful – with the collaboration of US agencies, which heavily funded all opposition activities.

Since the 1998 election, the opposition has played the democratic game by fielding candidates at most elections (regional, parliamentary and presidential), but it has not been prepared to accept the new institutional framework. Adopting the tactics displayed by the Chilean right between 1970 and 1973, it has thus far failed to obtain the same results, but this does not invalidate the point argued here – that its strategic aim is the complete eradication of *chavismo* and everything associated with it, particularly in terms of democracy and social progress. Many question the revolutionary nature of the advances achieved under Chávez, and although there are important deficiencies in the Bolivarian Revolution, it must be borne in mind that Latin American elites, in conjunction with Washington, have overthrown governments throughout the region for much less serious 'offences' (we might mention Guatemala in 1954, Brazil in 1964 and, more recently, Honduras in 2009). Thus, imperfections (or indeed lack of revolutionary depth of the transformations effected) have never been a reason not to overthrow a government. The fact remains, however, that the depth of the transformation of Venezuelan society and economy is, outside Cuba, the most profound in the region. The chapter now focuses on the key political crises unleashed by Venezuela's elite, so as to pinpoint the real nature of its strategic objective vis-à-vis the Chávez government. These are the crisis leading to the short-lived April 2002 coup; the 2002–03 oil lockout; the 2004 recall referendum; the boycott of the 2005 parliamentary elections; the constitutional referendum of 2007;

assassination attempts on the president; and the violence which followed the 2008 regional elections.

As mentioned previously, some members of the opposition hoped that they could co-opt the new government. Thus media tycoon Gustavo Cisneros suggested that one of his representatives should assume control of the National Telecommunications Commission, the state regulatory body, which would have greatly aided the expansion of his empire (Gott 2006: 155). Chávez refused to be taken prisoner in this way. He was determined both to transform the country without the assistance of its traditional rulers and to dismantle the whole edifice established by the Punto Fijo agreement. The turning point came in November 2001, when Chávez signed forty-nine decrees, one of which took PDVSA out of the hands of its AD/COPEI managers and transferred it to state control. When the elite realized the implications of the new legislation, PDVSA executives reacted vigorously and, in league with the Federación de Cámaras y Asociaciones de Comercio y Producción de Venezuela (FEDECAMARAS, Venezuelan Federation of Chambers of Commerce) and the corrupt leadership of the Confederación de Trabajadores de Venezuela (CTV, Confederation of Venezuelan Workers), launched the first general strike on 10 December 2001 (Wilpert 2003: 107). The strike sought both to prevent state control of PDVSA and to oust Chávez. The private media whipped up anti-government sentiments 'on a round-the-clock basis, a virulence unthinkable in Europe or North America' (ibid.: 102). The new laws were wide-ranging and challenged the privileged position of the Catholic Church, landowners, industrialists, corrupt trade unionists and functionaries. By 2002, the opposition was calling on the armed forces to end 'the Chávez "dictatorship"'(Buxton 2009: 67).

If the elite understood that losing PDVSA would jeopardize its survival as a class, Chávez knew that, without state ownership of oil revenues, the regeneration of Venezuela was impossible. The PDVSA management and the Venezuelan elite opposed his Hydrocarbons Law, and in this they coincided with the US's strategic interests. The law stipulated that royalties paid by private companies should rise from 16.6 per cent to 30 per cent, and that the Venezuelan state should control at least 51 per cent of new oil production and exploration. It also sought to stop overproduction (a policy that suited the US, in that it kept the price low) by convincing OPEC countries to adopt a more assertive stance. This led to a hike in the cost of a barrel of oil from $8.43 to $28. When Chávez then appointed new PDVSA directors, FEDECAMARAS and the CTV (themselves both recipients of generous 'grants' from the

National Endowment for Democracy (NED); see Lievesley's chapter) championed the old executives. FEDECAMARAS's president, Ernesto Carmona, wrote in *El Universal*: 'The crisis in PDVSA can be traced to the government's decision to create a managing board with political ends, thus shattering the meritocracy in high management' (cited in Kozloff 2007: 28). This 'meritocracy' had been involved in setting up joint ventures with private-sector contractors to pump oil and sell it back to PDVSA at a fixed rate, so that when oil prices collapsed their profits increased, because PDVSA was paying them high prices, thus leading to huge losses to Venezuela. This 'meritocracy' also sold PDVSA information technology to a US defence contractor for just $1,000 (Buxton 2009: 62), while its payroll included some 6,000 *gerentes* (managers) whose salaries amounted to $1 billion annually. Since 1995, PDVSA had paid some $500 million per year to its foreign branches but nothing to its Venezuelan branch, until Chávez forced it to do so in 2001 (Britto García 2008: 41, 46). The battle for PDVSA was crucial for both sides and was instrumental in the run-up to the April 2002 coup. In that month, the opposition arrested the 'illegitimate' resident of the presidential palace in Miraflores (that is Chávez), drove his ministers and government underground and abolished all the Bolivarian institutions, including the 1999 constitution, the National Assembly, the National Electoral Council, the ombudsman, the attorney general and the Supreme Court, and also suspended all elections. The police were unleashed to quell any resistance that would inevitably come from the *barrios*, where support for Chávez was strongest.

The world's corporate media welcomed the coup. To take just one example, in the UK the Blair government's minister responsible for Latin American affairs, Denis MacShane, wrote an article in *The Times* on 13 April in which he compared Chávez to Mussolini. So prominent was the role of the media in the crisis that the coup has been labelled the first media coup in history. On 10 April, various Venezuelan newspapers had openly called for a coup. Thus, the front page of *El Nuevo País* read: 'The military have to have their say'; *Tal Cual*, organ of the Movimiento al Socialismo (Movement towards Socialism) led by former Marxist guerrilla Teodoro Petkoff, called for 'civilian rebellion'; and *El Nacional* announced that 'The final battle will be in Miraflores', while also printing a statement from Primero Justicia (Justice First), a key member of the opposition coalition, which demanded 'the immediate resignation of the President'. On 11 April, *El Universal* was talking about 'total conflict'. As opposition marchers came face to face with *chavistas* who were congregated around the presidential palace to defend the government, snipers fired on demonstrators. Some thirty people, mainly *chavista* supporters, were shot in the space of thirty minutes (Palacios 2002). While the media reported that they had fainted from the heat, in fact most had been shot in the head. When it became impossible to deny that there had been shootings, the media charged Chávez with ordering the killing of innocent civilians. Members of 'civil society', former PDVSA executives, active and retired military officers, journalists, broadcasters, opposition politicians and even Venezuela's cardinal all called on the armed forces 'to please collaborate to re-establish law and order so that there are no more deaths' (Britto García 2008: 82). Their version of events was reiterated in Washington on 12 April, when the White House press secretary declared: 'We know that the actions encouraged by the Chávez government provoked this crisis; Chávez suppressed peaceful demonstrations, fired on unarmed peaceful protestors ... that's what took place and a civilian transitional government has been installed' (Bartley and Ó Briain 2003). However, CNN correspondent Otto Neusdalt had a different view: 'On 10 April evening I got a phone call and I'm told: "Otto, tomorrow you'll get a video about Chávez, the [opposition] march will go to Miraflores, there are going to be dead people, and you'll also see 20 high ranking officers speaking against the government and demanding his resignation"' (cited in Britto García 2008: 49). Thus, the plotters knew the chain of events in advance. Alternative versions were absent because all pro-government media had been suppressed. Chávez was finally arrested on 13 April, but the media reported that he had resigned. Otto Reich, US assistant secretary of state for the western hemisphere, would repeat this fabrication.

Venezuela's elite was elated by Chávez's ousting. It embarked upon a brutal repression of *chavista* ministers, MPs, governors and mayors (Antonio Ledezma, a leading opposition politician, appeared on television with an arrest list with 200 names); peasants were evicted from land distributed to them under the forty-nine laws (now abolished); privatization plans were put in place; oil sales to Cuba were halted; and the Cuban embassy was besieged by thugs led by Baruta's mayor, Capriles Radonski, with the excuse that Vice-President Diosdado Cabello was hiding inside (Palacios 2002; the siege can be seen in the 2002 documentary *Asedio a una embajada*). Total media censorship was voluntarily imposed by the media owners themselves. *El Universal* celebrated the coup ('a step forward') while *Tal Cual* said 'Chao Hugo' while their editorials gave their full support to every measure taken by the Carmona government. The private television channels were even more exuberant. A purge of *chavistas* working in the media began with the firing of some 500 journalists. All of these events took place within forty-seven hours!

The coup came to an end on 13 April, when the inhabitants of the *barrios* mobilized, surrounding the presidential palace and many military barracks, and Chávez was restored the following day (Britto García 2008: 86–99). However, its failure did not deter Venezuela's elite from continuing its campaign to reclaim PDVSA, to engineer the collapse of the economy and to destabilize the government. Thus, in July, *El Nacional* ominously announced that 'the government will not last beyond December'. The media talked regularly of a general strike, and in November 2002, Luis Giusti, former PDVSA head and a man closely associated with the privatization of the oil industry, predicted in *El Universal* that 'if PDVSA joins the stoppage, the country will collapse in about a week'. This hype was supplemented by the regular television appearances of masked soldiers telling audiences that when they acted 'nobody will have time to do anything' (Britto García 2008: 131). FEDECAMARAS joined forces with the CTV to organize the oil lockout, which began on 2 December; lasting sixty-four days, it brought untold suffering to millions of poor Venezuelans who were denied cooking fuel.

The opposition's Coordinadora Democrática received USAID assistance and was also helped by Venezuela's top public relations firms, which 'produced some of the most highly crafted anti-Chávez commercials Venezuela had ever seen' (Golinger 2007: 95). The central message was one of despair in the face of imminent catastrophe and irretrievable loss of freedom in a context of regime violence and descent into totalitarianism. One Venezuelan commented: 'Venezuelans are being subjected to a massive Chávez-aversion therapy programme, 24 hours a day, seven days a week, month after month, *ad nauseam*', while

> no less than four television channels [not to mention radio and newspapers] joined together 24 hours a day in December 2002 and January 2003, and broadcast 17,600 propaganda announcements against the government, dedicating all of their programming, without a second of rest, to denigrate the government through yellow journalism, to cause all classes of alarm and rumours to invoke terror. (Golinger 2007: 97, 100)

When dissident military officers rebelled, INTESA, the company in charge of running electronic operations in PDVSA, promptly joined the strike and sabotaged its systems, thus bringing the oil industry to a halt, with devastating losses. Venezuela was hard put to meet its contractual oil obligations and was forced to import oil to do so. Opposition PDVSA managers and employees destroyed or paralysed installations, oil wells and refineries, hijacked Venezuelan oil tankers and convinced insurance companies to declare Venezuelan ports unsafe, in order to prevent foreign tankers from unloading oil. On 13 December 2002, the US State Department called for early elections in order to 'end the political crisis' (Golinger 2007: 93–105). Even after the Supreme Court ordered the ending of the lockout, the private media continued to support it (*El Nacional*: 'The oil lockout will continue until Chávez is out', 21 December 2002). The economic cost to the nation was high: $14,400 million or 27.7 per cent of GDP (according to PDVSA in 2006), while unemployment, officially at 10 per cent, increased to 20 per cent (Weisbrot 2008b: 2). Trade union leader Orlando Castillo estimated that the oil stoppage led to the loss of 700,000 jobs and the closure of 10,000 small businesses (Britto García 2008: 151). In early January 2003, as the stoppage began to run out of steam, the opposition staged a march to the Tiuna Barracks in Caracas, with the deliberate aim of provoking a confrontation with *chavistas* and the forces of order, so as to have casualties for media propaganda purposes. Members of the Metropolitan Police, under the control of opposition mayor Alfredo Peña, shot dead several people (Britto García 2008: 138–52).

The oil lockout was defeated, but the elite did not give up: it now called for a recall referendum. Article 72 of the 1999 constitution provided for the president's legitimacy to be tested through a referendum, but only if 15 per cent of voters' signatures can be collected. Súmate, an NED-funded NGO, undertook the collection in November and December 2003 (barely eight months after the end of the oil lockout). The collection was riddled with irregularities: among those signing were dead people, minors, foreigners, names that did not match identity card numbers, and many evidently signed by the same hand. Deducting these irregularities from the total gathered left the opposition with insufficient numbers. Faced with this setback, the opposition, supported by the Catholic Church and the media, launched a violent campaign to intimidate directors of the Consejo Nacional Electoral (CNE, National Electoral Council) by publishing their photographs and telephone numbers, and to question their institution's impartiality and probity, in order to force the CNE to agree to the referendum. The Coordinadora also staged street marches that ended in clashes, and even tried to break the security perimeter of the G-15 summit taking place in downtown Caracas. Appeals for the military 'to act' resurfaced (Britto García 2008: 173). However, in March 2004, Colin Powell, in a speech to the US Congress, recognized both the CNE decision (to reject 800,000 signatures and to accept 1.9 million as valid) and the appeals process, saying that Chávez was the democratically elected president of all Venezuelans. The unrest came to an immediate end (Britto García 2008: 190).

This setback – and the fact that it had exposed its electoral weakness – led the opposition to adopt new tactics. In May 2004, Venezuelan security forces arrested 130 Colombian paramilitaries, wearing Venezuelan army uniforms, at the Daktari hacienda, near Caracas, the property of Cuban-Venezuelan Roberto Alonso, an individual with strong connections to Colombia and to anti-Castro Cubans in Miami and a leading light in the Coordinadora (Ministerio del Poder Popular para la Comunicación y la Información 2004). The paramilitaries were being trained by Venezuelan army officers. The then governor of Miranda (where Daktari is located), Henrique Mendoza, had already announced that there would be surprises and actions 'about which we cannot comment because we could jeopardize them' (Britto García 2008: 200). Chávez announced that the plan had been to attack both Miraflores and military barracks, and that the wearing of military uniforms had sought to suggest this was an army uprising. When the government asked the private media to broadcast this information to the public, they refused and instead waged a campaign to minimize the plot and distort its purpose. On 10 May, *Tal Cual* talked of 'manipulation', and, despite the evidence, the *Daily Journal* said that 'Chávez alleges coup plot', and a BBC World Service headline noted 'two paramilitaries assassinated', emptying the event of its subversive nature. On 16 May, Globovisión quoted opposition leader, Felipe Mujica, who described the plot as 'the comic strip that the government mounted with the paramilitaries'. The opposition parties also alleged a government plot. US Ambassador Shapiro took a full week to comment, despite an appeal from Venezuela's vice-president. The Church was totally silent (Britto García 2008: 203–4).

With the paramilitary plot foiled, the opposition turned its attention to the recall referendum. It launched a two-pronged attack by questioning the impartiality of both the electoral system and the CNE, hinting heavily that fraud was about to be committed by the government. It also circulated the rumour that the country was on the verge of civil war. Thus, RCTV and other private media showed a commercial that depicted 'a Revolutionary Manual to rob elections' (Britto García 2008: 215). The charges of electoral fraud (before the election actually took place) were strident and repetitive. The Coordinadora – which was still in receipt of NED and USAID support – based its campaign on 'an alternative plan for a transitional post-Chávez government' that was widely believed to have been drafted by officials from the Bush administration (Golinger 2007: 110–11, 114–15). This campaign continued to be accompanied by appeals for violence. In July, Carlos Andrés Pérez, now exiled in Miami, sent the following message: 'Referendum to get Chávez out? Violence will allow us to get rid of him. It's the only way we have. Method? Chávez must die like a dog' (cited in *El Nacional*, 15 July 2004). Some sections of the opposition advocated the suspension of democracy for three years, the abolition of the Supreme Court and a drastic restructuring of the armed forces.

On polling day, Chávez won with a handsome 59 per cent, while the opposition polled 41 per cent – figures confirmed by both the Carter Center and the Organization of American States (OAS). Opposition politicians saturated the airwaves with denunciations of a 'gigantic fraud', and on 25 August were still rejecting the result: 'The people voted SI, the international community voted NO' (Britto García 2008: 258). Calls to take to the streets 'to defend the victory of the people' were made by all Coordinadora leaders, but not a single formal complaint of fraud was lodged with the CNE, the OAS, the Carter Center or any other body. When the US recognized the result of the referendum, one newspaper editorialized that 'Bush has abandoned us' (*El Nuevo País*, 19 August 2004).

The opposition was now uncomfortably aware that it would contest the 2 December 2005 National Assembly elections defeated and in disarray. Its response was to continue to question the probity of the whole process: 'The CNE is discredited to conduct any election' (*El Universal*, 26 September 2004). Thus, it failed to engage in regional elections held on 31 October 2005, preferring to concentrate its fire on the digital fingerprint machines deployed by the CNE as part of the computerization of elections. As a result, *chavistas* won the governorships of twenty out of twenty-two states, and 229 of 355 mayoralties (Britto García 2008: 279). Prospects for the National Assembly did not look at all promising for the opposition, and thus it decided to boycott the election process. The opposition argued, incorrectly, that there were software irregularities in the electronic voting machines, and that the digital fingerprint machines threatened voter confidentiality and should be withdrawn. It expected that its objections would be rebuffed by the government, giving it a good excuse to pull out of the election. It was, therefore, surprised when the complaints were accepted. Nevertheless, the opposition decided to continue with its withdrawal. According to the *New York Times*, the real reason was that 'government candidates would crush them in the election' (Forero 2005). This was an observation confirmed by official EU observers (Degutis 2005). With the opposition abstaining, *chavista* candidates won all 167 National Assembly seats on 2 December. The Coordinadora, having suffered a stream of setbacks since 1998, split into factions. Reflecting on this political meltdown, the Venezuelan elite realized that it would be better to participate in the coming 2006 presidential elections than to maintain its policy of abstention, even if this meant confronting a massively strengthened Chávez.

Chávez received 63 per cent of the vote in 2006, thus resoundingly defeating Manuel Rosales, the opposition candidate, who was forced to concede defeat. This was the first time that an opposition politician had recognized a *chavista* victory. Turnout was 75 per cent, a historic high (Hurtado 2010: 91). *Time* magazine, perhaps unwittingly, interpreted Rosales's acceptance of defeat as a pause in the quest to overthrow Chávez: 'Rosales' brief concession speech suggested the opposition may have resolved to accept that Chávez won't be ousted any time soon' (Gould 2006). Nevertheless, despite grudging acceptance of the result, any conclusion that the opposition had finally embraced democracy would soon be dispelled. In the run-up to the constitutional reform referendum of December 2007, called by the president to reform the 1999 constitution in a radical direction, Venezuela's elite embarked on a semi-insurrectionary strategy aimed at destabilizing the government. It began hoarding food and other daily essentials (including milk, rice, toothpaste, bread and meat), and, in a move that was highly reminiscent of the tactics used by the Chilean right against Allende, students and thugs became involved in 'violent street clashes; targeting pro-Chávez students, police and the National Guard; smashing windows; turning over and setting cars alight; starting other fires; burning tires; throwing rocks and bottles; engaging in a shootout at Caracas' Central University' (Lendman 2008).

Thus, the right's seeming acceptance of the democratic rules of the game was easily substituted by tactics aimed at causing chaos through a national wave of unrest and confrontation. A US Congress report recognized the significance of the students' actions: 'with their ability to mobilize demonstrators, students emerged as perhaps the most prominent and visible opponents of the constitutional reform effort and some observers believe that the reform would not have been defeated had it not been for the students' (Sullivan 2009: 17). Inexperience, inefficiency and corruption among some *chavista* officials no doubt contributed to the sense of uncertainty felt by broad sections of the middle class and the poor. This was relentlessly exploited by the opposition's propaganda machine. However, the opposition was mostly responsible for the atmosphere of crisis and violence. Besides mobilizing students, it persuaded individual shoppers to hoard foodstuffs in opposition to price controls. The Church helped by condemning constitutional reform as morally wrong, while the private media waged their customary incendiary campaign, depicting the proposal as a lethal threat to freedom, human rights, the family, Christian values and such like (Sullivan 2009: 17). An anonymous two-page spread in *Ultimas Noticias* claimed: 'If you are a Mother, YOU LOSE! Because you will lose your house, your family and your children (children will belong to the state)' (Young 2008; and see Ludlam below). It also put the fear of God into readers, arguing they would lose their religious freedoms, their jobs, their businesses; that peasants would lose their land and students their right to decide what to study; that the armed forces would be replaced by militias; and that the Venezuelan currency, the bolívar, would be devalued (Fox 2007). The media also predicted that Chávez would become president for life and, as in Chile in 1970–73 and Nicaragua in the 1980s, Venezuela would be subject to a process of 'Cubanization'. These scare stories were replicated by the world's media, which depicted a government unleashing wanton repression against a rebellious civil society (Young 2008).

The constitutional referendum was defeated, by the smallest of margins, thus becoming the first opposition electoral victory against an otherwise unbeatable Chávez. An analysis of the results shows that, while the opposition vote barely increased, the *chavista* vote went down: 3 million people who had voted for Chávez in the 2006 presidential election did not vote in the constitutional referendum of 2007. That is, the opposition did not win the referendum; the government lost it. With the opposition emboldened, sections of it began to hatch a plot to assassinate the president either by blowing up the presidential plane or the Miraflores Palace in September 2008. Earlier, in January 2008, thirty-seven Colombian paramilitaries had been arrested in the state of Zulia, on the border with Colombia, and found to have all sorts of weapons, including anti-tank missile launchers. It was clear that sections of the opposition did not believe they could win the November regional elections. This proved to be the case, although the opposition's municipal representation was enhanced by victories in key urban areas, notably Caracas, Maracaibo, Miranda, San Cristobal and La Asunción – that is, in the largest cities and in the most economically developed states of the country. This contest was immediately followed by an orgy of wanton violence and destruction, carried out by opposition thugs who went on the rampage, destroying facilities (buildings, computers, vehicles, ambulances and so on) and attacking everything associated with the Bolivarian missions (schools, health centres, educational establishments, community centres for the third age, and especially Cuban doctors). In Caracas itself, newly elected Mayor Antonio Ledezma arbitrarily sacked about 6,000 City Hall workers for being associated with the social missions. Similar sackings took place in other local authorities where the opposition won, affecting thousands more workers. The world's corporate media barely reported these ugly events. It is well to remember that, in all these battles, not only did the opposition have an abundance of resources (funding from the US and private Venezuelan sources, the support of the national and international media, and control over large chunks of the economy, including the banking and commercial sectors) which facilitated its ability to sabotage any policy initiative, but it also had control over important institutions of the state apparatus, such as governorships and municipalities and, crucially, substantial police forces (as we saw above, the Metropolitan Police was the decisive mechanism utilized during the short-lived coup against President Chávez in April 2002, while regional police forces were complicit in the rioting and street battles unleashed by the opposition). It could also count on the assistance of the large number of Colombian paramilitaries operating in the border areas and, according to some reports, in Venezuela's main cities, particularly Caracas (VTV 2009).

On 16 January 2009, key opposition figures met secretly with US State Department officials in Puerto Rico, weeks before the Obama inauguration. On their return to Venezuela, they prepared to contest the 15 February referendum called to pass judgement on the government's proposal to lift term limits on all elected officials, including the president. Two days before the vote, Chávez went on television to announce that a coup involving retired army officers had been foiled (PressTV 2009). The elite obviously feared that it would lose the referendum – a view confirmed when the government received 54 per cent, to the opposition's 45 per cent (Consejo Nacional Electoral 2009). The opposition was also active in mobilizations in the state of Zulia against the government's plan to take control of the nation's ports. In tactics reminiscent of the Bolivian elite (see Tsolakis below), the governor Manuel Rosales led calls for a referendum on whether Zulia should separate from Venezuela. Given that Zulia borders Colombia, this initiative raised deep concerns in Caracas. The Zulia separatist movement is part of the US's promotion of NED-funded 'regional autonomies' in Latin America.

Conclusions

The Venezuelan elite's repudiation of democratic practice began with the overthrow of Pérez Jiménez and its accession to political power in 1958 following the Punto Fijo Pact. Since the election of Hugo Chávez to the presidency, it has explored all possible avenues to overthrow him and his government. There is irrefutable evidence that its methods have involved the traditional coup d'état, bringing about the economy's collapse, ousting through referendums, assassination, and vigorous attempts to discredit the legitimacy of electoral results favourable to the government as a prelude to its overthrow. Venezuela's elite is a highly integrated political and economic class, whose privileges, status, standing and wealth depend on its control over the levers of political power and, crucially, the executive branch of the state. Its dislodgement from national political power since 1998 and its loss of control over the colossal wealth emanating from the country's oil industry have threatened its very existence as a class. What compounds its predicament is the Chávez government's determination to redistribute this wealth among millions of hitherto socially, politically and economically excluded Venezuelans, thus creating a national consensus, in which the elite's previous privileges are not only questioned but rejected by a growing body of politically aware citizens.

Furthermore, whatever its shortcomings – and it has a few – the Bolivarian Revolution is a process involving the massive transformation of the lives of millions of individuals; without such mass support, the government could not have survived the sustained attack of a powerful elite, which enjoys the active complicity of the US. The Bolivarian Revolution's aim of building twenty-first-century socialism, however foggy some of its tenets may be, is substantially more than an abstract aspiration. It involves the restructuring of the economy, including the distribution of millions of hectares of land and the nationalization of the commanding heights of the economy (electricity, steel, transport), which has led to a dramatic reduction in the power of multinational capital (particularly of finance capital and its multilateral bodies, the IMF and the World Bank). Although the Venezuelan economy remains fundamentally capitalist, the logic of neoliberalism is being challenged. The Venezuelan state is being steadily transformed, and many of its permanent institutions no longer protect the interests of the ruling class in a way they used to a decade ago. The objectives of Venezuela's elite and its class interests are fundamentally incompatible with the Bolivarian project – not because the latter is undemocratic, but because its logic points to the elimination of all the elite's privileges. Finally, although Venezuela's elite has been dislodged from national political power and has been greatly weakened by the democratic encroachments of the Bolivarian Revolution, it maintains powerful political and economic levers, which it has deployed effectively to prevent the development of the Bolivarian Revolution. Rather than its self-presentation as a group of beleaguered democrats resisting the authoritarian thrusts of *chavista* populism, the Venezuelan right is more realistically to be viewed as a movement intent on the overthrow of a democratically elected government. To achieve this aim, it has been ready to use any means.

8 | Multilateral lines of conflict in contemporary Bolivia

ANDREAS TSOLAKIS

The election of Evo Morales in December 2005 signalled the conclusion of a long crisis that had defined, for a quarter of a century, the interrelated developmental cycles of political and economic liberalization in Bolivia. Bolivia's society and state are undergoing significant transformations – stimulated by the Morales administration's renationalization of the hydrocarbon, telecommunications and mining sectors, land reform and the struggle for a new constitutional order (Dunkerley 2007). These transformations, however, have generated systematic and sometimes vicious resistance by the Bolivian elites, both within and beyond the state (Eaton 2007). Business organizations, regional civic committees and conservative political parties entrenched in the *Media Luna* (Half Moon) departments of Santa Cruz, Tarija, Beni and Pando in the south and east of the country have spearheaded resistance to Morales-sponsored reforms. Furthermore, bastions of the opposition in the state – the Senate, the prefectures, some municipal administrations and, less blatantly, the Banco Central de Bolivia (BCB, Bolivian Central Bank) – have also resisted social and institutional change. Incessant struggles beyond, but also within the state, have regularly threatened to overwhelm the Morales government (Tsolakis 2008).

These domestic developments must be placed within worldwide and macro-regional processes of change. The election of Evo Morales has formed part of a hemispheric rejection of neoliberalism and US imperialism. It has therefore significantly changed relationships between the Bolivian state, the US and multilateral development institutions (MDIs). This chapter addresses the following questions: how have the US government, the multilateral donor community and transnational capital reacted to Morales' election and his reform project? How, in turn, has the Morales government managed its relationship with transnational elite forces? How have alternative macro-regionalist projects such as the Alianza Bolivariana para los Pueblos de Nuestra América (ALBA, Bolivarian Alliance for the Peoples of Our America) transformed Bolivia's foreign relations?

Despite its substantial shift of military and financial capabilities towards the Middle East, and despite its professed neutrality towards democratically elected governments shaping a 'pink tide' against imperialism, the George W. Bush administration perpetuated the Cold War strategy of antagonizing populist/left-wing governments in its historical backyard (Robinson 1996). I argue that a distinction must be made between the destabilizing tactics of the US and engagement with the Morales administration by the rest of the donor community. The latter has been far more effective in facilitating the Bolivian state's protection of private property and fiscal and monetary discipline. The process of the internationalization of the Bolivian state, begun in 1985, continues and has shaped Morales' reforms. However, this clashes with Bolivia's membership of ALBA alongside the Venezuelan, Cuban, Nicaraguan and Ecuadorian governments, among others. Concurrent internal and external institutional struggles are thus placing the Bolivian state on new, unpredictable developmental paths.

Evo Morales and the Movimiento al Socialismo (MAS, Movement towards Socialism) have demonstrated the capacity to build a hegemonic movement, despite the protracted resistance of Bolivia's elites. Thus, the Bolivian electorate ratified the new constitution by referendum in January 2009, and the MAS won the elections of December 2009 by a landslide, returning Morales to the presidency and securing more than two-thirds control of both houses of representatives (Corte Nacional Electoral 2009). However, its effective containment of the destabilizing actions of business elites has not freed the Morales government from the underlying class and inter-ethnic contradictions, in part because it relies on transnational production networks and the support of global governance institutions to sustain its hegemony.

Contextualizing contemporary changes in Bolivia's foreign relations

The Bolivian state has undergone far-reaching transformations since the 1985 hyperinflationary crisis, which laid bare the insoluble contradictions of state capitalism, and heralded a wave of liberalization under the Paz Estenssoro (1985–89), Paz Zamora (1989–93), Sánchez de Lozada (1993–98; 2002–03) and Banzer/Quiroga (1998–2002) administrations. A radical programme of social restructuring was engineered by the staff of MDIs, in collaboration with a small transnational faction of Bolivian businessmen and technocrats. The latter were considered model students of the Washington Consensus, not merely for their orthodox approach to economic management but also for their creative implementation and elaboration of orthodox macroeconomic policies (Tsolakis 2010).

Neoliberal restructuring sought to reconfigure capital–labour relations, in order to sustain global capital accumulation. Restructuring involved the privatization of accumulation, the creation of a consensual capitalist order and the liberalization of the state. Restructuring was underpinned by a process involving the internationalization of the state, which itself stimulated multilateralism – defined as 'mechanisms for arriving at general policy consensus' through 'cooperation and dealing collectively with conflict' (Cox 1992: 27). I define internationalization broadly as the integration of the state into a global organizational or governance complex, built through intergovernmental collaboration, enjoying supranational authority and tending to 'privilege the investor as dominant political subject' (Gill 2000: 3).

Restructuring created its antithesis in the resistance, which has challenged the transnational bloc both within and beyond the Bolivian state. Attempts to depoliticize the state were systematically undermined by its re-politicization by domestically oriented elites and labour forces (Conaghan and Malloy 1995). Some policies were implemented successfully, while others remained in limbo or were rolled back; some institutions were transformed or eliminated, others remained bastions of continuity. Post-1985 restructuring may be understood as an elite attempt, with the active support of MDIs, to graft modern capitalism and liberalism on to a corrupt, nepotistic and statist social organism. For the implementation of liberal reforms, Bolivian elements of the transnational bloc were part of, and were dependent on, clientelistic social networks, and this explains their failure to legitimize the high social costs of world market integration.

The transnational bloc failed to generate neoliberal hegemony because restructuring impinged on customary elite practices, and because the policies conditioning private-sector development not only failed to increase per capita GDP but also accentuated the concentration of Bolivia's social surplus in transnational capital (World Bank 2000). Social polarization and insufficient growth, compounded by the worldwide economic crisis of the late 1990s, the repression of *cocaleros* (coca farmers) in the Chapare region by paramilitary forces, and the re-composition of labour around indigenist movements in the highlands conditioned the form of subaltern resistance that emerged and eventually overwhelmed elite forces (Hylton and Thomson 2007).

The failure of restructuring was symbolized by the landslide election of Evo Morales. Morales promised to deconstruct the entire political and economic edifice painfully constructed since 1985, by refounding Bolivia through the renationalization of its strategic jewels (gas, mining, telecommunications); by sponsoring the election of a Constituent Assembly; by ridding the state of its corrupt and inefficient ruling elites; by promoting traditional coca production; and by redistributing Bolivia's social surplus to subaltern forces. Morales promised a dual decolonization, by challenging external neo-colonialism and by ending the internal colonialism perpetuated by *criollo* elites (white, of Spanish descent) through the defence of indigenous sovereignties (Webber 2008).

The interconnections between internal and external forms of 'colonialism' identified ought to be emphasized. In this chapter I focus primarily on the latter. I contend that we must break down the apparent unity of the agents of such colonialism, as there are substantial differences between the strategies and policies elaborated and implemented by the US State Department, the transnational corporations (TNCs) and the MDIs towards the Morales government. However, before analysing multilateral lines of conflict, a short exposition of the contemporary domestic balance of social forces is required.

The MAS, the 'plebeian mass' and the conservative opposition

The MAS emerged in the late 1990s, just as Bolivia was undergoing accelerating social change that transformed a self-consciously working-class movement into a heterogeneous and multiple 'plebeian mass' (García Linera, Gutierrez, Prada and Tapia 2000). This compelled the trade union confederations to share centre stage with a plethora of smaller associations, giving a multifaceted and fluid form to subaltern resistance and consequently to *criollo* domination itself. The organizational core of the MAS, the union of *cocaleros* from Chapare, many of them relocated miners who retained their organizational capacity (Crabtree 2005) is only one element in an array of organizations. The MAS won the elections when the lines of conflict had multiplied into innumerable local, sectoral and national/ethnic struggles, and had become potentially unmanageable.

The principal achievement of the MAS has been to harness these various lines of resistance and become the overarching organizational force opposing neoliberal restructuring, internal colonialism and indigenous exclusion (Movimiento al Socialismo 2008). The MAS leadership has achieved the seemingly impossible feat of channelling nationalist, class-based and indigenist discourses into a discursive whole centred on two fundamental issues reminiscent of the National Revolution of

1952: agrarian reform and the renationalization of privatized corporations (Do Alto and Stefanoni 2008). However, just as the MAS was generating this hegemonic movement, the conservative opposition, battered in the 2005 general elections but entrenched in the Senate, in five out of nine prefectures, and in key municipalities, including Cochabamba, Santa Cruz and Tarija, began to coalesce into a liberal, business-oriented political front.

Bolivian *criollo* elites are not immune from internal struggles; transnational and domestic elite blocs have been historically split between the *Altiplano* (Western highlands), the valleys, and the *Oriente* (Eastern lowlands) (Grebe 1983). A significant section of *Cruceño* (Santa Cruz) elites has been demanding sovereignty for its region since the 1950s. The objective of the Comité Civico Pro-Santa Cruz (CCPSC, Civic Committee of Santa Cruz) was to defend the (successful) appropriation of 11 per cent of oil export revenues. This generated significant income for the departmental administration and fed into the regional bloc's separatist sentiments, as its influence over the national government, political parties and business confederations grew. The CCPSC leadership has not bothered to hide its white supremacism: its close relationship with the fascist Falange Socialista Boliviana (Bolivian Socialist Falange) is well documented (Dieterich 2006).

Overshadowing these regional elite rivalries, the election of Morales has arguably unified the class interests of domestically oriented and transnational business groups, and the caste/racial consciousness of *Paceño* (La Paz) and *Cruceño* elites. Convergence against a broader enemy fostered their coalescence around civil and state institutions such as the Poder Democrático Social (PODEMOS, Social Democratic Power) and Unidad Nacional (National Unity) political parties, the Senate, the prefectures, the CCPSC and business organizations. Indeed, a National Democratic Council was formed as an opposition bloc, made up of five provincial governors, business associations, conservative civic groups and PODEMOS legislators. The strategic nucleus has, however, become the CCPSC, which is linked to conservative political parties and business organizations grouped in the Cámara de Industria y Comercio (CAINCO, Council of Industry and Commerce) and the Cámara Agropecuaria de Oriente (Eastern Council of Land and Cattle), among other organizations (Eaton 2007). These business federations constitute a flexible framework for the union of foreign TNCs (primarily in hydrocarbons and banking) and domestic export-led agribusiness, and constitute a formidable anti-MAS platform. The CAINCO and CCPSC have also engineered a strategy of direct diplomatic visits by business leaders to the European Commission, the US government, Brazil and Argentina, to muster support for the protection of private property and to expound the autonomist demands of the *Media Luna* (interview with European Commission official, 30 March 2007).[1]

The CCPSC does not merely resist the MAS through formal channels and an autonomist discourse, but has also employed terrorist tactics through its youth organization, the Unión Juvenil Cruceñista (UJC, Santa Cruz Youth Union). Since 2003, the UJC has intimidated indigenous immigrants and particularly MAS supporters, and has kidnapped and beaten Cuban doctors who are providing medical services to low-income patients in Santa Cruz. On 10 September 2008, it raided state-owned agencies in the city, including the television station, the telecommunications corporation Entel, and the tax-collection agency. Described by the media as 'isolated' acts by 'uncontrolled' youth, these actions were designed to provoke a coercive government response and thereby generate international and domestic support for the CCPSC (Council on Hemispheric Affairs 2008).

The concurrent upheavals in the *Altiplano* and the entrenchment of *criollo* elites in the *Media Luna* increased the centrifugal tendencies of the nation. The *criollo* bloc galvanized a significant section of the urban population in the *Media Luna* in 2007 and 2008 by emphasizing the racial distinction between *cambas* ('natives' of the lowlands) and *kollas* (indigenous peoples from the highlands), denouncing the invasion of their territory by the latter and proposing internal migration controls. *Criollo* secessionist ambitions have been undermined by Aymara and Quechua immigration from the *Altiplano* since the 1970s. Those latter communities' support for the MAS, at least in rural areas and in the extensive shanty towns surrounding Santa Cruz, stems from Morales' reform programme, including renationalizations, land reform and an increase in the legal minimum wage to 577 bolivianos (BOB) ($77). The government has also introduced the universal *Renta Dignidad* (dignified pension), involving a monthly payment of BOB 200 ($26), financed by gas profits and costing $260 million annually. It has implemented the *Bono Madre-Niño* (the Mother-Child Voucher): free healthcare to pregnant women and BOB 1,800 ($234) over two years for the child. This is expected to cost $100 million per year, and has secured World Bank financing. Finally, it has created the *Bono Juancito Pinto,* which allocates BOB 200 to each primary schoolchild to encourage attendance. These

1 Interviews referred to in the text were conducted with current or former high-level European Union officials and delegates. All sources remain anonymous.

reforms have been instrumental in restraining labour demands and securing the electoral support of the poor.

US interference

The domestic opposition was defused by the recall referendums in August 2008, the January 2009 ratification of the new constitution and the December 2009 re-election of Morales (Crabtree 2008; 2009b). Before the Constituent Assembly opened, the opposition had been demanding the *capitalia plena* (full capital) – the transfer of the executive and legislative branches of the state from La Paz to the nineteenth-century capital, Sucre. The object was to shift the administrative centre of gravity away from La Paz and undercut Aymara influence. It would also add prefectural support to the *Media Luna* and create difficulties for the MAS, which controlled the prefecture of Sucre. The strategy galvanized the Civic Committee of Sucre, which duly initiated a debate in the Constitutional Assembly, which convened in Sucre. The MAS delegates' rejection of its demand incensed the committee, which organized violent protests in the city, leading to four deaths and hundreds of injuries in August 2007. This forced the Constitutional Assembly's suspension for one month in September. As violence was spiralling out of control, in November 2007, Morales announced a recall referendum – on the president, vice-president and all prefects – to be held in August 2008. The outcome – an endorsement of the Morales government – bolstered the MAS and its commitment to constitutional reform.

Domestic struggles do not occur in an international vacuum, but must be directly related to US policy in the region. The US government financed the repression of coca farmers and backed repressive Bolivian governments in the late 1990s and early 2000s. As a consequence, it can be blamed for the persistence of poverty and inequality in Bolivia. Popular anger propelled Morales on to the national and international political stages, and led his administration to indiscriminately – and perhaps inappropriately – link neoliberal restructuring to US dominance over the IMF, the World Bank and the Inter-American Development Bank (IDB). Since Morales' election, the US government has maintained a relatively low public profile, which observers have interpreted as a 'wait and see' approach (Gamarra 2007: 3). Empirical evidence nonetheless demonstrates that the US State Department has sought to covertly undermine the Morales administration. On 1 September 2008, Morales expelled Philip Goldberg, the US ambassador, for seeking to conspire against democracy and destabilize the country. This prompted Venezuela's Hugo Chávez to follow suit in solidarity, and the US to declare the Bolivian envoy in Washington, DC *persona non grata*. Morales later expelled Ambassador Goldberg's successor and the Drug Enforcement Agency (DEA). The Bush administration responded with a series of aggressive actions, further souring relations. In September 2008, it placed Bolivia on a counter-narcotics blacklist, and later suspended the country from the Andean Trade Promotion and Drug Eradication Act, the preferential trade agreement through which, between 2002 and 2007, the US became Bolivia's second-largest trading partner in the region, for failing 'to cooperate with the United States on important efforts to fight drug trafficking' (Council on Hemispheric Affairs 2009). How did US ambassadors and the DEA conspire against democracy in Bolivia?

A string of gaffes by US embassy staff that revealed the covert activities of the United States Agency for International Development (USAID) led Evo Morales to declare, in August 2007: 'I cannot understand how some ambassadors dedicate themselves to politics, and not diplomacy, in our country ... That is not called cooperation. That is called conspiracy' (Dangl 2008a). In July and again in November 2007, at least three Peace Corps volunteers and a Fulbright researcher were asked by US embassy staff to provide information on the identity, whereabouts and residence of Venezuelans and Cubans they met in Bolivia (*Democracy Now!* 2008). Ambassador Goldberg held secret meetings with the prefect of Santa Cruz, Rúben Costa, and the leadership of the CCPSC, directly prior to a wave of opposition-sanctioned violence in August and September 2008 following the recall referendum. The takeover of factories, roadblocks, the sabotage of gas pipelines and the unprovoked killing of thirty indigenous farmers by individuals whom the government described as 'hit men' employed by the opposition, justified Morales' decision to declare martial law in the northeastern department of Pando. The meetings between Goldberg and the CCPSC leadership suggested that these terrorist activities had at least received the US ambassador's blessing, if not the US embassy's financial and organizational support (Council on Hemispheric Affairs 2009).

After the 2002 presidential election, when Morales came second, the MAS was identified by the US government as Bolivia's most powerful anti-systemic force. A declassified 2002 memo explained that a 'USAID political party reform project aims at implementing an existing Bolivian law that would ... over the long run, help build moderate, pro-democracy political parties that can serve as a counterweight to the radical MAS or its successors' (Dangl 2008b). Thereafter, the Bush administration provided direct financial support and strategic advice to conservative parties and associations. In 2004, USAID established a special Office of Transition Initiatives (OTI) in Bolivia which, in its own words, 'intervenes rapidly and undertakes quick-impact interventions through short-term grants that catalyze broader change' (Weisbrot 2008a). Since 2006, this 'support for democracy' has taken the form of strategies promoting administrative and fiscal decentralization, in order to consolidate state institutions that challenge the central government. The OTI transferred at least $4.5 million to foundations and NGOs used by the opposition and white separatist organizations, and to the four autonomist prefects of the *Media Luna*. Juan Ramón Quintana, minister of the presidency, calculated that, of the $134 million of USAID financial assistance provided in Bolivia in 2007, $89 million was spent on such activities (Bolpress 2007). This funding was spent undermining the legitimacy of the government through media campaigns soiling Morales' image and introducing issues such as the *capitalia plena*, departmental autonomy and the Venezuelan 'conspiracy', seeking to galvanize parochial 'popular' movements and foster instability, and supporting the main opposition bodies, PODEMOS, the civic committees and departmental prefects (Center for Economic and Policy Research 2008). The US-based National Endowment for Democracy, active in the coup d'état against Venezuelan President Hugo Chávez in 2002, has also organized workshops and panels to promote decentralization and polarization in Bolivia. The US ambassador's personal role in the 1990s in the transitions in Croatia and Bosnia (where regionalist discourses acquired more political weight) and the active participation in the workshops of *criollos* of Croatian descent and of Catalan researchers fuelled accusations of attempts to Balkanize Bolivia (Chossudovsky 2008). Additionally, since the 1980s, both USAID and the DEA have funnelled assistance funds and provided training and weapons to special police units, purportedly to fight narco-trafficking. However, in light of its spying and subversive activities, it may be inferred that the US government has actually been trying to divide and destabilize the coercive apparatus of the Bolivian state (Weisbrot 2008a).

The MAS has dealt with these provocations in a number of ways. It signed a Complementary Accord to the Basic Technical Cooperation Agreement on Defence between the Republic of Bolivia and the Bolivarian Republic of Venezuela – a mutual defence agreement, which promises the support of the Venezuelan military in the case of an invasion or a civil war (Council on Hemispheric Affairs 2006). Additionally, many Venezuelans and Cubans are undertaking humanitarian work in Bolivia. These include 2,000 Cuban doctors, who provide free services in rural areas, in particular in the Santa Cruz region, the bastion of *criollo* opposition to land reform. It is possible that some of these activities are not strictly humanitarian, but are designed to provide military and strategic support to the government in the *Oriente*. According to sources close to the president, at least fifty Venezuelan economic and military advisers were active in the presidential palace and key ministries (personal interview, summer 2007). Bolivia also began an ambitious military procurement programme, using Venezuelan loans of at least $50 million. Securing the support of the army has been the cornerstone of the government's struggle against the destabilizing activities of the opposition and the US government. Until now, the army has obeyed Morales' orders. It took over the facilities of private hydrocarbons corporations upon the announcement of their nationalization in May 2006; it deployed in mining areas to restore order in the face of violent skirmishes between mining cooperatives and state-employed miners in February 2007; and it implemented the government's state of siege in Pando in September 2008.

TNCs, the donor community and the ALBA: multilateral lines of conflict

By contrast, European policymakers and the staff of MDIs have exhibited a more subtle response and have worked towards stabilizing Bolivia. There appears to be reluctance on the part of the donor community to endorse the fragmentation of Bolivia. Instead of antagonizing the new, democratically elected government, they have engaged with it, waiving more than half of Bolivia's foreign debt (from $4.942 billion in 2005 to $2.142 billion two years later), including the entire stock of debt outstanding to the World Bank, the IMF and the IDB (Gamarra 2007: 43). The European Commission has increased its annual grants to the Bolivian Treasury and NGOs since the mid-1990s. While ostensibly respecting the will of the people, MDIs have restricted their role to locking Bolivia into the structure of global capitalist production, by securing the government's commitment to fiscal and monetary stability, free trade and the defence of private property, as well as fighting against the expropriation of the assets of TNCs and promoting public–private partnerships between private and state-owned mining and hydrocarbons corporations (International Monetary Fund 2009). Depoliticized state agencies, chief among them the BCB, have continued monetarist economic management and price control policies. Indeed, Article 327 of the new constitution enshrines the depoliticization of the BCB (Asamblea Constituyente de Bolivia 2007). The international exchange system remains free of restrictions on current payments and transfers, and no significant controls on capital flows have been imposed (International Monetary Fund 2009). Interestingly, a pillar of the MAS's programme has become macroeconomic stability, in stark contrast to its more radical electoral rhetoric (Movimiento al Socialismo 2008). The ghost of hyperinflation and the debt crisis of the early 1980s continues to haunt the government, which is 'fully aware of the need to maintain macroeconomic stability' and 'to continue with fiscal consolidation efforts' (International Monetary Fund 2009: 3). Far from delinking from the multilateral institutional complex it inherited, the Morales government cooperates with MDIs and the European Commission, in part to undercut US dominance (interviews with officials of the European Commission in Bolivia, May–December 2007).

The MAS's economic programme may be said to have deepened the structural presence of capital in the Bolivian economy. Its macroeconomic programme recalls Bolivia's pre-1985 state capitalism model, but it is now couched in new rhetoric calling for the invention of a vague transition to socialism in the form of 'Andean-Amazonian capitalism'. This would be founded upon large private and public corporations; a primitive capitalism centred on family and kinship networks based on artisan and small commerce; and a communitarian economic organization shaped by autonomous territorial sovereignties. The cornerstone of this form of capital accumulation would remain, as in the 1930s, 1950s and late 1960s, the nationalization of strategic resources. Vice-President García Linera boasted in 2007: 'the Bolivian state has thus increased its control of the GDP by 6–7 per cent, to 19 per cent today. Our objective is to reach 30 per cent' (Do Alto and Stefanoni 2008: 99). It is thus no surprise that the IMF (2007; 2009) lauded the MAS leadership's fight against corruption and waste in state institutions and the increased efficiency of tax-collecting agencies, while noting persistent patronage. Speaking on Bolivia's national day in 2007, Morales emphasized that international financial institutions are no longer imposing conditions for economic and state restructuring, because Bolivia is already achieving responsible fiscal and monetary policies. The core tenets of neoliberalism – monetary and fiscal discipline and free trade – remain intact (International Monetary Fund 2007; 2009). This does not preclude an improvement in the conditions of workers, but only so long as terms of trade remain positive. Low economic growth between 1985 and 2005 barely matched population growth, signifying the stagnation of real wages. The principal historical constraints on accumulation in Bolivia have been deteriorating terms of trade, corruption and legal insecurity, and above all social instability

(World Bank 2005). Returns on investment outside the hydrocarbon and banking sectors have historically been hindered by tense Bolivian labour relations. Low levels of foreign direct investment (FDI) and domestic capital formation as a proportion of GDP were characteristic of the entire 1985–2005 era, and this reflected low business confidence.

What does this tell us about the relationship between the Morales administration and transnational capital? First, that the Morales government did not cause low business confidence, nor did it exacerbate already highly volatile social relations. Secondly, that the threat of capital flight and economic collapse – brandished by right-wing newspapers and European leaders in May 2006 in the face of nationalization – remains low, considering the quasi-exclusive dependence of growth on hydrocarbons and mining, and the unprecedented global upsurge in demand for oil, gas, minerals and metals – an upsurge that has only been partially halted by the global financial crisis. Even without significant private domestic capital formation – a situation prevalent before Morales' election and not caused by the MAS government – GDP growth has been more robust (4.5 per cent in 2007; 6.1 per cent in 2008; 3.4 per cent in 2009), as the value of exports quadrupled to $6.5 billion between 2004 and 2008, generating an unprecedented positive trade balance, at the same time as corporate taxation was increasing significantly. Nationalization does have international repercussions, as it affects the interest of TNCs controlling the strategic hydrocarbons, telecommunications and electricity sectors. The nationalization of extractive industries by Supreme Decree was regarded as an exercise in redistributive justice against abusive exploitation by TNCs. Resistance by US and European governments to the nationalization of oil and gas was lukewarm, in part because of the awareness that privatization contracts signed in 1996 had grossly underestimated natural gas reserves. And TNCs have already multiplied the returns on their investments while continuing to infringe workers' rights and cause large-scale environmental damage. Most importantly, nationalization does not constitute a full-on expropriation of foreign property – a distinction Morales emphasized. The Bolivian administration implemented a Venezuelan-style nationalization, by which those TNCs that operate gas fields and transfer ownership of the gas produced to the Yacimientos Petrolíferos Fiscales Bolivianos (YPFB, Bolivian State Petrol Reserves) must pay 82 per cent of their profits to the state, instead of 50 per cent before nationalization and 18 per cent before the 2004 gas referendum (Gray 2007). For Jorge Alvarado, president of the YPFB, 'The days of superprofits are over. But even at 18 per cent of the value of gas being produced, the foreign companies will enjoy 20–25 per cent profits' (Lewis 2006). Moreover, the government took a controlling stake in four TNCs operating in the energy sector, and on 1 May 2008 announced the renationalization of the telecommunications company Entel (owned by Italy-based Stet) – a move that antagonized both the European Commission and the Italian government. In 2007, the government withdrew from the World Bank's International Centre for Settlement of Investment Disputes, evading arbitration in favour of Stet (International Institute for Sustainable Development 2007). The timing of these waves of nationalization demonstrated an assertion of government power and a commitment to reform in the face of opposition forces.

Despite threats of capital flight and legal challenges, all TNCs investing in the hydrocarbons sector remained in Bolivia and accepted the new contractual terms, an important political victory for Morales. FDI increased consistently, to $1.302 billion in 2008 – back to the record levels of the years of capitalization and privatization ($1.026 billion in 1998) (Instituto Nacional de Estadísticas 2009). Although FDI was significantly lower in 2009 (only $322 million by the end of the second quarter), it remained relatively high by Bolivian standards. TNCs appeared to have understood that the legitimacy of the new Bolivian administration would enhance the social stability necessary for profitable investment. Most importantly, booming Chinese and Indian demand has rendered such ventures highly profitable. Indeed, with oil prices well above $70 a barrel (affecting the price of gas, too), legal conflicts between the MAS and the opposition (with accompanying roadblocks and regional protests) did not affect TNC investment plans and have barely impinged on output in the energy industry (International Monetary Fund 2009). TNCs have also been lining up to invest in the mining sector, with contracts for future investments worth $2.9 billion. This was highly important for a national economy valued at $18 billion in 2009. Crucially, the current revival of mining production in Oruro and Potosí (with regional growth rates of around 18 per cent and 24 per cent, respectively, in 2008), plus the potential exploitation of globally significant deposits of lithium in the Salar of Uyuni, may aid in rebalancing the economic relationship between *Altiplano* and *Media Luna* (Agencia Bolivaniana de Información 2009).

The extent to which the global economic crisis will affect Bolivian production relations in the future remains to be seen, but it is bound to undermine the transient hegemony achieved by the MAS. Bolivia's limited integration into global capital markets has partially insulated it from the global turmoil. This was demonstrated by the fact that GDP growth fell to 3 per cent in 2009, yet Bolivia did not enter recession. Sharp, if temporary, declines in commodity prices for its main exports began to have a negative impact on FDI and fiscal revenue, although exports maintained adequate levels through 2009 and the country achieved a trade surplus, and Bolivia narrowly avoided deflation for the year, with a 0.29 per cent inflation rate at year end (Banco Central de Bolivia 2010). The IMF expected growth to rebound in 2010, accompanied by moderate inflation, though it suggested that any current account deficit would reduce the government's margins of manoeuvre in its ambitious social programmes and mean that the government, in order to control inflation and sustain GDP growth, could be disciplined into implementing wage restraint and improving the investment climate (International Monetary Fund 2009: 4).

ALBA

The continued integration of the Bolivian state into global governance networks contradicts the alternative macro-regional project it has built in collaboration with Venezuela, Cuba, Nicaragua, Ecuador and others. The ALBA, the alternative to George W. Bush's proposed Free Trade Area of the Americas, is founded on a creative approach to regional integration that aims to dissolve the cash nexus binding the world market, through the creation of alternative, de-monetarized and expanding circuits of international exchange, based on solidarity and welfare provision – the exchange of oil for medical services is the conventional example (Harris and Azzi 2006). However, three fundamental constraints have undermined this project. First, ALBA's exchanges of services are quantitatively too limited to remove the pressure of monetary discipline – they are just drops of water in a sea of market relations. Secondly, the other regionalist Chávez–Morales initiative, ALBA's Banco del Sur investment bank, which seeks to provide an alternative to IMF lending, undermines the ALBA by incorporating a notoriously conservative government (Colombia) and by offering microcredit to small entrepreneurs. This latter factor is a striking example of the expansion of capital and capitalist class formation (primitive accumulation) into rural areas (Chu 2005), including indigenous communities, which undermines the communitarian production purportedly defended by the MAS. The Banco del Sur's capital of $8 billion is tiny by comparison with that of conventional development institutions, and its political impact is likely to be minimal. Thirdly, and most importantly, the Bolivarian bloc intersects with a multilevel regional and global governance complex which dwarfs it and its potential. Bolivia remains linked to global institutions, notably the United Nations, the IMF and the World Bank, along with regional institutions such as Mercosur and the Andean Community, and this legally constrains Bolivian state policy. Furthermore, most Latin American governments have refused to join ALBA, preferring the consolidation of Mercosur and continental energy integration (the construction of a pipeline from Venezuela to Argentina being an example).

It is worth remembering that, especially since the late 1970s, Bolivia's most fundamental economic constraints have been generated by Argentinian, Brazilian and Chilean imperialism rather than US dominance. Until the mid-1990s, 40 per cent of foreign exchange reserves depended on gas exports that were directed exclusively to Argentina. Following the construction of a gas pipeline to Brazil in 1997–98 using a $130 million World Bank loan, Brazil became Bolivia's largest trade partner and Petrobras (the state-owned Brazilian company) one of its principal sources of FDI. Commodity exports (agricultural products and gas) are primarily targeted at Bolivia's direct neighbours, notably Argentina and Brazil. The latter's interests lie in sustaining a cheap, steady supply extracted from the Bolivian gas fields by Petrobras. Bolivia antagonized Brazil in 2006, when it demanded a substantial increase in oil prices; it then forced Petrobras to sell Bolivia's two biggest refineries to the YPFB in 2007. In geo-economic terms, Brazil and Argentina are far more relevant than Venezuela and Cuba, or indeed Chile (the historic enemy) – a reality that is borne out by the increasing cooperation between Bolivia and Mercosur.

The principal impediment to Bolivia's economic development remains its relationship with its direct neighbours. Morales' nationalist logic of emancipation confronts neighbours with higher levels of development and hence far greater economic, institutional and military power. Crabtree (2006) rightly emphasizes the tensions generated by a nationalistic social model infringing the economic interests of bordering national elites. In this context, the support of Chávez has been important in securing regional acquiescence to Bolivia's reforms – in particular nationalization – and multilateral support against the secessionist ambitions of the *Media Luna*. It is also difficult for governments in Brazil and Argentina, themselves struggling against US imperialism (albeit in a reformist manner), to justify their own societies' unequal relationship with Bolivia.

Latin American regionalization is therefore bolstered by the participation of the Bolivian government in Chávez's Bolivarian federation, and by the official acquiescence of Argentinian and Brazilian administrations (Sader 2005). An unprecedented movement towards inter-state cooperation and peaceful conflict resolution among new Latin American elites may sustain the formation of a macro-regional bloc with enhanced power in the global appropriation of social surplus, recasting the existing internationalization of the Bolivian state.

Conclusions

The internationalization of the Bolivian state has been distorted by new, regional lines of governance and by the penetration of subaltern social forces into state institutions. In turn, these new and unpredictable institutional relations have stimulated US attempts to interfere in the reform process. The MAS has suffered from protracted resistance to the implementation of its short-term policy objectives by elites entrenched in various state institutions (prefectures, the Senate and minority groups in the Constituent Assembly) and civil organizations (regional civic committees and business associations). The destabilizing tactics employed by the opposition have received systematic technical and financial support from the US government, which has taken the dangerous path of fuelling racist movements and discourses that promote civil war. The MAS leadership has faced important threats to its survival, yet it has remained in government and maintained its authority. This resilience has been fostered primarily by unprecedented favourable terms of trade, and by implementing popular social reforms, including a new constitution, land reform, nationalizations à la Chávez, a universal pension scheme, and increases in the legal minimum wage. However these reforms have, in part, been made possible by the generosity of the donor community. I have argued that its continued collaboration with MDIs has safeguarded the Morales government against the subversive activities of the US embassy and business elites in Santa Cruz. Morales' willingness to sustain fiscal and monetary discipline, free trade and joint ventures between state-owned and privately run companies induced MDIs to gradually reduce Bolivia's external debt burden, which in turn has released the fiscal resources required for the social investments currently galvanizing mass support for the government. The institutional interlocking of MDIs with key central government ministries – in particular the finance, commerce and planning ministries, the BCB and depoliticized regulatory agencies – has persisted and has provided a much needed buffer against US-promoted subversion (International Monetary Fund 2007; 2009). This trajectory is likely to continue and intensify with an ongoing worldwide economic crisis, which has bolstered the political weight of the IMF and the World Bank and which is leading Latin American governments (including the Bolivian) to adopt a more conciliatory tone towards the 'instruments of the Empire'. Indeed, supranational 'legal padlocks' have effectively neutralized the revolutionary changes desired by some members of the Morales government.

Although the financial, technical and diplomatic support provided by the Venezuelan government has interfered with the smooth functioning of collaborative practices with MDIs, Bolivia's alliance with Caracas has offered relative protection from US encroachment and valuable support in its claims against its neighbours. It has also sustained macro-regional integration and stability. Neighbouring governments – in particular Venezuela – and MDIs have helped to undercut the articulation of a right-wing autonomist project in the *Media Luna*. Their overt opposition to any form of secessionism in Bolivia's lowlands has thus neutralized the destabilizing tactics employed by the US. There were hopes that the Obama administration would inaugurate a new partnership with Bolivia, and the conciliatory words of Assistant Secretary of State for Western Hemisphere Affairs Thomas Shannon during a visit to Bolivia in May 2009 helped to bolster this belief; but bilateral negotiations failed to result in a single concrete agreement on any of the issues dividing the two governments. These included the reinstatement of the DEA, the extradition of Gonzalo Sánchez de Lozada (the former Bolivian president accused of genocide against the indigenous nations) and the continuation of US technical and financial support for conservative movements and political parties (Council on Hemispheric Affairs 2009).

Multilateral lines of conflict, created by geo-economic shifts and transnational political alliances, are currently in flux. It is a matter for conjecture whether the Morales government will be able to foster a sustainable form of Andean capitalism in an unpredictable economic and international environment defined by ecological degradation, US overstretch, European stagnation, unstable Chinese and Indian growth and the social experiments engendered by the 'pink tide' in Latin America. We can, however, expect that the progressive policies implemented by the MAS will continue to generate protracted resistance from conservative elites and will remain conditioned by the vagaries of world market prices and the goodwill of MDIs. Furthermore, knowledge of leaps forward, stagnation and retreats in neighbouring countries will affect expectations and action in Bolivia (and vice versa), reflecting the transnational interconnections between domestic contexts. The political prospects for conservative forces in Bolivia appear dire. To use Gramscian terminology, the ratification of the new constitution closed a cycle of wars both 'of position' and 'of movement'. The firm control of both houses of congress by the MAS following the 2009 elections, buttressed by the indubitable popularity of Morales on the one hand and by unprecedented capital accumulation on the other, temporarily stabilized the political scene and crystallized a (transient) hegemonic order organized by the MAS. The right is divided, subdued by the MAS's electoral victories (including unexpectedly high levels of support in Bolivia's lowlands, considered bastions of conservatism), by the apparent success of Morales' nationalization and welfare measures, and by the delegitimization of neoliberal discourse in the wake of the global economic crisis. Its activities are currently confined to a protracted defence of property rights (particularly of land resources), to media attacks on the government and to a slow and painful political reorganization involving the rearticulation of liberal ideas. However the economic reverberations of a possible 'double-dip' global recession and emerging protests linked to the government's inadequate or sluggish investments in certain localities may help to accelerate the eventual reconstitution of Bolivia's conservative forces (Hatheway 2010).

9 | Right-wing opposition as counter-revolution: the Cuban case

STEVE LUDLAM

Neither the left in Latin America nor its supporters elsewhere need history lessons about the reactions of which the right is capable when ruling-class interests are threatened, especially when, as has frequently been the case, the right has the active partnership of, or acts directly as the agent for, the US government. The 2002 coup in Venezuela, the 'Pando Massacre' in Bolivia in 2008, the 2009 coup in Honduras and the attempted coup in Ecuador in 2010 are but the most recent and extreme examples (at the time of writing) of the continuing vulnerability of the left, especially the electoral left, in the face of such reaction. The mere fact that Cuba has successfully resisted decades of violent right-wing opposition justifies its inclusion in this book. In this chapter, the term 'right wing' is preferred to conservative. Right-wing Cuban exiles had hoped that by now the term 'conservative' would have come to apply to irreconcilable Stalinists in a post-communist Cuba, in the same way as it has been applied to the remnants of Soviet-bloc communist parties. Here, though, 'right wing' refers to Cuban political forces seeking 'regime change': the replacement of Cuba's constitutional 'socialist state of workers' with a capitalist state and multiparty liberal democracy. It would, of course, be foolish to imagine that social conservatism has disappeared on the island: any regular visitor can observe it in deep-rooted attitudes to religion, race and gender, in everyday conversation about the music played on buses, the behaviour of young people, and gay storylines in the Cuban TV soap opera.

Politically, though, Cuba's right has been exceptional in several ways. First, and most obviously, Cuba has not held multiparty elections since 1948. None was held in the wake of the 1959 revolution, and since its constitutional referendum of 1976 Cuba has had a no-party electoral system within a one-party state, in which the Communist Party enjoys the status of 'the highest leading force of society and of the state' (Republic of Cuba 1992: 5). With social ownership of the economy and most media, right-wing politics cannot take the forms familiar in liberal-democratic states. Secondly, in the context of US hostility and US-based terrorist attacks, right-wing opposition inside Cuba is treated by the state as counter-revolutionary. Since the defeat of the last counter-revolutionary guerrillas in the Escambray mountains in the 1960s, there has been no serious right-wing presence inside Cuba. And although some internal dissidents distance themselves from US intervention, the commitment of US 'Cuba transition' funds to oppositional civil society activity makes right-wing activism inside Cuba easy to classify as mercenary and treasonous. So Cuban right-wing politics have been led overwhelmingly by US-based exiles, who have forged a powerful lobby to influence a US Cuba policy that is characterized by the principal objective of 'regime change' and restoration of exiles' properties. As a study written for the US Army War College in the early 1990s put it:

> It would be going too far to say that our Cuban policy has been 'made in Miami'. Nevertheless, Cuban American influence – primarily through the Cuban American National Foundation (CANF) – has been palpable and has strengthened the hard-line inclinations already dominant in US foreign policy circles. This influence has been all the more potent because there is no political constituency for a 'safer' or more flexible line on Cuba ... The upshot is that the Cuban American community has been able to exercise a virtual veto over US policy. (cited in Arboleya 2002: 202)

Thirdly, US-based intervention against the Cuban revolution gives it a wider significance in Latin America, since its forms, ranging historically through destabilization and attempted invasion, sabotage and terrorism, to strategies based on promoting an oppositional 'civil society', have for decades constituted some of the principal US methods against the left across the region. This chapter will outline the origin of Cuba's counter-revolutionary right and its domination of the Cuban exile community; factors underpinning its domination; and signs of cracks in the right-wing exile monolith in the twenty-first century.

Empires and dictators

Historically, Cuba's right, as elsewhere in Latin America, was associated with loyalty to the Spanish empire and other strong states (notably the US); with the dominance of landowners; with an anti-Enlightenment alliance with the Catholic hierarchy; and with murderous defence of slavery. In the republic, such politics produced the 1912 slaughter of the black protest party, the Independent Party of Colour, and the emergence of fascist groups under the dictatorship of Machado, the 'tropical Mussolini' (Castro Fernández 2008; Cupull and González 2005). The practice of normal electoral politics was regularly crushed by US occupations and by the Machado and Batista dictatorships and their assassins (Gott 2004: ch. 4; Thomas 2001: books 4–7). Cuba's elitist governance was further debauched by corruption and clientelism, by the US mafia and by home-grown political *gangsterismo* (Cirules 2004: 89, 156; Pérez 1995: chs 8–10). The absence of a mass Catholic vote underpinning a particular conservative party may have been partly a consequence of the unpredictable opportunism of politicians in the 'pseudo-republic', but it also reflected the Catholic hierarchy's elitist alliances with Cuba's ruling class.

Post-revolutionary right-wing exile leaders were notoriously competitive as they jostled for US support. But they shared one determination: the restoration of their property and power, by any means necessary. Normalization of relations between the US and revolutionary Cuba has been violently opposed. Initially, exiles quickly produced hundreds of armed groupings, inextricably linked to the CIA's secret 'dirty war' against Cuba and featuring hundreds of bombings and arson attacks on Cuban targets, as US and Cuban agencies have detailed (Kornbluh 1998; Elliston 1999; Rodríguez 1999; Escalante 2004; 2006). The chief executive of the Bacardí rum company actually bought a B-26 bomber to attack Cuba's oil refineries (Calvo Ospina 2000: 19). When preparing the 1961 Bay of Pigs invasion, the CIA organized armed groups inside and outside Cuba. Prominent exile families sent their young men to join the invasion force, and the ensuing fiasco left a tenth of the invasion force dead and over 1,100 taken prisoner. An inflamed right blamed President John F. Kennedy's refusal to commit the US air force to battle.

Kennedy's agreement with the USSR to end support for invasion plans – part of the 1962 missile crisis settlement – ended right-wing hopes of a rapid restoration of their rule in Cuba. But right-wing violence simply changed form. Some joined the US Special Forces (H. Jones 2008: 151). Many became freelance terrorists. Terrorist attacks on revolutionary Cuba have claimed 3,478 lives and have injured 2,099 people (Rodríguez Cruz 2005: 271). Proportionately, this is as if some 95,000 US citizens had been killed by Cuban attacks (none has). Attacks have included chemical and biological weapons, from napalm bombs to crop viruses and deadly human viruses which affected over 300,000 Cubans in 1981 and killed 158, including 101 children (Rodríguez Cruz 2005: 134; Bolender 2010: 113–21). In 1976, a bomb destroyed a Cuban airliner, killing all seventy-three people on board (León Cotayo 2006). It had been planned by the two most prominent Cuban-American terrorists, whose involvement with the US state is detailed by a former US Head of Interest Section (de facto ambassador) in Cuba:

> Many Cuban exile terrorists got their start by working with the CIA on acts of violence against targets in Cuba. But as the CIA closed its base in Miami and de-emphasized such tactics, its former 'operatives', among them Orlando Bosch and Luis Posada Carriles, turned freelance. Declassified CIA and FBI documents leave no doubt that Bosch and Posada were then involved in acts of terrorism, such as the bombing of a Cubana airliner in 1976 with the loss of 73 innocent lives ... Posada acknowledged to *The New York Times* that he was responsible for the 1997 bombings of tourist hotels in Havana, resulting in the death of an Italian tourist and the wounding of several other people. (Smith, Harrison and Adams 2006: 1)

It would thus be a mistake to imagine that the right abandoned terrorist tactics in the 1960s. As expectation grew in Miami in the 1990s that Cuba would collapse, new terrorism campaigns against Cuban tourism and visiting foreign tourists began, in an attempt to cut off a potential economic lifeline. The Cuban National Assembly reported over sixty such incidents in the 1990s and into the 2000s (National Assembly of Cuba 2006). As one Cuban anti-terrorism agent reported, Cuba, its tourists and their aircraft became targets in a 'free fire zone' (Ludlam 2009).

Right-wing hegemony in 'Exilio City'

While united over Cuba policy, the growing exile community was ideologically diverse (García 1996: 122–3). But public exile politics have rarely reflected this diversity: 'Perhaps the main characteristic of the diverse Cuban American community in Miami over the past forty years has been the domination by the exile minority waging permanent war against Castro' (Levine 2001: 218). This domination was ruthlessly forged to ensure that the Cubans in 'Exilio City' perceived themselves as 'exiles' rather than mere 'immigrants' (Ortega 1998: 45). The first exiles were the *batistianos*, officials and supporters of Batista's dictatorship, determined to recover their power and property (Portes 2007: 123–37). Yet these ultra-rightists reportedly made up only some 5,000 of the 200,000 migrants who entered the US before the missile crisis, and an even tinier minority of the 700,000 or so who had arrived by the mid-1990s (Levine 2001: 55). 'Exilio City' remained true to pre-revolutionary *cubanidad* (Cubanness) – socially reactionary, preserving racism, sexism and class discrimination (Sawyer 2006: 159; de la Torre, 2003: 117, 126).

Right-wing hegemony rested, first, on economic and political power: 'a mass of resources and opportunities available to friends and allies. Fellow Cubans stood first in line as recipients of this largesse but only on condition that they adhered strictly to the ideological outlook of the enclave' (Portes 2007: 131–2). This hegemony was enforced by the 'official pulpit' of exile radio stations, leaving '[a] million Cubans ... blackmailed, totally controlled, by three radio stations', according to one exile businessman (cited in de la Torre 2003: 47–9). Confronted by anti-Hispanic prejudice, the community was mobilized to capture local political power, as 'Cuban-American entrepreneurs contributed to the campaigns of Cuban-American politicians who, once in office, reciprocated the favor' (Portes 2007: 127). The right 'turned the city into a one-issue community in which candidates for positions ranging from school boards to judges are assessed by their political beliefs regarding Cuba' (Levine 2001: 218). The level of corruption became legendary.

Political power has been underpinned by *exilio* social and religious ritual and commemoration, reinforced by the Catholic hierarchy, whose messianic anti-communism intensified during the Cold War, in a Cuban Church only too aware of the fate of some of their colleagues in the Spanish Civil War (Kirk 1989; Alonso Tejada 1999). When official Catholic proclamations welcomed the Bay of Pigs invasion, foreign priests were deported from Cuba (Kirk 1989: 94). The Church fought the revolutionary government's childcare programme, claiming that Catholic families would lose custody of brainwashed children, and its Operation Peter Pan saw some 15,000 children rushed into exile unaccompanied, many never to see their families again (Torreira Crespo and Buajasán Marrawi 2000). An astonishingly similar right-wing media scare was launched in Venezuela in 2009, the similarities so pronounced that the Venezuelan minister of education broadcast footage of the Cuban events.

Enforcing hegemony by terror

A second crucial factor underpinning right-wing hegemony has been terror and intimidation within the US. The right-wing culture of Miami 'is the product of four decades of seething betrayal, suspicion and conspiracies ... [It] was out of such thinking that the boundaries of the Castro War were drawn: any individual or business viewed as sympathetic to Havana became fair game for vigilante justice' (Bardach 2002:

113). From the mid-1960s, the receding prospect of early restoration of the old order led some to facilitate family travel to Cuba, and even dialogue with the Cuban government. In the 1960s, Cuban exiles carried out 156 terrorist actions within the US and in other countries (Arboleya 2002: 141). Moves under Carter in the 1970s to ease relations with Cuba further alarmed the right (García 1996: 140). In 1973–76 alone, the FBI investigated 103 bombings and six murders within the US that were credited to Cuban exile groups. Those who promoted dialogue found their businesses bombed (including one whose Cuba visits secured the release of 3,600 political prisoners) and several were assassinated (Levine 2001: 183; de la Torre 2003: 49). The president of the Bay of Pigs veterans' association was murdered after publicly attacking exile terrorism (García 1996: 142). At the turn of the century, the *Miami New Times* listed sixty-eight terrorist acts in the city, including six murders, commenting that 'lawless violence and intimidation have been the hallmarks of *el exilio* for more than 30 years' (Mullin 2000).

Academics and cultural industries were similarly targeted. The human rights group Americas Watch and the Fund for Free Expression found that 'suppression of dissent in Miami takes a variety of forms, including attacks on artistic freedom, academic freedom, the press, and human rights activists' (Human Rights Watch 1993). The Institute for Cuban Studies, at Miami-Dade University, was bombed for holding unapproved conferences, and the Cuban Museum of Arts and Culture for displaying works by Cubans from the island. A few years later, when Cuba's 'Miami Five' anti-terrorism agents appealed against their conspiracy convictions, the US Court of Appeal noted many reports of exile bombings and killings. It ordered a new trial, concluding that it 'was mandated by the perfect storm created when the surge of pervasive community sentiment, and extensive publicity both before and during the trial, merged with the improper prosecutorial references' (US Court of Appeals 2005: 91). In 2005, the UN Working Group on Arbitrary Detention also noted that men in paramilitary uniforms had appeared in the courthouse, and it declared that the Cubans' imprisonment was 'arbitrary, being in contravention of article 14 of the International Covenant on Civil and Political Rights' (United Nations 2005). The appeal verdict was later overturned, and the Supreme Court declined to consider the case. But in 2010, defence lawyers discovered that some of the journalists reporting the trial had apparently been on the US government payroll in anti-Cuba projects, raising new constitutional issues about the case (Amnesty International 2010: 7).

Tolerated terrorism

A third factor in the longevity of right-wing domination has been the protection offered by the relationship between the Cuban right, US government agencies and their clients in Latin America. When, in 1998, Cuba gave the FBI evidence, at the latter's request, about terrorist activity in Miami, the information was not used to arrest terrorists, but to arrest Cuba's anti-terrorism agents. Human Rights Watch reported in the 1990s:

> The official response to the violence and intimidation in Miami has been marked by a notable failure to prosecute criminal acts directed against dissidents. While in the last few years there have been over a dozen bombings aimed at those who favor a moderate approach to the Cuban government, there has not been a single arrest or prosecution in that time. (Human Rights Watch 1993)

Networks of Cuban exiles served right-wing Latin American regimes across the death-squad decades (Dinges 2004: 128). Orlando Bosch was security adviser to the Pinochet regime in Chile. Luis Posada Carriles ran Venezuela's intelligence service. Both Bosch and Posada Carriles were later jailed in Venezuela for masterminding the 1976 airliner bombing. Bosch served eleven years. Posada Carriles escaped, allegedly with bribes funded by Miami right-wing leaders (Calvo Ospina 2000: 43–4). He went back on to the CIA payroll, helping run US Colonel Oliver North's 'Irangate' operation with the Contra armies in Nicaragua (National Security Archive 2005; 2006).

Bosch later entered the US and was arrested. The attorney general opposed political asylum, declaring that Bosch had been 'resolute and unwavering in his advocacy of terrorist violence' for thirty years (cited in Bardach 2002: 202). His release became a key demand in the 1988 congressional campaign of Miami-Cuban Ileana Ros-Lehtinen, managed by Jeb Bush, the future governor of Florida, whose father, President George H. W. Bush, overruled the Justice Department and released him. Having escaped from Venezuela, Posada Carriles continued to organize terror attacks against Cuba. A Cuban agent, recruited in Miami to bomb Havana's Tropicana nightclub, records that Posada Carriles gave him the C-4 explosives for the bombing (Alvarado Godoy 2004: 129–30). Pardoned for an attempted bombing of Fidel Castro in Panama, Posada Carriles re-entered the US in 2005 and was arrested for illegal entry. The US Justice Department declared him 'an unrepentant criminal and admitted mastermind of terrorist plots and attacks on tourist sites' (cited in Lacey 2006). Released and welcomed in Miami as a hero, he was eventually tried on immigration-related charges, and acquitted in 2011.

The 1999 FBI report *Terrorism in the United States 1999: 30 Years of Terrorism, a Special Retrospective Edition* catalogued 'terrorist activity in the United States 1980–89', including twenty-seven acts, mostly bombings, attributed to Cuban-American groups (Federal Bureau of Investigation 1999). Yet, in sixty-two pages of analysis, there is no mention of the Cuban connection. The report completely neglects terrorist attacks launched against Cuba in violation of the Neutrality Act. One FBI agent complained: 'Every day we have a Neutrality Act violation because people leave to do runs on Cuba. But no one will allow us to do our job' (cited in Bardach 2002: 117).

Invading the Hill

The protection of terrorists reflected a wider Cuban-American mutuality, anchored in a formidable exile lobby based in Washington. The election of President Ronald Reagan and his hard-line anti-communist officials transformed the Cuban lobby. Prompted by Reagan's national security advisers, and federally funded by his National Endowment for Democracy, the heart of the lobby from 1981 was the Cuban American National Foundation. One hundred right-wing exiled business leaders paid a joining fee. Through its Political Action Committee, CANF rewarded and relied on hundreds of national politicians, distributing some $400,000 in the 1992 elections alone (Arboleya 2002: 198). The public voice of right-wing Cuban America was now speaking about human rights diplomacy, and pursuing legislative means to lock US policy into exile strategy.

Reagan's Democracy Project and Clinton's 'Track 2' strategy focused on the promotion of oppositional civil society in Cuba, enabling CANF to participate directly in federal projects. CANF placed itself at the heart of the Reagan White House's secret war in Nicaragua, and forged ties with the South African-backed rebel forces fighting the Angolan government and its Cuban ally. CANF announced: 'We support President Reagan's initiative to lend moral and material assistance to freedom fighters in Cuba, Afghanistan, Ethiopia, Cambodia, Nicaragua, Angola and other countries' (Calvo Ospina 2002: 43).

CANF grew strong enough to initiate policy. In the 1990s it mobilized its legal expertise and its political clout to drive through two laws that embedded key right-wing exile objectives: the 1992 Cuban Democracy Act (Torricelli Act) and the 1996 Cuban Liberty and Democratic Solidarity (Libertad) Act (Helms–Burton Act). These tightened the embargo by internationalizing it further: introducing sanctions on countries that provided 'assistance' to Cuba, banning US multinationals' subsidiaries from trading with Cuba, prohibiting merchant vessels from entering US ports within six months of docking in Cuba, and making it possible to expel from the US non-US citizens who 'traffic in property', if their businesses with Cuba involved property nationalized in the 1960s (Title III of Helms–Burton). Cubans who were not US citizens at the time of the nationalizations were also given retrospective rights to compensation. The laws also banned remittances, severely limited travel by US citizens to Cuba and made humanitarian medical aid subject to 'on-site' inspection by US officials of their use in Cuba. They removed most of the president's discretion to lift the embargo, passing the authority to Congress; and they made lifting the embargo dependent on prior 'regime change' in Cuba. They also authorized and required the expenditure of federal funds to build civil society inside Cuba and to run programmes to prepare for Cuba's 'transition' to a liberal capitalist democracy. A measure of the effectiveness of the CANF lobby is that, in the passage of both laws, the incumbent presidents rejected the legislation, but flip-flopped in election years when their principal opponent supported the CANF position.

A measure of the ruthlessness of this Cuban right is the extent to which its strategies rely on the suppression of the human rights of other Cubans. In the first place, they have removed the rights of Cuban Americans (and US citizens in general, of course) to send money or goods to help Cuban families and others, and to travel freely to the island, and have imposed penalties on those who have defied these restrictions (US Government Accountability Office 2007: 56).

In the second place, the ruthless pursuit of restoration through economic strangulation has had, as intended, a dire impact on the mass of Cubans. The UN Human Rights Council itself has recorded 'the disastrous and lasting economic and social effects ... of the embargo imposed on the Cuban population over 40 years ago, as well as its impacts on civil and political rights' (United Nations 2008: 10–11). The American Association for World Health, after a twelve-month study in the 1990s, reported that 'the U.S. embargo of Cuba has dramatically harmed the health and nutrition of large numbers of ordinary Cuban citizens ... [It] is our expert medical opinion that the U.S. embargo has caused a significant rise in suffering – and even deaths – in Cuba' (American Association for World Health 1997).

In the third place, right-wing policy has had a direct adverse impact on civil society activists inside Cuba. In the 1990s, Cuba's internal opposition groups were, one US diplomat in Havana noted, woefully small and disunited, in spite of exile attempts to unite them under the umbrella of the Concilio Cubano (Cuban Council) (Moses 2000: 126). The right-wing strategy made their position even more precarious. Amnesty International, a severe critic of Cuba, has made this point succinctly:

> The embargo legislation contains provisions for 'democracy building' in Cuba which include the allocation of significant amounts of aid and support for Cuban NGOs and individuals opposing the government … The Cuban authorities portray non-violent political dissidents and human rights activists as foreign sympathizers supporting US policy against Cuba. The embargo has helped to undermine the enjoyment of key civil and political rights in Cuba by fuelling a climate in which fundamental rights such as freedom of association, expression and assembly are routinely denied. (Amnesty International 2009: 6)

Amnesty's perception is shared by a former US head of interest in Havana (Smith 2006) and by former President James Carter, who, following his own investigations inside Cuba, noted that dissidents

> were unanimous in … opposition to any elevation of harsh rhetoric from the United States toward Cuba and to any funding of their efforts from the U.S. government. Any knowledge or report of such financial support would just give credibility to the long-standing claims of President Castro that they were 'paid lackeys' of Washington. (Carter 2002)

Arguably the most effective internal opposition movement of recent years has been the Varela Project, which in 2002 collected some 20,000 signatures on a petition to the Cuban National Assembly, seeking to change the law in order to permit private enterprise and political parties. However, the US-orchestrated international campaign in support implicated activists on the island, some of whom were prosecuted in 2003 for receiving funds and materials from the US (Amnesty International 2003). The strategy of organizing oppositional groups and of staging provocations to justify coups d'état and external intervention is a well-known CIA approach used in Guatemala in the 1950s, Chile in the 1970s, Nicaragua in the 1980s, Venezuela in the 2002 coup and since, and in Bolivia since 2006. Cuba is permanently on alert for such plots, given the history of the US's planning of violent pretexts to justify invasion (National Security Archive 2002). One of CANF's attempts to form an internal branch in 1991 collapsed when the Cuban Democratic Coalition's leader emerged as a Cuban security official (Arboleya 2002:

209). Cuban laws passed in retaliation to the Helms–Burton provisions were used against the dissidents arrested in 2003, after US diplomats toured Cuba organizing, funding and supplying activists, providing the Cuban courts with the evidence that individuals had been collaborating with US subversion (Pérez Roque 2003; Elizade and Báez 2003). This baleful connection is acknowledged in Amnesty's report on the 2003 cases (Amnesty International 2003).

US human rights diplomacy has also given Cuba's right-wing exile leadership an international platform, both in informal diplomacy and in the human rights arena. The early 1990s saw CANF working alongside the US government in the Geneva sessions of the United Nations Commission on Human Rights, funding the participation of ex-political prisoners. Initial US attempts to win a vote condemning Cuba had failed. So CANF and others had launched Human Rights 88 to mobilize at the 1988 Geneva sessions, coordinating hunger strikes in Miami and in Cuba. CANF established an office in Moscow, and its leaders accompanied US senators to Moscow in the early 1990s to offer trade deals in return for ending subsidies to Cuba and for Russia to switch its vote against Cuba in Geneva (Calvo Ospina 2002: 49–50).

Helms–Burton enabled the US to drive a new bargain with the European Union: suspending implementation of Title III and the threat of having EU business executives arrested, in return for the EU 'Common Position' on Cuba, whose objective is 'to encourage a process of transition to pluralist democracy and respect for human rights and fundamental freedoms' (European Union 1996). This gave CANF an arena in which to fight for tougher sanctions. Right-wing political parties in the former Soviet bloc, as well as in states like Sweden and Spain, were eager allies. The Cuban Liberty Council boasts of its meetings with Václav Havel, Lech Wałęsa, Ronald Reagan, Boris Yeltsin, George H. W. Bush, George W. Bush and José María Aznar. Such personal meetings are manifestations of links with international foundations working for regime change in Cuba, such as Aznar's Fundación Hispano Cubana (Spanish Cuban Foundation). Václav Havel helped launch the International Committee for Democracy in Cuba, which campaigns to hold governments to account for their implementation of the EU Common Position. Its elite members include prominent right-wing politicians and many ex-presidents from Latin America and Eastern Europe. Three times between 2002 and 2010, such lobbying operations have helped secure the award of the European Parliament's Sakharov Prize to Cuban dissidents.

In all of this human rights activism, the Cuban right stands shoulder to shoulder with US human rights diplomacy, in which the charges against Cuba are brought in a manner that is – in the light of truly horrendous abuse elsewhere in the Americas and the world (and, of course, in US-occupied Guantánamo Bay) – wholly disproportionate. This right-wing discourse similarly rejects the equal status of economic and social rights in the UN Declaration of Universal Rights – rights mostly enjoyed in far higher measure in Cuba than in most other states on the planet.

A further advantage accruing to the Cuban right from the activities of its lobbying strategy has been access to state funding. This is not a new phenomenon in the exile community, but the scale of support has grown greatly. The US Government Accountability Office recorded that:

> To support independent civil society groups and individuals, State and USAID awarded 44 grants and cooperative agreements between 1996 and 2005 to three types of grantees: (1) democracy and human rights NGOs focused specifically on Cuba, which received about 51 percent ($37.3 million) of the assistance; (2) democracy and human rights NGOs with a worldwide or regional focus, which received about 39 percent ($28.7 million); and (3) universities, which received about 10 percent ($7.6 million). (US Government Accountability Office 2006: 3)

One historian of the Cuban right wrote that 'being a dissident has become a business', and recorded the view of one ex-political prisoner that the 1995 Cuban Council, promoted by CANF as an umbrella group inside Cuba, was 'eaten up by its members' personal greed' (Calvo and Declerq 2000: 143). According to one account, more than $200 million in US federal funds were channelled through CANF leader José Mas Canosa after the foundation's creation (Bardach 2002: 140). So lucrative (but corrupt, extreme and ineffective) has been the virtually uncontrolled, right-wing Cuban management of US government-funded Radio and TV Martí that a Senate report in 2010 recommended it be moved out of Miami and managed by the state-run Voice of America service (US Senate 2010b). The University of Miami's Cuba transition studies programme was a direct creation of the CANF's Endowment for Cuban Studies, with matching state funding (Calvo Ospina 2002: 38–9).

Cracks in the monolith

Although the Cuban right clashed furiously with the US government over migration policy in the mid-1990s, historians may come to see the period as the high tide of exile right-wing influence. They were able to take the moral high ground in 1996, after the Brothers to the Rescue

(BTTR) shoot-down. BTTR had initially searched for Cuban rafters, but after US migration policy changed, it began flying militarized Cessna aircraft illegally into Cuban airspace, dropping leaflets and threatening to provoke a civilian air incident. After twenty-five Cuban warnings to the US Federal Aviation Authority following intrusions, two Cessnas were shot down. Within ten days, President Clinton had signed off Helms–Burton, the legislation that arguably represents the greatest achievement of the right-wing lobby.

But in the twenty-first century the exile monolith has begun to reveal significant cracks. There have certainly been more victories. President George W. Bush went to 'war on terror' and listed Cuba as a terror state. His appointment to key foreign policy positions of hard-liners from the 1990s Contra teams was welcomed. Bush delivered far more than the frequent White House photo opportunities. The hundreds of pages of the reports of his Commission for Assistance to a Free Cuba detailed plans for 'regime change', privatization of Cuban welfare services and, above all, property restitution, the core right-wing demand (Commission for Assistance to a Free Cuba 2004; 2006). As noted above, Bush's diplomats in Havana travelled the island organizing and supplying dissidents. The 2006 commission report called for an $80 million 'Cuba Fund for a Democratic Future', of which $31 million was earmarked for 'support to independent civil society on the island' (Commission for Assistance to a Free Cuba 2006: 20). In 2007, in the presence of family members of imprisoned Cuban dissidents, Bush announced the creation of an international Freedom Fund to offer Cubans post-regime-change loans. The policy traffic was not all one way, however. Bush continued to suspend the implementation of Helms–Burton Title III (which would have allowed the arrest of foreign businessmen 'trafficking' in nationalized Cuban property). Nor did he repeal the 2000 Trade Sanctions Reform and Export Enhancement Act, which opened the way to what became a $700 million trade in sales of food to Cuba.

But the real challenge to Cuba's right has come from within its own community. Some of this shift is routinely associated with the changing class composition of the later waves of Cuban-American migrants, and with less extreme younger generations. The death in 1997 of CANF leader José Mas Canosa began a process of splintering. A more moderate CANF stance emerged, opposed bitterly by the new Cuban Liberty Council. Some of the shift is clearly linked to the behaviour of the right-wing machine. Its opposition to the pope's historic visit to Cuba in 1998 reopened, in a highly sensitive part of the *exilio* soul, the dilemmas about engagement (Erikson 2008: 119–20). An oversubscribed Catholic Church-organized cruise to Cuba to join the pope's visit was abandoned in the face of right-wing hostility. Soon after, the right's image was damaged by the case of Elián González, who survived a raft crossing from Cuba during which his mother drowned. A politically charged custody battle ensued between the boy's father in Cuba and family relatives in Miami, noisily backed by the exile right. When the US courts found for the father, the exiles refused to release the boy. He was eventually seized by heavily armed police, prompting violent right-wing protests in Miami. In the aftermath, a more moderate Cuba Study Group emerged. One of its members explained that its purpose was to reclaim a moral right for exiles to participate in a reformed Cuba and to overcome 'the image of Miami as being vengeful and anxious to get back to establish the old order, as opposed to a new Cuba. The image of Miami as trying to get back to Cuba and control things, and reclaim property and all these things' (cited in Erikson 2008: 122).

Bush's 2004 restriction on family support, curtailing visits to one every three years and limiting the money and goods that could be sent, was a victory for the right, but one that revealed deep divisions in 'Exilio City', just as right-wing opposition to remittances had in the past (García 1996: 140). Fraudulent use of federal Cuba Program funds did further damage. In 2008 the federal Government Accountability Office reported fraud involving the USAID Cuba Program's two largest democracy aid grants – to the Center for a Free Cuba and the Grupo de Apoyo a la Democracia (Democracy Support Group) (US Government Accountability Office 2008: 15). The US has recently turned to paying private contractors to distribute material aid to internal dissidents (see Lievesley above).

And, significantly, more policy think tanks in Washington, and a report to Congress, have wearily pointed out that the embargo has failed (US Senate 2009; Stephens and Dunscomb 2009). Even the CANF cautiously weighed in along similar lines (Cuban American National Foundation 2009). Fidel Castro's illness in 2006 and his retirement as president in 2008 had so little immediate effect on politics in Cuba that the long-awaited 'biological solution' now appeared bankrupt, too. And in the wider foreign-policy arena, all the states of Latin America now opposed the embargo, and in 2009 invited Cuba to rejoin the Organization of American States. The emergence of the Bolivarian Alliance of the more radical states in the so-called 'pink tide' of left Latin American presidents has given Cuba crucial political and economic allies (Lievesley and Ludlam 2009a). Boosted by sales of medical services, above all to Venezuela, by 2005 Cuba had restored its GNP to the levels it had enjoyed before the Soviet collapse.

Straws began to blow in the electoral wind. Two of the three right-wing Republican Cuban Americans in the House of Representatives in South Florida, the Diaz-Balart brothers and Ileana Ros-Lehtinen, faced prominent Cuban-American Democrat challengers in 2008. All three held their seats, but with margins of victory that fell by 7 percentage points on average from the 2006 results – to 16 percentage points in two cases and 6 percentage points in the third. (In the 1990s they had enjoyed majorities of between 30 and 50 percentage points.) A major Brookings Institute survey of opinion in the Cuban-American community at the end of 2008 found 55 per cent opposed to continuing the embargo – the first such majority since the Brookings series began in 1991; even among supporters of the embargo, 55 per cent wanted the US government to open dialogue – that dirty word – with Cuba (Brookings Institute 2008).

Conclusions

This chapter has focused overwhelmingly on the Cuban right in exile. Some of the factors identified here as underpinning the strength of the Cuban right remain significant; others have weakened. It remains immensely well funded, but its political and cultural domination of 'Exilio City' has significantly weakened, and it has lost the automatic protection it once seems to have enjoyed for violent intimidation of other strands of exile political thought. Its rejection of all compromise with the Cuban government is no longer shared by most Cuban Americans, and the culture of terror in Miami has finally damaged its wider legitimacy.

It remains active internationally, though, and still contains functioning terrorists. The international right-wing networks that the Cuban right has been prominent in for so long remain busy. The image of Cuban totalitarianism meticulously disseminated by the US and the Cuban right has been part of the propaganda machinery that, two decades after the end of the Cold War, has been repackaged in the face of the 'pink tide' in Latin America, and notably in Venezuela, Bolivia and Honduras. In each of these cases, the threat of the Cuban example has been prominent – in the run-up to the coups in Venezuela and Honduras and in the attempted armed secession in Bolivia. The darker side of this network is also still active. In 2010, one of the terrorists recruited by Posada Carrilles to plant bombs in Havana hotels in 1997 was arrested entering Venezuela. Extradited to Cuba, he told television journalists that he had been sent to Caracas by a right-wing group in Miami to organize the assassination of Hugo Chávez and to bomb oil tankers going to Cuba. Cuba's media were quick to construct the man's terrorist family tree, in order to demonstrate the continuing terrorist ambitions of some in Miami.

The voice of the Cuban right, however unrepresentative it may have become, remains loud and uncompromising. Hard-line opposition quickly emerged to the intervention of the Catholic Church to improve the prison conditions of political prisoners in Cuba, and then to secure the release of the dissidents imprisoned in the 2003 crackdown. When the latter group of prisoners called on the US government to lift the embargo, a longer list was quickly issued in Miami of ex-prisoners who supported the embargo. When the Catholic Church's mediation secured prisoner releases to Spain, the right attacked the Church's deal because it forced the prisoners into exile (even though those who refused the offer of asylum in Spain were released in Cuba anyway, on early parole).

In 2008, President Barack Obama took Florida from the Republicans by 2 percentage points: the first presidential victor since 1959 to win without the Cuban lobby's support. He had incurred right-wing wrath by pledging to lift Bush's 2004 controls on family visits and remittances, and by hinting at new talks with Havana (although he rejected a lifting of the blockade until Cuba met the standard 'regime change' conditions). But even if he had not lost his majority support in Congress in the 2010 mid-term elections, he was highly unlikely to risk a 1 per cent swing in the Florida vote in the battle for a second term by launching a prolonged congressional battle to lift the embargo. And in the aftermath of the right-wing revival in the 2010 mid-terms, two prominent members of the hard right on Cuban policy, Ileana Ros-Lehtinen and Connie Mack, took the chairs of the House Foreign Affairs Committee and the Foreign Affairs Subcommittee on the Western Hemisphere, respectively. So, though there had been steady progress in Washington towards a gradual lifting of the ban on US citizens travelling freely to Cuba, the prospects for this once again seem dim. Many with an interest in US Cuba policy saw open travel as initiating a wider economic reoccupation of the island and its strangulation with dollar bills – always the preferred option of a significant minority of US politicians since 1959.

So the Cuban right, its forces still concentrated in Miami, retains a loud and insistent voice in US debate, and is still in a strong position to block legislative change. It also maintains its voice in international right-wing networks. But as the monolithic representative of Cuban America and guardian of an unchallenged embargo policy, the right's time appears to be passing. Its classic modelling of the lawless Latin American oligarchic tradition – a tradition equally at home in the southern states of the US when the exiles arrived in the 1950s – has long outlived its legitimacy. It has failed.

10 | Right-wing politics in contemporary Brazil

MARCOS COSTA LIMA

Owing to Brazil's economic significance and the high esteem in which ex-president Luiz Inácio Lula da Silva is held by the Latin American left, the Partido dos Trabalhadores (PT, Workers' Party) administration that has governed Brazil since 2002 – first under Lula and then under Dilma Roussef – has been a target for conservative forces within the country, as well as in the region as a whole, in the US and elsewhere. The Brazilian right has its origins in an authoritarian, property-owning oligarchy whose power rested on slavery and which was able to cast a long shadow over society, even as the country went through the processes of industrialization and modernization. Thus the oligarchy was able to survive the abolition of slavery in 1888 and to weather the Vargas revolution, which began in 1930. Between 1930 and 1945, and again in 1950–54, the populist Getúlio Vargas and his Partido Trabalhista Brasileiro (Brazilian Workers' Party) created the corporatist *Estado Novo* (New State), whose objective it was to achieve state-led industrialization and social reform. Vargas led a coalition of the new urban working class, segments of the middle class and the peasantry seeking a democratic system. Opposing them were the forces of reaction, represented by landowners and other groups closely linked to international commerce and capital and the US. The right-wing União Democrática Nacional (National Democratic Union) led the political fight against Vargas. Having survived this populist challenge (Vargas committed suicide in 1954), the oligarchy would later support the military coup of 1964, which ousted the democratically elected government of João Goulart and established a dictatorship that lasted until 1985 and that transformed Brazilian political institutions. The political parties which emerged during the struggle for the end of military rule and for a transition to democracy continue to dominate the political scene today, not least the PT, which emerged in 1980 as a heterogeneous alliance of trade unionists, left-wing intellectuals, feminists, grassroots activists and liberation-theology Catholics. On the right, the Partido da Frente Liberal (PFL, Liberal Front Party) – known as the Democratas (Democrats) since 2007 – emerged as the pre-eminent force. In the

2010 election, conservative forces attempted to end PT control. The right desired a government more closely identified with the interests of international capital and the socio-economic elite, and one that would bring to an end the PT's domestic reforms, which aimed at improving the living conditions of the poor through social assistance and investment, while also seeking greater South–South cooperation and autonomy vis-à-vis foreign capital (for a critical assessment, see Branford 2009). This chapter will focus on the right's political activities and its ideas about how Brazil should be inserted into the international financial system, as well as its resistance to the recent leftward shift in Latin America's continental alliances.[1]

The military dictatorship and the politics of transition

The contemporary right emerged from a process of political realignment during the twenty-one years of military rule. The 1964 coup interrupted the national-popular project of development, including land reform and control over profit repatriations by foreign corporations – initiatives that had been introduced by President Goulart – and in their place formed policies closely in line with the needs of domestic capital and its foreign allies. The military immediately closed Congress and ruled by decree. The harshest periods of military control – the administrations of Costa e Silva (1967–69) and Garrastazu Médici (1969–74) – provoked armed insurgency by communist and Maoist guerrillas in 1968. The military's response was to impose a 'state terror [which] suppressed all opponents – generally left-wingers but also many liberals' (Weffort 1984: 94). Such was the ferocity of the repression that all insurgents were eliminated by 1971. Once the left had been defeated, the regime then permitted the creation of two pro-regime political parties, the Acçao Nacionalista Renovadora (ARENA, National Renewal Party) and the Movimento Democrático Brasileiro (MDB, Brazilian Democratic Movement), which were intended to act as safety valves for societal pressures – that is, as proof that the regime believed in democracy. After 1974, the governments led by generals Geisel and then Figueiredo assumed less hard-line positions and embarked upon a slow political liberalization, allowing the restoration of *habeas corpus* and freedom of the press, as well as a political amnesty; furthermore, in 1982 direct elections for state governments were permitted. This opening facilitated the creation of the Partido Democrático Trabalhista (PDT, Democratic Labour Party) led by

1 This chapter is dedicated to my friend Gildo Marçal Brandao (1949–2010), political scientist at the University of São Paulo.

Leonel Brizola (a veteran southern politician and disciple of Vargas), the PT and the Partido Socialista Brasileiro (Brazilian Socialist Party). It was at this time that Lula emerged as a trade union leader (he represented the metalworkers) as labour mobilization intensified. Changes were also taking place within the two tame official parties. ARENA was renamed the Partido Social Democrático (PDS, Social Democratic Party); it then suffered a schism, from which the PFL emerged. The latter would become the dominant conservative force in contemporary politics, whereas the PDS became discredited as a consequence of its identification with a military regime denounced as incompetent and corrupt. The MDB, now called the Partido do Movimento Democrático Brasileiro (PMDB, Party of the Brazilian Democratic Movement) experienced a major defection, resulting in 1988 in the formation of the Partido da Social Democracia Brasileira (PSDB, Social Democratic Party of Brazil) led by José Serra and future president, Fernando Henrique Cardoso. The opposition to the military was thus wide-ranging and increasingly vocal, particularly in the 1983–84 campaign demanding the election of the president by direct popular vote, rather than by the regime-dominated electoral college. Although the military won that particular argument, the opposition, led by the PMDB and the PDT, nominated Tancredo Neves as its presidential candidate in the 1985 elections, which he subsequently won. Neves died before his inauguration and was succeeded by his deputy, José Sarney, a politician who, though close to the military, led the re-democratization movement. He introduced a new constitution in 1988, which allowed for the direct election of the president for the first time since 1960. Despite the opposition's strength, the transition to democracy in 1985 was very much a case of being managed 'from above' – that is, being carefully controlled by the military, particularly under the leadership of General Golbery do Couto e Silva.

Although dos Santos has asserted that 'in contemporary Brazil, the archaic, patriarchal world is peripheral and in a process of accelerated obsolescence' (1985: 268), oligarchs and local chieftains still retain considerable political power. This is despite the fact that the Brazilian right has suffered a greater degree of fragmentation than other Latin American conservative parties, the result of which is that it needs to negotiate and accommodate in order to move forward (Mainwaring, Meneguello and Power 2000b: 54). In the 1990, 1994 and 1998 elections, conservative parties accounted for 51.2 per cent, 45.3 per cent and 42.3 per cent, respectively, of the total vote for congressional seats (Mainwaring, Meneguello and Power 2000b: 48). These electoral results demonstrate how much power the PFL (later the Democratas) and the PMDB (plus others) have exercised in Congress. Thus, the PMDB remained the largest party up to the 2010 election. The situation was further complicated by the fact that, as well as having to accommodate one another, the four largest parties – the PMDB, PT, PSDB and PFL – also needed to consider the *partidos nanicos* (tiny parties), which were generally devoid of ideological intent but were willing to be bought. Up to 2010, a government of the left or right needed to adopt these tactics in order to get legislation through. An example of the potentially catastrophic political consequences of this method of governing occurred in 2005–06, when the first Lula administration was almost brought down by the *mensalão* (monthly allowance) scandal, which cost the president his chief of staff, José Dirceu (essentially, the PT had been bribing opposition politicians to support its parliamentary bills). Obviously progressive reform was constrained by these circumstances, as well as by other factors, domestic and international. Thus, during the period of liberalization, both the PT and the PDT hoped that, if elected to government, they might be able to move in a socialist trajectory; once in power, however, this aim was dropped from the PT's agenda, as Lula was compelled to consider the demands of large domestic and foreign capital and the right-wing oligarchy. This would lead to a diminution – some would say to the disappearance – of the radical content of the PT's programme.

Despite the retention of oligarchic influence, the elite has not been able to hold back the rapid pace of change in Brazilian society since the mid-twentieth century. The urban population has risen from 31.2 per cent in 1940 to 67.6 per cent in 1980 and 80 per cent in 2010, as a result of rapid rural-to-urban migration, industrialization and huge population growth (from 70 million in 1960 to 190 million in 2010). Although the country has thus undergone a dramatic transformation, it has not been able to overcome the problem which Buarque de Holanda has identified: 'Democracy in Brazil always was an unfortunate misunderstanding. A rural and semi-feudal aristocracy imported it and tried to adapt it wherever possible to its rights and privileges' (2006: 160). This contradiction between Brazil's democratic and modern needs and the interests of the oligarchy, as represented by the political right, would become ever more apparent as post-transition governments implemented monetarist structural adjustment policies.

The right after the transition

The neoliberal model – so beloved of the Thatcher and Reagan governments in the UK and the US – was applied to economies across the world in the context of the debt crisis and under the aegis of the IMF restructuring packages that responded to it. It was driven by the imperatives of the Washington Consensus. The ideological objectives of the consensus were rolled out by the corporate media as 'the end of history', as if there could be no alternative to them. Thus even social democratic parties – such as the Socialists in France and Labour in the UK – reduced public spending and moved away from inclusive social policies. There now seemed to be little political difference between 'left' and 'right'. This phenomenon affected Brazil and the rest of Latin America, as a broad array of left-wing parties began to behave as parties of order, and not as parties of change. Thus, in order to get elected in 2002, Lula reassured domestic and international capital that he would not undertake structural reforms and would not default on Brazil's foreign debt. Once in office, he continued Cardoso's macroeconomic strategy.

Sarney governed Brazil at the head of an alliance of regional leaders and political clans. Unable to curb the massive inflation, he became increasingly unpopular, as did his successor, Fernando Collor de Mello, who, having narrowly beaten Lula in the 1989 election (by 49.9 per cent of the vote to 44.2 per cent), escaped impeachment for corruption by resigning in September 1992 (he was impeached *in absentia* in 1993). The interim president, Itamar Franco, appointed Fernando Henrique Cardoso as his finance minister. Cardoso presided over a programme of privatization and huge public spending cuts and the introduction of a new currency, the Real, in 1994. Cardoso's political ascendancy first at the Treasury and then as president (1994–2002) was welcomed by multinational capital, the Brazilian elite, the middle classes and even significant sections of the poor, particularly because of the dramatic reduction in inflation by 1997. He was able to defeat Lula in two presidential elections: in 1994, he obtained 54.3 per cent (to Lula's 27 per cent) and in 1998, 53.1 per cent (to 31.7 per cent). However, the central thrust of his policies was not to promote autonomous development through domestic industrialization, but rather to restructure the economy so as to attract foreign investment by eliminating tariff barriers and exchange controls – measures that were complemented by a comprehensive policy of privatization. As a result, imports climbed to 52.7 per cent in 1994 and many Brazilian businesses closed or went into partnership with foreign companies; this accounted for 70 per cent of mergers and acquisitions between 1995 and 1999. It led even the pro-neoliberal *Veja* magazine to comment 'the history of capitalism has rarely seen the transfer of control on such a scale in such a short period' (Lambert 2009). Brazil went through a rapid process of deindustrialization, affecting much of São Paulo's automobile industry, the PT's birthplace (Sader 2005). Unemployment doubled to 9 per cent, while the balance of payments fell from a surplus of $10.5 billion in 1994 to a deficit of $3.5 billion in 1995. It was to remain in the red until 2000. In short, Brazil's sovereignty was being seriously compromised. To stem the haemorrhage, Cardoso borrowed heavily; the external debt rose from $150 billion in 1994 to $250 billion in 2002 (Lambert 2009). Critics of Cardoso have argued that he deliberately created the conditions for the 'recolonization of Brazil', which turned the country 'from a liberal raw material exporting country to a dynamic industrializing country and emerging industrial power ... to a regressive stagnant foreign owned subsidiary of overseas credit holders and investors dependent on the largesse of international financial institutions' (Petras and Veltmayer 2003: 4–5). In other words, Lula inherited a financial crisis, which had horrendous social consequences.

The pre-eminent conservative party, the PFL, and the pre-eminent centre-right party, the PSDB, worked together during the late 1980s and the 1990s. They were instrumental in obtaining congressional approval of the Plan Real, under which the new currency was pegged to the dollar in an effort to secure financial stability, as well as in securing the constitutional amendment that guaranteed Cardoso's second term as president in 1998. Former PFL governor of Pernambuco, Marco Maciel, was vice-president during both Cardoso's terms in government. Falling out in 2002, the parties resumed collaboration for the 2006 elections, when the PFL's José Jorge was the vice-presidential running mate of the PSDB's Geraldo Alckmin. Over the years, and despite the fact that a number of their members had opposed the military dictatorship, the PFL and the PSDB grew increasingly conservative and ever more closely aligned with agribusiness and the financial and industrial sectors. Their agenda centred on the need to reshape the relationship between the state and the market, which they believed necessitated opening the Brazilian economy to foreign investment and privatizing its commanding heights, as well as the education, health and social insurance sectors (under the advice of the World Bank). These were the policies pursued by the Cardoso government, which also set about dismantling labour legislation, allowing employers maximum flexibility in matters of hiring and firing, and cutting social expenditure. The right also repudiated agrarian reform and measures to protect the environment, which it regarded as creating unnecessary limitations on economic growth. In terms of ethical policy, it opposed abortion and equal rights for homosexuals, and supported the death penalty; in foreign-policy terms, it sought preferential relationships with rich countries, particularly the US. It is easy to imagine the Brazilian right's displeasure when it perceived that the Lula government was going to implement the exact opposite of these policy preferences following the 2002 election. Despite not challenging the neoliberal economic model, the PT introduced extensive social provision programmes and agrarian reform.

The Lula government and the Brazilian right

One of the mainstays of the right's influence over Brazilian politics was its traditional electoral hold over the poorest states of the north and northeast, where conservative politicians enjoyed clientelist relations with many voters. The epitome of this was the state of Bahia, which was the fiefdom of the PFL's Antônio Carlos Magalhães from 1985 until his (and other conservatives') strongholds began to be challenged by the PT after 1998. In the 1990s, the PFL controlled 90 per cent of the 417 mayoralties and 75 per cent of local state deputies. Today, the northeast is a bastion of PT support and, following the 2010 elections, the Democratas lost most of its Congressional representation there. The success of the PT and its allies was initially based on competing for seats in state parliaments that historically had had what Borges describes as 'low electoral competitiveness', given the dominance of local chiefs in Amazonas, Bahia, Ceará, Goiás, Paraíba, Maranhão and Tocantins. Of these, five had been controlled by a single party – either the PFL, the PMDB or the PSDB – between 1982 and 1998, during which time each party was a member of a national government coalition, and the PFL was crucial to Cardoso's policy of savage neoliberal restructuring (Borges 2010: 169–71, 177). The PT also made inroads into governorship elections in these states, obtaining an average 8 per cent in 1994, 34 per cent in 2002 (coinciding with the PT's national electoral thrust) and 25 per cent in the 2006 elections (Borges 2010: 171).

The key to understanding this electoral volte-face, which saw the left (principally the PT) in ascendancy and the right in massive decline, is the impact of the Lula government's social programmes, particularly the *Bolsa Familia* (Family Grant). Under this scheme, the poorest families receive a monthly grant for each of their children (up to a maximum of three) provided they are sent to school and are vaccinated. By 2010, it had benefited 52 million people – almost half of the beneficiaries of all such programmes in the region put together (Economic Commission for Latin America 2010b). Other initiatives included *Fome Zero* (Zero Hunger), which was designed to combat urban and rural malnutrition; employment stimulation; and limited agrarian reform and resettlement. The slowness of this final element was criticized by radicals within the PT and outside it by the militants of the Movimento dos Trabalhadores Rurais Sem Terra (Rural Landless Workers' Movement), while the reform's progress through Congress was blocked by lobbyists for large agribusiness concerned with the export of soya, beef, ethanol and coffee. The political effect of Lula's reform agenda was to dismantle the traditional clientelistic networks that historically had aided right-wing political parties (Borges 2010: 175).

Despite its efforts, the PT government failed to resolve the huge social problems inherited from the Cardoso administration (and, of course, from Brazil's previous history). Although this is unsurprising, given the scale of the problems, it did offer opportunities for critiques of the PT's political trajectory. By 2008, Brazil was one of the most unequal countries on earth. According to the United Nations Development Programme, income inequalities, as measured by the GINI index, were as high as in very poor African countries, such as Sierra Leone, Swaziland, Lesotho or Namibia. However, the World Bank ranks the Brazilian economy as among the ten richest in the world – the country has a GDP of $1.7 trillion, similar to Italy (Beghin 2008: 1). The reason for this disparity was income distribution. As Beghin shows,

> 1 per cent of the population – less than 2 million people – have 13 per cent of all household income. This percentage is similar to that of the poorest 50 per cent – about 80 million Brazilians ... 30.3 per cent of the population or 54 million are considered poor and, within this group, 20 million people or 11.5 per cent of the population are ranked as extremely poor. (Beghin 2008: 1)

Levels of rural poverty are even more marked, and the living conditions of a large proportion of the urban population are woefully inadequate. UN Habitat drew attention to the fact that

> 38.5 per cent of all urban households were 'precarious' in 2005 [and] 31.8 per cent of households in the southern region and 26.7 per cent in the southeast region are inadequate [while the figures rose to] 70.1 per cent in the northern region, 59.7 per cent in the mid-west ... and 53.5 per cent in the northeast. (UN Habitat 2010: 40)

However, in the period 2000–10, Brazil was able to improve the living conditions of an estimated 10.4 million people. The main factors behind this were improving incomes for poor urban households; slower population growth; slowing rural-to-urban migration; the development of low-income housing policies that subsidize construction costs and slum upgrading (UN Habitat 2010: 40). The remaining housing deficit mainly affects those 'with an income of less than 3 minimum wages a month'. For Beghin,

> Poverty in Brazil has a colour and a location: it is black, urban and concentrated in the northeast region. Two-thirds of all the poor are black, 70 per cent of the total population living in poverty ... are city dwellers and 51 per cent ... live in the northeast. (Beghin 2008: 2)

This is compounded by the fact that some 45 million male and female workers do not enjoy labour rights, formal wages or minimum social protection, and that there is a highly regressive tax system, with the poor paying far more as a proportion of their wages than the rich.

The PT's critics have argued that, in order to get elected in 2002, it made an historic compromise with finance capital, both domestic and international, and the consequence of this was that it did not attempt to initiate structural socio-economic transformation. The result was continuing poverty and exclusion, as detailed above (despite the positive accomplishments of the *Bolsa* and its sister programmes), along with deepening insecurity, rising violent crime and allegations of corruption against the government (Sader 2005). However, from an entirely different viewpoint, the *Economist* hailed Lula's achievements:

> Brazil's circumstances and its standing in the world have been transformed during Lula's presidency ... Poverty has fallen and economic growth has quickened. Brazil is enjoying a virtuous circle: soaring Asian demand for exports ... is balanced by a booming domestic market, as – partly thanks to better social policies – some 20m new consumers have emerged from poverty. No wonder foreign businesses are piling in, while a swelling group of Brazilian multinationals is expanding abroad. (*Economist* 2010a)

At the same time, it was highly critical of the expansion of the role of the state in economic management, particularly over Petrobras, the national oil company. Lula ended his term of office with a staggering 80 per cent approval rating, giving the Brazilian right little space for manoeuvre. Its own credibility was particularly affected by the fact that, using its parliamentary majorities, it had attempted to obstruct the PT's social legislation as it passed through Congress. Its spoiling tactics discredited the entire party system. A 2009 Supreme Court report on the state of the country's party system concluded that, in 2008, almost 90 per cent of Brazilians had no formal party links; the figure rose to 91.6 per cent in 2009: that is, 119.7 million people, in a context where 2.9 million more people registered to vote. This disconnectedness contrasts sharply with Lula's personal popularity, and is explained by his political style, which was to appeal direct to citizens over the heads of the right-dominated Congress and Senate, and his efforts to build links with state governors in order to ensure implementation of the social programmes.

The 2010 election: a resounding defeat for the right

Dilma Rousseff, Lula's preferred PT successor, began her campaign for the 2010 presidential election amid a shower of media accusations that she was linked to corruption scandals, narco-trafficking and organized crime. The attacks reached such levels of intensity in newspapers like *O Estado de S. Paulo* and *Folha de São Paulo*, the magazine *Veja* and TV Globo that the São Paulo branch of the journalists' trade union held a protest rally against the possibility of a 'media coup' (see Tsolakis, above, and Díaz Echenique, Ozollo and Vivares, below, for other examples of media interventions in politics). At the same time, the right-wing parties attempted to block discussion of any substantive matters during the campaign (Nogueira 2009: 24, 30).

No candidate won outright in the first round of voting, and during the second round Rousseff and José Serra of the PSDB faced each other in a number of televised debates. The *Economist* argued that Serra's dilemma was that 'attacking Lula's record would go down badly, and ... dwelling on his own would be little more successful, because that would mean reminding voters of his ties to ... Fernando Henrique Cardoso'. While the magazine lauded Cardoso for conquering 'Brazil's endemic hyper-inflation ... he is usually remembered for high unemployment, a succession of crises not of his making, and political scandals no worse than those that have rocked the current government'. As the journal concluded, the consequence was that 'Mr Serra was left with almost nothing to talk about' (*Economist* 2010b). Serra was normally described in the corporate media as being a centrist or a social democrat, but in fact his views were extremely right-wing. During the second round, he accused the Bolivian government of being 'complicit' in drug trafficking; accused Venezuela of 'sheltering' the Fuerzas Armadas Revolucionarias Colombianas (FARC, Revolutionary Armed Forces of Colombia); and castigated Lula for failing to recognize the Honduran regime installed after the coup against President Manuel Zelaya in June 2009 (Weisbrot 2010). The right's propaganda campaign notwithstanding, Rousseff won the second round comfortably, with 56 per cent to Serra's 44 per cent. Furthermore, the PT and its coalition allies won majorities in the Chamber of Deputies (68 per cent) and the Senate (67 per cent) and gained a number of state governors and local state deputies. In Congress, the PT commanded 311 seats out of a total of 513, but if one adds the seats of the broad array of its nine coalition partners, that figure rises to 402; this represents the largest majority since the transition to democracy in 1985. In the Senate, Rousseff had the support of fifty-four out of eighty-one senators. The PT also won the popular vote in sixteen out of twenty-seven states (*Folha de São Paulo* 2010).

Concluding thoughts

The 2010 election results were a clear indication that the process of democratization, integral to the PT's policies of social inclusion, has substantially eroded the right's traditional clientelistic support base. It is also evident that a majority of Brazilian voters identify right-wing policies with debt, unemployment, growing social inequalities, rising poverty and severe loss of sovereignty, and view the PT in a highly positive light. For this situation to crystallize into a permanent political shift, there would need to be a deepening of the PT's redistributionist policies, a continued democratization of society and polity, and a renewed affirmation of national sovereignty.

It is also essential to situate Brazil within the context of the region's political changes, where, after the resounding failure of the Washington Consensus, popular movements underpinned the elections of left-leaning governments, beginning with Hugo Chávez in 1998, continuing with Lula in Brazil in 2002 and then successes in Argentina, Uruguay, Bolivia, Chile, Ecuador and Paraguay (see Lievesley and Ludlam 2009a). This trend explains why the Brazilian right has consistently attempted to obstruct regional integration by, for example, trying for ten years to block Venezuela's entry into Mercosur (a move that was finally approved by the Brazilian Senate in December 2009). Opposition senators had 'argued that under Chávez, Venezuela had lost its democratic character with regards to the press, courts and legislature, disqualifying the country from membership' (Rabello 2009). Nevertheless, Brazilian capitalists were keen to invest in the Venezuelan economy (Márquez 2010).

To conclude, the two PT governments led by Lula embarked upon a development model based on the redistribution of wealth. Although this did not tackle the structural roots of inequality or the capitalist nature of the Brazilian economy, it did garner huge popular support.

This drastically reduced the political standing of conservative politicians and the electoral prospects of their parties. The latest financial crisis, which erupted in August 2008, has demonstrated that the economic and political practices pursued by global capitalism require profound changes if individuals are to live in a world where the fruits of their labour and wealth are not appropriated by an elite, and where the vast majority of people benefit from the wealth they themselves produce. With the election of Dilma Rousseff and the legislative dominance the PT government enjoys, Brazil is in an optimum position to deepen its socio-economic reforms and overcome the country's oligarchic tradition.

11 | Undermining the new dawn: opposition to Lugo in Paraguay

PETER LAMBERT

The election of Fernando Lugo at the head of the Alianza para Cambio (APC, Alliance for Change) coalition in April 2008 was a historic event in a number of ways. First, it put an end to over sixty years of uninterrupted rule by the Colorado Party, which had governed Paraguay since 1947. Second, it brought about the first peaceful handover of power between political parties in the history of the country. And third, it brought an ex-bishop to power. What was perhaps even more astonishing in a country ruled by deeply conservative and authoritarian regimes for most of its history, Lugo was a strong advocate of liberation theology, the progressive Catholic doctrine that emerged in the 1960s. It argued that the Church had a moral obligation to defend and promote the interests of the poor, and advocated profound socio-economic and political reform. Indeed, Lugo's platform was based on a series of progressive social and economic reforms, including an unprecedented land reform programme, judicial reform and state-sector reform to address rampant corruption. These initiatives were to be accompanied, and in part financed, by tax reform, as well as by a renegotiation of the 1973 Treaty with Brazil relating to the Itaipú hydroelectric dam. Lugo's victory and the scope of his electoral promises led to huge expectations and gave him significant political capital when he took office. When he promised a 'new dawn' for Paraguay of justice, peace and solidarity, many believed that he would deliver it. Yet three years later, Lugo could point to very few tangible successes or reforms.

This chapter will examine why Lugo was unable to implement the most important elements of his electoral platform and will analyse the array of powerful and entrenched interests that stood against him, blocking his reform agenda and undermining governability in Paraguay. Concretely, it will first analyse the nature and context of his victory and the constraints they imposed on his programme. It will then consider the successes enjoyed in the first two years, before examining the strategies employed by the opposition to block four key elements of his reform agenda: judicial reform, tax reform, anti-corruption and land reform, before assessing the role of the opposition in Congress and the media. What becomes clear from this analysis is that opposition behaviour not only reflects the entrenched and conservative structures of power that have been a legacy of the dictatorship, but also the very real limitations of a transition that has stagnated in a state of 'defective democracy', characterized by clientelism, authoritarian enclaves and inequality (Merkel 2004).

The victory in the context of the transition

The overthrow of General Stroessner in February 1989 by his erstwhile military ally, General Andres Rodríguez, ushered in a transition to democracy, but not a significant change in the structures of power in the country. Without doubt the transition brought advances in terms of democratic procedures and institutions, including elections (national, municipal and regional), and a new constitution in 1992; yet it was essentially limited, conservative and unconsolidated (Lambert 2000).

The political dominance of the Colorado Party was a central reason behind the limitations of the transition process. The party had come to power via the bloody civil war of 1947, rapidly transforming itself into the pillar of the infamous Stroessner dictatorship (1954–89), and then into the initiator of, and dominant force in, Paraguay's transition to democracy. During this time it constructed a political system based on vast networks of patronage and clientelism at the local level (as well as in the highly inefficient and politicized state sector), on widespread corruption and on an effective electoral machinery, all of which were key to its development as 'one of Latin America's most powerful and best organized political movements' (Sanders 1989: 3). These factors, far more than actual performance, explain how the Colorado Party managed to hold on to power in successive elections in 1989, 1993, 1998 and 2003. Indeed, the Colorado governments until 2003 were particularly inept in terms of levels of corruption, economic mismanagement and ineffectual governance. Between 1996 and 2002, Paraguay endured a prolonged period of economic stagnation, during which per capita income dropped by over a third to just over $1,000 and poverty rose to 48 per cent (Lambert 2000: 400), while corruption, contraband, arms and drugs trafficking increased; indeed, in 2002 Paraguay was categorized as the most corrupt country in Latin America, and the third most corrupt in the world (Transparency International 2002), while indictment charges were brought against three former presidents of the transition period. The party itself was beset by internal factionalism – a factor that contributed to attempted coups d'état allegedly involving ex-General Lino Oviedo in 1996 and the infamous *marzo paraguayo* (the Paraguayan March) of 1999, which witnessed the assassination of the vice-president, Luis Maria Argaña, and pitched battles involving thousands of civilian pro-democracy demonstrators outside Congress that led to the death of seven pro-democracy demonstrators and to dozens of others being wounded (Abente Brun 1999).

The quality of democracy in the Colorado-dominated transition remained poor in terms of good governance, democratic legitimacy and active citizenship, while the political and judicial systems were undermined by clientelism and corruption (Lambert 2007). Furthermore, social exclusion in the form of high levels of poverty, inequality and discrimination undermined democratic citizenship, participation and access to basic services (UN Development Programme 2008). As a result, Paraguayan democracy might have advanced further than merely a semi-authoritarian regime, but it was certainly tentative and unconsolidated, with clear signs of what Merkel (2004) termed a 'defective democracy', with long-term deficits in areas of rule of law, accountability and inequality. By the early 2000s, democracy appeared less threatened by the 'sudden death of military intervention than by the slow death of decay' (O'Donnell 1994), as the legitimacy of democracy as a system was steadily eroded by poor performance, low quality and widespread disillusionment.

This dangerous trend was clearly reflected in a series of polls by Latinobarómetro. In 2007, for example, only 33 per cent of Paraguayan respondents supported democracy as a system, and only 9 per cent were satisfied with its performance. Paraguay also scored lowest in Latin America on almost all other ratings of attitudes towards democracy, including support for and trust in politicians and political parties, and government performance and improvement to welfare (Latinobarómetro 2007). Meanwhile, the 2005 survey found that 69 per cent of respondents would support authoritarianism under certain circumstances, with almost 70 per cent of respondents replying that the nature of government, whether authoritarian or democratic, was less important than performance (Latinobarómetro 2005). Such low levels of legitimacy and support for democracy raised the possibility of the rise of social conflict on the one hand, and on the other authoritarian populism, reflected in the prolonged popularity of the controversial figure of Lino Oviedo.

The outcome of the 2008 elections

Lugo's electoral victory, with 41 per cent of the vote, ended six decades of 'maladministration and pillage' (O'Shaughnessy 2009b: 7) by the Colorado Party. In the words of the new president, it was a victory by 'the little ones', the end of 'an exclusive Paraguay, a Paraguay of secrets, a Paraguay known for its corruption', promising a 'new dawn' of reformism in Paraguay (*Diario Ultima Hora* 2008). However, the triumph was not as clear cut as some have suggested.

First, Lugo's victory did not imply the collapse of the Colorado Party. Indeed, it remained the largest party in terms of membership, seats in the Senate (fifteen out of forty-five), seats in the Chamber of Deputies (thirty out of eighty), departmental governorships (ten out of seventeen) and local government (with control over 70 per cent of municipalities). Moreover, its mechanisms and structures of informal power (clientelism, patronage and corruption) remained largely intact, not least in the highly politicized public-sector bureaucracy, and, via domination of the Supreme Court, in the judiciary as a whole. Secondly, the outcome of the 2008 elections 'did more to rearrange the electoral map than to transform it' (Abente Brun 2008: 150). Rather than a large shift of votes from the Colorado Party to the APC, there was a shift (of about 8 per cent) to the Unión Nacional de Ciudadanos Eticos (UNACE, National Union of Ethical Citizens), the highly conservative, populist party of Lino Oviedo, which broke away from the Colorado Party in 1998. The combined Colorado/UNACE vote was 53 per cent, reflecting a continued high level of support for conservative and right-wing parties that were based on clientelistic relations and that were virulently opposed to Lugo's reforms (Nickson 2009).

Thirdly, the APC was not a solid, ideologically based coalition, but rather a marriage of convenience between Lugo and the main, traditional opposition to the Colorados, the centre-right Partido Liberal Radical Auténtico (PLRA, Authoritarian Radical Liberal Party), which was by far the largest party in the APC coalition. Once the election had been won, the structural weakness of the coalition became increasingly evident. While Lugo could count on the support of only a handful of centre-left parties with minimal representation in Congress, the PLRA was itself sharply divided between competing, highly personalized factions. This was exacerbated by the deeply conservative views of many in the PLRA, especially on issues such as land and tax reform, which were integral to Lugo's reform programme. To complicate matters further, from the outset Lugo's relations with his vice-president, Federico Franco of the PLRA, were difficult, leading Lugo to ally himself with anti-Franco majority factions in the PLRA, while Franco increasingly positioned himself as a source of opposition. Fourthly, the nature of Lugo's reforms challenged entrenched elite interests in Paraguay that held significant power and influence in all major parties. Significantly, the initial reform efforts of the previous Colorado administration of Nicanor Duarte Frutos (2003–08) in the crucial areas of tax and land reform had been effectively opposed and blocked by a powerful alliance of interest groups with cross-party representation, even though the Colorado Party at the time held a clear majority in Congress.

Lugo was therefore backed by a fragmented, ideologically divided coalition which lacked an absolute majority in Congress. This, combined with the weak presidentialist system established under the 1992 constitution, which grants Congress extensive powers, meant he would have to negotiate support not only with sections of the political opposition in Congress, but also with elements within his own coalition. Yet his victory gave him considerable political capital, extremely high approval ratings (over 90 per cent when he took power) and high expectations of positive change (Latinobarómetro 2008: 31–2). He also had a clear reform programme that promised substantive improvements in the quality of democracy in terms of governance, rule of law and far-reaching socio-economic reform. Given his lack of a solid support base, his popularity and legitimacy would be dependent on performance and on his ability to address the longstanding and pressing issues of poverty, inequality, corruption and landlessness highlighted in his electoral programme.

Successes

In the first two years of Lugo's presidency, his government made significant gains in the areas of healthcare, poverty-alleviation programmes, foreign relations and the negotiations over Itaipú. In healthcare, despite traditional low levels of service and coverage, Paraguay had made progress since the mid-1990s due to a long-term coordinated strategy based on the creation of social pharmacies, local health councils and preventive healthcare. Lugo built on this success through the introduction in the first months of his administration of free access to medical attention in public hospitals, free maternity care, free emergency treatment and free access to certain medicines, with free dental treatment added in 2009. He also expanded the highly successful primary healthcare pharmacy project. Initial poverty-alleviation measures were based on the establishment of a system of conditional cash transfers, which, modelled on the Brazilian system of *Bolsa Familia*, aimed to provide the poorest families with a monthly cash subsidy of up to $60 in return for commitments to child vaccination and school attendance. The coverage included 13,000 families in 2008, rising to

65,000 in 2009, with a target of 200,000 families by the end of 2010 (Arce 2010).

Lugo also managed to create a strong, pragmatic and proactive foreign policy, establishing trade and aid agreements with a wide range of international partners from across the political spectrum. While he maintained good relations with the US, which was generally supportive of the administration in terms of reforms to improve areas of governance and rule of law, he also received strong support for his reform agenda from centre-left governments in Latin America. Meanwhile international donors and financial institutions were key to important innovations in areas such as customs, the financial control system, the civil service and the police.

Perhaps Lugo's most significant success was over the issue of the 1973 Itaipú Treaty with Brazil, which had long been a source of contention in Paraguay. Although each country owns an equal (50 per cent) share of the energy produced, the treaty obliges Paraguay to sell any unused electricity at an established cost price to Brazil, rather than at market value or to third parties. In practice, Paraguay uses barely 7 per cent of the energy output and so sells the remainder of its half share to Brazil. Although Paraguay receives a 'compensation' fee of $120 million per year, it has long argued that this is a 'scandalously unfair' treaty, by which Paraguay provides a subsidy on approximately 20 per cent of Brazilian domestic energy use – put at $3 billion per year (Nickson 2009). After repeated refusals by Brazil to renegotiate conditions until 2023, constant pressure from Lugo, including veiled threats to take the matter to the International Court of Justice, led to an unprecedented agreement in July 2009. Brazil promised to triple 'compensation' royalties to Paraguay to $360 million per year, to complete the substation and transmission line to Asunción, to agree to auditing and transparency, to allow Paraguay to gradually begin to sell electricity to Brazil (but not other countries) at market price, and to share management (Comisión de Entes Binacionales Hidroeléctricos 2009). This was seen in Paraguay as a major victory, since the extra annual revenue could potentially double public investment from central government and finance major poverty reduction and social expenditure programmes. However, it took until May 2011 for both houses of the Brazilian legislature to approve the agreement.

Blunting the key reforms

By Lugo's own admission, the first two years of his administration were disappointing, largely because of the successful strategies employed by the opposition to block his reform agenda. This can be seen in the four key policy areas that formed the basis of his electoral programme: judicial reform, anti-corruption, tax reform and land reform.

Almost twenty years after the beginning of the transition, the judiciary was still widely regarded as corrupt, inefficient and unable to combat corruption or impunity or to protect citizens' rights (Lambert 2007). It was also highly politicized, due to a quota system established under the 1995 *Pacto de Gobernabilidad* (Governability Pact), under which appointments and promotions were decided by political negotiation between the major parties, and hence on the basis of political service, allegiance and loyalty, rather than on merit, expertise, experience or qualification. Reform of the Supreme Court was seen as the starting point for any overhaul of the corrupt judicial system. Faced with a Colorado majority in the Supreme Court, Lugo required a two-thirds majority in both chambers of Congress to push through reform. Without the political support from Congress to undertake a major overhaul of the system, and unable to convince the PLRA to abandon the quota system, Lugo was forced to continue the practice of negotiation of individual appointments. In January 2009 he failed to garner enough support to replace a retired Colorado member of the Supreme Court with his own preferred candidate, which would have given the government a majority of five to four. This reflected deep divisions in the ruling coalition, as well as Lugo's inability to negotiate with the opposition. More revealing of the opposition to Lugo, in January 2010 the *Sala Constitucional* (Constitutional Tribunal) voted to reinstate two members of the Supreme Court who had been suspended in 2003 but had not been replaced because of repeated impasse in Congress. Although there was no evidence that Lugo had intervened in the decision, Lino Oviedo of UNACE declared that Lugo was 'taking the first steps towards the establishment of a dictatorship', following in the steps of Hugo Chávez and Evo Morales 'to personally manage Judicial Power and annul the power of Congress', while ex-President Nicanor Duarte termed the decision a 'coup d'état against Congress' (*La República* 2010). The decision was subsequently rejected by Congress and annulled by the Supreme Court. Unable to negotiate reform in Congress or challenge the quota system imposed by the two major parties, by 2010 Lugo had tacitly accepted defeat in his campaign to overhaul the judicial system.

In terms of increased transparency, anti-corruption and professionalization, reform of the inefficient, corrupt and Colorado-dominated public sector (Nickson and Lambert 2002) made initial progress in a number of areas, including customs, the ports administration, the telephone company and Itaipú. The Ministry of Finance also continued the work begun in 2003–05 to transform itself into an 'island of integrity' in terms of greater transparency and accountability (Abente Brun 2008). Initiatives by the secretariat of the civil service also made some headway in introducing standardized norms for merit-based appointments, promotion and accountability. However, by 2010 there had still been no implementation of the progressive Public Administration Law of 2001, beyond a few isolated ministries. This was not so much a question of financial resources as of political will: control of ministries has long been seen in Paraguay as a political prize, enabling parties to establish clientelistic structures within the state sector. While between 1947 and 2008, the Colorado Party had almost sole access to such power, the 2008 electoral victory allowed the PLRA to gain a foothold in the public sector for the first time and begin to appoint its own political allies throughout the state bureaucracy. Against such established political practice, efforts to reform the system made slow progress.

The key element of Lugo's anti-corruption campaign was tax reform, which would also provide essential funding for proposed social welfare and poverty-alleviation programmes. Paraguay is the only country in the region with no system of direct income tax; furthermore, it has the lowest tax burden (under 12 per cent) and has no effective agricultural export tax, instead relying heavily for revenue on regressive, indirect taxation (chiefly VAT). Nor does it have any system of declaration of assets and income, which is seen as a contributing factor in the growth of the informal sector and corruption, including money-laundering, contraband and narcotics trafficking. The tax reform bill, originally drawn up in 2004 by Finance Minister Dionisio Borda, was modest, in that, as well as establishing a declaration of assets, it would only directly affect approximately 10,000 of the country's wealthiest people (0.3 per cent of the economically active population) with a top rate of 10 per cent (Ministerio de Hacienda 2010). However, it had twice been postponed (2006 and 2007) due to political opposition from UNACE and the PLRA and intense lobbying from powerful interest groups, such as soya exporters. Having reappointed the reformist Borda as finance minister, Lugo attempted to push through the reform in January 2009; when this was blocked, he launched a high-profile (but unsuccessful) campaign to get it through Congress in April 2010, when it was postponed for a further three years.

Opposition to such a key measure reflects three factors: first, the ability of legal and illegal economic interest groups, including soya producers, cattle farmers and those involved in illicit activities, such as contraband and narcotics, to use their cross-party influence to block a reform that was clearly in the national interest; secondly, the tribal nature of Paraguayan politics, reflected in the number of Colorados who had supported reform while in government in 2006 and 2007, but who voted against it in opposition in 2009 and 2010; and thirdly, a clear opposition policy of macroeconomic destabilization as part of its efforts to undermine the government. The opposition was well aware that failure to gain congressional approval for tax reform would represent a major blow to Lugo's ability to fund his key reforms designed to address inequality, poverty and corruption.

According to government figures, 38 per cent of Paraguayans (some 2.3 million people) live in poverty, rising to 49 per cent in rural areas; 19 per cent live in extreme poverty (Dirección General de Estadídisticas, Encuestas y Censos 2008). These figures have changed little since the mid-1990s. Paraguay is also one of the most unequal countries in Latin America, with a GINI index coefficient of 0.58. Nowhere is this more evident than in the area of land ownership, with 1 per cent of landowners owning 77 per cent of the cultivable land (Alderete 2009), making Paraguay the most unequal country in Latin America in terms of distribution of land. The combination of traditional inequality, increased land concentration since the 1990s (due to the uncontrolled expansion of soya production) and increased landlessness (which affected approximately 30 per cent of the rural population) led to growing tensions between landowners and landless peasant organizations throughout the first decade of the new millennium. The promise of agrarian reform was central to Lugo's electoral platform and provided him with a strong base of support among Paraguay's increasingly well organized peasant movements. However, despite the creation of a new state body for land reform, the Coordinadora Ejecutiva para la Reforma Agraria (CEPRA, Executive Coordinating Committee for Agrarian Reform), the crucial first step – the conducting of a cadastral survey to establish land value and ownership – had still not been carried out by the end of 2010, allegedly due to the lack of funds to cover the cost, estimated at $300 million. Reform efforts such as investigating, expropriating and redistributing *tierras malhabidas* (lands gained through corrupt practice under the dictatorship) also foundered due to the legal complexity of ownership and opposition by powerful groups. By 2010, land reform appeared to have stagnated and Lugo had reverted to the previous expensive policy of buying land at commercial prices for redistribution.

The inability of the government to implement its agrarian reform programme was the consequence not so much of a lack of will or even resources, but rather of the existence of a coordinated, well resourced and powerful opposition. Landowners' groups, especially the Asociación Rural del Paraguay (ARP, Paraguayan Rural Association) and the Asociación de Productores de Soja (APS, Association of Soya Producers), comprise some of the wealthiest and most influential elites in the country, and enjoy a strong lobbying presence, with representation in all major political parties. The APS, for example, represents the richest economic group in Paraguay, looks to Brazil for representation, support and protection, and has proved under successive administrations to be able to block tax and land reform, not only through lobbying, but also through the threat of direct action in the form of *tractorazos* (road-blocking of major routes by tractors). Such a *tractorazo* early in December 2008 sent a clear signal to Lugo that land reform efforts would be met with significant opposition. The slow pace of reform under Lugo led to a rise in land occupations, an increasingly militant discourse among peasant organizations and clashes with armed, often Brazilian, security guards. The deterioration in the situation led Claudia Ruser, the controversial hard-line leader of the APS, to accuse Lugo of alleged support for the landless movement, which she went on to classify as a proto-guerrilla organization, supported by President Chávez (Oxford Analytica 2008). As Lugo's land reform project stagnated, social conflict became increasingly likely.

Opposition in Congress

Opposition in Congress was the key element in the failure of these four key reform packages. While this opposition came mainly from the Colorado Party and UNACE, it also came from within the PLRA, in the form of Vice-President Federico Franco, who, in mid-2009, formally led the PLRA out of the APC, although the two majority PLRA factions remained in government. The opposition strategy in Congress was three-fold. First, it sought to block key legislation pertaining to Lugo's reform agenda through alliances between the Colorado Party, UNACE and dissident PLRA members. This included voting to block vital funding streams (most notably the tax reform bill, but also initially a key foreign aid package), while also voting against a wide range of reforms and proposals supported by Lugo, ranging from reform of membership of the Supreme Court to Venezuela's membership of Mercosur. In a party system predominantly composed of non-programmatic parties, party loyalty rather than ideological opposition was an important contributory factor.

Secondly, the opposition sought to destabilize the government by generating a fiscal deficit and undermining macroeconomic stability. The government's initial five-year plan for 'sustainable growth with justice' was immediately undermined by attempts in Congress to subject both the 2009 and 2010 budget proposals to huge increases in spending, generating the possibility of an unsustainable deficit. In June 2009, Congress voted to further postpone the tax reform bill, thus cutting a key revenue stream; while on the same day it also voted to increase state pensions and double the salaries of departmental governors and members of the National Electoral Commission, at a combined cost of $118 million. Likewise, in October 2009, it voted to increase its own budget by 52 per cent and that of the judicial system by 20 per cent. Such measures had the clear aim of undermining the government by 'prising open a tailor-made fiscal gap' and suggested that the Colorado Party was 'intent on macroeconomic destabilisation as part of its plan to regain power at any cost in 2013' (Oxford Analytica 2009b).

Thirdly, it sought to undermine Lugo's social welfare and poverty-alleviation programme in an attempt to prevent him from establishing a political base among the poor. Revealingly, at the same time as Congress increased spending in June 2009, it refused funding to CEPRA, the land reform agency, to finance new settlements for landless farmers. Meanwhile, in October 2009, Congress cut the budgets of the key institutions for poverty alleviation, including the Secretaría de Acción Social (Social Welfare Secretariat), and the Secretaría de Emergencia Nacional (National Emergency Secretariat), while a congressional commission voted to cut funds for Paraguay's internationally respected conditional cash transfer programme. With limited executive powers, Lugo found his room for manoeuvre highly constrained. When he raised the possibility of 'popular consultations' as a means to pressure Congress to cooperate with the government (referendums are expressly permitted in the 1992 constitution), Congress alleged 'creeping authoritarianism' and insisted he signed a 'Democratic Pact' to support representative – rather than participatory or Bolivarian – democracy. When Lugo refused, the opposition in Congress and the media adroitly manipulated his discourse to accuse him of plotting to introduce a totalitarian, Chávez-style 'twenty-first-century socialism' to Paraguay.

Fourthly, throughout 2008 and 2009 rumours of an impending military coup in Paraguay were rife. These were heightened or reflected by Lugo's replacement in his first fifteen months in office of a total of forty-three generals – as well as of the heads of the army, navy and air force on no fewer than three occasions. Strikingly, while he rejected the idea of any imminent military uprising, he did state that there might be 'small groups' of military personnel that 'could be used by the political class' (Smink 2009). Indeed, despite the constant rumours, few believed that the military would act alone, but might briefly intervene in a Honduras-style coup on behalf of an opposition faction. Lugo's administration was perhaps even more vulnerable to a coup by Congress, in the form of almost constant threats of impeachment. Indeed, by the end of 2009 Lugo faced highly publicized calls for impeachment from the opposition on four separate grounds: for alleged corruption in the management of lands for redistribution; for promoting the class struggle; for alleged links with guerrilla movements; and for failing to protect citizen security.

Given how close the opposition was to the two-thirds majority in Congress required to impeach Lugo, his survival was due principally to the deep divisions in the opposition, and to its separate strategies to gain power. While Vice-President Franco might have relished the opportunity to take over the presidency and strengthen his own position, and that of the PLRA, before the 2013 elections, this was virulently opposed by factions in the Colorado Party, which had their eyes set on the same elections. This would suggest that the constant threat of impeachment was more a strategy employed by the opposition to destabilize the government, gain concessions from Lugo, or simply undermine his attempts to implement his reform programme (Arce 2009).

The opposition in Congress was driven not only by party political concerns, but also by a shared ideological opposition to many of the reforms proposed by the government. Although none of the three major parties in Paraguay is programmatic, all are heavily weighted towards conservative and right-wing interests, and all benefit from the current socio-economic status quo. It is this unity, in terms of class, economic and social interests, that is most striking in the case of the Paraguayan Congress. When a right-wing PLRA senator, Alfredo Jaeggli, stated in November 2009 that 'we have a six-month window in which to remove Lugo before the social organizations are strengthened', he revealed the cross-party fears among the political elites in Paraguay of the growth of peasant and other social movements and of overdue socio-economic reforms that would threaten the status quo (Benegas 2010). There is a striking consensus among political elites in Paraguay: they view both reform and social movements as a very real threat to their interests.

The media

Although the media became important unofficial sources of investigation into corruption, impunity and crime during the transition, they were far from objective or non-partisan. The lack of regulation in the 1990s led to a concentration of media control in the hands of a very small group of figures with shared business and political interests, and a resulting integration of the print media with television and radio outlets. Moreover, the print media strongly influenced the coverage and analysis of news for radio, television and digital services. In this sense, the press not only reported political events, but had the power to manipulate, limit and set the political agenda (Ortiz 2009). In the case of Lugo, this resulted in the emergence of a powerful and influential source of opposition.

Even before the 2008 election, there appeared to be a concerted campaign to associate Lugo with the radical left, linking him not only with Hugo Chávez and Evo Morales, but also with landless peasant organizations, and, by extension, with the incipient Paraguayan guerrilla movement, the Ejército Popular Paraguayo (EPP, Paraguayan People's Army) and even the Colombian Fuerzas Armadas Revolucionarias Colombianas (FARC, Revolutionary Armed Forces of Colombia). From August 2008, this association between Lugo, landless but allegedly armed peasants, Chávez and the threat of 'twenty-first-century socialism' constituted a central part of the opposition campaign in the majority of the media. Most notably, *ABC Color*, Paraguay's most widely read and influential daily newspaper, adopted a consistently anti-government line in its headlines, editorials and comment pieces. Political analysis involved emphasizing, repeating and exaggerating the weakness of the government, the inexperience and ineptitude of Lugo and the growth of social tension, instability and insecurity in order to create a climate of fear and anger directed at the president. In addition, the press gave extensive coverage to the opposition to Lugo's reform programme, presenting it as sensible, responsible, led by elite consensus and acting in the national interest.

On the other hand, proponents of reform were presented as irresponsible, naïve and dangerous (Arce 2009) – and, in the case of peasant organizations, as corrupt, a threat to law and order, and even linked to guerrilla groups (Ortiz 2009). The fact that the press effectively set the parameters of debate meant that Lugo increasingly strove to portray himself as a moderate centrist, adopting a more cautious rhetoric that led to accusations from supporters that he was responding to opposition criticisms of creeping socialism and imminent government collapse, rather than sufficiently promoting his own reform programme.

The case of the EPP

A further destabilizing element in Lugo's administration was the continued activities of the EPP. This very small guerrilla group operated primarily in the poor regions of Concepción and San Pedro, which, from the 1990s, had seen growing conflict between an increasingly militant movement of landless peasants and an alliance of powerful cattle ranchers and Brazilian soya bean producers. While the activities of the EPP were sporadic and relatively limited (Oxford Analytica 2009a), they were exploited by the media and opposition politicians to reflect an alleged deterioration in national security and public order, becoming a rallying cry of anti-Lugo opposition. Days after the kidnapping of cattle-rancher Fidel Zavala in October 2009, Lino Oviedo threatened Lugo with impeachment for failing to protect citizen security, while Mario Abdo Benítez, vice-president of the Colorado Party, went further, as did sections of the press, accusing the president of having direct links with leaders of the EPP. While there was little evidence, the repeated accusations left permanent negative associations.

The true nature of this nascent armed group remains shrouded in mystery. Isolated and disowned by the left, it is a small group with a very limited field of action. While it is perceived by many in the ARP and the APS, by the press and by politicians in the three major political parties as evidence of a wider subversive movement with links to the Paraguayan landless movement and the Colombian FARC, others have raised questions regarding its aims and financial backers, and whether these are at all what they seem. It is plausible, for example, that the EPP is financed and supported by powerful drugs mafias that have established themselves in the north and east of the country and wish to keep the area 'out of bounds' for the authorities (Oxford Analytica 2009a). Whatever their real identity, the issue of the EPP was used to further undermine the embattled president's legitimacy. In a reaction that was indicative of the power of the right and the media to establish the political agenda, in April 2010 Lugo declared an ultimately futile thirty-day state of emergency in five departments, in response to the killing of four people, including a policeman, by the EPP. The measure, unprecedented in the transition, was widely criticized as a dangerous overreaction by Lugo and evidence of his susceptibility to the constant allegations of his sympathies towards the guerrillas and his inability to provide security in the areas in which they operate.

Undermining the new dawn

By the end of 2010, the administration of Lugo was widely perceived simply to have run out of steam – a perception perhaps exacerbated by the revelation in August of that year that Lugo was suffering from an advanced but treatable form of lymphatic cancer. In the municipal elections of November 2010, the Colorado Party emerged triumphant, with over 55 per cent of the vote, winning 132 out of 238 municipalities – including, narrowly, Asunción. But it was the unprecedented 54 per cent abstention rate and the renewed dominance of the two traditional parties – which together won nearly 94 per cent of the vote – that most clearly reflected the extent of popular disillusionment with the failure of Lugo to implement his promised reform programme.

To some extent this was due to personal failings. His highly individual style of leadership and informality in decision-making led to prevarication, improvisation and back-tracking on certain issues, and made it more difficult to establish a working coalition in Congress or to turn widespread support among the poor into a clearly articulated political base of support beyond the fractious APC. Furthermore, his integrity came under scrutiny with the emergence of three paternity suits in the first sixteen months of his presidency, one of which he accepted. The issue was not so much one of a senior member of the Church fathering children, but rather his refusal to recognize paternity or to support the (impoverished and single) mothers and offspring in question. Additional accusations of corruption, affecting him and some of his inner circle, as well as nepotism further undermined his image as a 'clean' and therefore different kind of politician (Oxford Analytica 2009c). Yet, despite personal inadequacies, the clearest cause of the failure of the reformist programme lay with what Lugo characterized in November 2009 as an orchestrated campaign to undermine his presidency and impede his policies. This was due not, as he claimed, to 'mafia' organizations or *golpistas* (coup plotters), but to a conservative elite that was threatened by the nature of his reforms. The form and success of this campaign are notable for a number of reasons.

First, the opposition, ranging from members of the traditional agrarian and political elites, modernizing agrarian elites, the soya producers and sectors of the business elite, was characterized by a complicit agreement to oppose reforms that threatened the socio-economic and political status quo. In this sense, the opposition showed itself to be more united by class considerations than by party allegiance. Despite factionalism and cross-party mistrust, the elites from all major parties were able to unite to oppose reforms of the tax system, the judiciary and land ownership, which would have adversely affected their class interests. Secondly, given the large body of consensus on the need for socio-economic reform both within the international financial and development community, and among the Paraguayan population, it would appear that the opposition was more motivated by the desire to regain and retain political power at almost any cost, than by any overriding concern for the national interest. This reflects the historical tendency of politicians in Paraguay to act strategically to further their own power and that of their party (in terms of capture of the state, public posts and state revenues and resources), rather than to act in the interests of their constituents.

Thirdly, the elites were able to adopt a multi-layered strategy to undermine Lugo's popular legitimacy. This consisted of constant opposition through often shifting alliances in Congress, which sought not only to block key legislation and government initiatives but also to undermine government fiscal balance. This was supported by a media campaign that criticized the performance and character of Lugo by portraying rumour and supposition as fact, most notably by associating Lugo with left-wing radicalism, 'twenty-first-century socialism', and the spectre of imminent social breakdown. Such opposition was supported most forcefully by the powerful rural landowners' associations, the APS and the APC, which also threatened direct action in the form of *tractorazos* to block legislation.

Fourthly, the opposition reflected the limitations of an unconsolidated and 'defective' democracy. While democracy is often judged by the performance of the administration in office and by its relationship with democratic procedures and institutions, equally revealing are the behaviour, alliances and strategies of the opposition. In the case of Paraguay, the opposition acted within the constitutional framework, but it did not act as a responsible opposition in a consolidated democracy. Threats of impeachment, the use of rumours of impending coups, macroeconomic destabilization and the blocking of moderate reforms even against the clear national interest reflect a political class accustomed to power within a defective rather than a consolidated democracy.

The nature of Lugo's proposed reforms and the virulence of the opposition campaign to destabilize his administration suggest that the roots of this conflict go deeper. Much of the mainstream writing on democratization in the 1990s stressed the importance of caution and accommodation in democratic transitions in terms of socio-economic reform, emphasizing the political nature of democracy and the need not to provoke elite reaction. Adam Przeworski argued that democratization was best served by the 'docility and patience' of marginalized sectors and the preservation of existing socio-economic relations, including the distribution of income and wealth (Przeworski 1986: 63), while Alan Rouquié stated the need for 'constructing democracy before changing society' (Rouquié 1986: 136). Others, of course, have argued of the dangers of such a narrowly institutional and procedural approach, maintaining that, in countries characterized by poverty and the highly unequal distribution of wealth and resources, reform is central to democratic consolidation. Atilio Borón, for example, has argued powerfully that significant social reform programmes to reduce inequality and poverty are as necessary as elections in terms of the stabilization and consolidation of democracy (Borón 1995: 192). The case of Paraguay in the 1990s, with a transition stagnating in a mire of corruption, mismanagement, disillusionment and lack of reform, highlighted the very real dangers of a model of democracy limited to institutions and procedures. It also demonstrated that, if democracy is to survive and progress, it must be founded on a far greater degree of social and economic redistribution, attainable only through a programme of socio-economic reforms, along the lines of those proposed by Lugo.

Lugo's reforms were more consistent with 'moderate social democracy' than radical socialism (O'Shaughnessy 2009b: 122). Yet from the outset he was confronted by a broad opposition, composed of entrenched economic, media and political elites, which, determined to defend their class interests, sought to undermine the legitimacy of his administration and hence his reforms. In the first three years of the administration, the opposition managed to block almost every aspect of Lugo's reform programme, blunt his ambitions and hence neutralize and then undermine his popularity. As a result, Lugo was unable to develop his base of support, form a coherent political movement, push through his desperately needed social reform agenda or significantly move Paraguay towards a more consolidated – and less defective – democracy.

12 | The new Argentine right and the Cristina Fernández administration

LEONARDO DÍAZ ECHENIQUE, JAVIER OZOLLO AND ERNESTO VIVARES

The process of change in Argentina and the country's regional reintegration, initiated after the deep crisis of 2001, did not take place without a reaction from the social forces that underpinned the neoliberal model consolidated in the 1990s. In 2007, President Cristina Fernández de Kirchner succeeded her husband, Néstor Carlos Kirchner Ostoić (2003–07). It was in exceptionally favourable political, economic and social conditions that she came to power with the goals of consolidating the ongoing reform of conservative and neoliberal structures and pursuing new domestic and regional policies (Vivares, Díaz and Ozorio 2009). It seemed that no opposing force could halt this programme of reforms. However, the first attempt to tax the extraordinary profits of grain exporters, in order to insulate domestic food prices from international trends, culminated in an institutional and democratic crisis and represented a national confrontation between alternative models of development. Opposing the government, the leaders of Argentina's four major agricultural producers' organizations launched a national strike and mounted road blockades, paralysing the country, causing widespread food shortages and producing a growing atmosphere of political crisis that was intensified by the media monopolies.

Unexpectedly, the government coalition fractured, casting doubt on the sustainability of the Cristina Fernández administration, which faced not just electoral defeat but even a Honduras-style coup. Suddenly, confronting the previously unbeatable administration was a resilient and unified coalition, capable not only of halting the reform process, but even of restoring the conservative and neoliberal order. In response to new domestic, regional and international patterns of politics and development, a new Argentine right has emerged. It is a complex political-economic force, consolidated through three decades of development by powerful political and economic actors in agribusiness, finance and the media. This new right retains strong features from its past, but its composition and strategies constitute a new identity that is more aligned with current conservative and neoliberal tendencies in the hemisphere: working within democratic settings, supported by media monopolies and networks linked to multilateral financial institutions.

This chapter analyses the composition and behaviour of this conservative and neoliberal opposition in Argentina in the light of the major conflicts over agrarian taxation and over the 2009 reform of media regulation that have consolidated the right.

From world granary to soya nation

Argentina is an agri-exporter, especially of meat and grains. This is uniquely profitable, thanks to the natural conditions of the famous *Pampa húmeda* (humid Pampas) and to the insertion of the agrarian sector into the value chain of global agribusiness. This sector is developed and capitalist, with highly concentrated and absentee landownership, and has been shifting in recent decades towards financial forms of control of land and production. Within this model of accumulation, Argentina ranks today as the world's third-largest soya bean producer, behind the US and Brazil. The agrarian sector has historically enjoyed decisive political and economic influence, and its elites have opposed all projects of social transformation.

The golden age of the agricultural sector, which made Argentina the 'world granary', spanned the end of the nineteenth and the beginning of the twentieth centuries, when the country occupied a key role in the international division of western labour as a producer and exporter of food. The dominant social force was an oligarchy of landowners, who consolidated their domination by exterminating the indigenous population and promoting European immigration. The political order, its institutions and civil society were forged on the back of the needs of this economic model, and on the basis of positivist and Darwinist ideas. However, with modernization in the twentieth century, this model declined, eroding the political power of the agrarian sector, which sustained the status quo through a long alliance with pro-fascist military groups, intellectuals and the hierarchy of the Catholic Church. The Argentine right would become the core anti-democratic force during a long period of the country's political and economic instability, enjoying the decisive external support of various industrialized countries.

This phenomenon, in similar forms, occurred throughout the region, and the study of the Argentinian experience produced major interpretations of authoritarianism and political instability in Latin America involving the struggles between agri-export and import-substitution-industrialization coalitions (O'Donnell 1978; McGee Deutsch 1999). Years later, without the support of the US and after the decline of the dictatorship in the wake of the Falklands/Malvinas war, a rapid process of regional democratization prompted a retreat by the traditional authoritarian and conservative forces. In parallel, the agrarian sector lost its decisive economic importance. As a result of falling international food prices and sector profitability, the green revolution in agriculture ended the myth of Argentina as the granary of the world. Revenues for meat and grain (particularly wheat) dropped from 30 per cent of national income in the 1960s to 10 per cent in the 1980s (Teubal, Domínguez and Sabatino 2005). The power of the agrarian sector declined with the loss of the military option of seizing power, with classic divisions between business interests and with its inability to build a political party. In the 1980s, the sector became a secondary factor in a new political-economic complex, now led by highly internationalized financial and industrial sectors.

However, in the 1990s, complex transformations occurred in the political and economic domains. These transformations were driven by an increase in demand for food; by the use of grain for other products, such as bio-fuels; by the continued incorporation of technology; and by the accelerated integration of industry and agribusiness, which strengthened internationalized agribusiness sectors. The food sector in Argentina is highly integrated into world trade via global value chains, with strong vertical integration controlled by international corporations such as Dreyfus, General Lagos Cargill, Noble, ADM, Nidera, Bunge and Born, Aceitera General Deheza and Vicentín (Bisang, Anlló and Campi 2008; Economic Commission for Latin America 2009).

At the domestic level, institutional changes have played a central part, with the Menem administration's (1989–99) neoliberal policies making the Argentine agricultural sector one of the most deregulated in the world. This popular market economy sought to emulate a Thatcherite social alliance between the different sectors. The Menem government's populist discourse turned out to be a Trojan Horse for conservative and neoliberal political forces. At the heart of these forces was the Unión del Centro Democrático (Union of the Democratic Centre). A conservative, neoliberal and anti-Peronist party, it became the key ideological ally of the administration as it sought to increase market confidence. The chief executive of the transnational agribusiness corporation Bunge and Born was appointed minister of economy, and the Sociedad Rural (Rural Society) was given extensive and valuable real estate in the capital city of Buenos Aires. Reinsertion of the country into the global order was completed with Menem's pardoning of members of the military responsible for gross human rights violations, his alliance with the most conservatives sectors of the country and his foreign policy of subordination to the United States. These changes marked the reconfiguration of social forces behind a market-led model of development, designed to dismantle the welfare state, open the economy, commodify labour and produce a significant shift in the balance of power between labour and capital in favour of the latter.

Agrarian transformation during the Menem administration

During the Menem administration, the last stage in a long process of liberalization and internationalization of the agricultural sector witnessed the dissolution of regulatory committees, changes to leasing laws, privatization of grain silos and ports, and the opening up of the market to genetically modified (GM) products. The objective was to promote outsourcing and to anchor the sector in international markets. The process strengthened the major economic groups in the country, whose members became key players in the confrontation with the government in the conflict over agricultural product export taxes. With currency convertibility facilitating outsourcing, competition policy before the 2001 crisis put the sector in a favourable export position.

Within this internationalized sectoral model, it is possible to identify various levels of actors. Companies such as Cargill, Dreyfus, Bunge and Deheza are at the first level, as market leaders controlling 27 per cent of the export market. The second level consists of large groups of farms, controlled by investment trusts, which lease and hire intermediaries to harvest large tracts of land. Between 1997 and 2002 alone, these trusts increased their holdings from 400,000 to 2,000,000 hectares. The third level is composed of international actors in control of agro-technology, particularly seeds and chemicals. A strategic feature of this structure is the small landowner, who, with insufficient capital to access the new value chain of the agribusiness, rents land to larger businesses. Completing the structure of the sector are the oil and machinery supply industries, creating an agribusiness sector that is highly integrated from production to commercialization, but that has low levels of employment of labour.

In these conditions, the agrarian political reaction was triggered by an increase in the price of international grains and industrial derivatives, such as bio-fuels, which put GM soya at the centre of the agribusiness, thanks to easy harvesting, low labour costs and huge profits. In just a few years, the conversion to soya yielded exponential growth in terms of production and land usage: from 3.7 million tons in 1980 to 46.5 million tons in 2008; the area of land affected went from 7 million hectares to 12.5 million hectares in the same period (Instituto Nacional de Estadística y Censos 2010).

TABLE 12.1 Growth in production and price of main grains 2001–08*

Year	Wheat		Maize		Soya	
	million tons	$/ton	million tons	$/ton	million tons	$/ton
2001	16.0	132	15.4	87	26.9	186
2002	15.3	127	14.7	90	30.0	203
2003	12.3	160	15.0	107	34.0	237
2004	14.6	169	15.0	105	31.6	230
2005	16.0	158	20.5	99	38.3	262
2006	12.6	178	14.4	110	40.5	235
2007	14.6	209	21.8	165	47.6	299
2008	16.0	500	20.4	240	46.5	590

Note: * Price Gulf of México (International Price Index for Commodities).
Source: INDEC; Secretaría de Agricultura, Ganadería y Pesca, Gobierno de Argentina.

In 2007, agribusiness, primary production and manufacturers of agricultural origin represented 56 per cent of total Argentine exports. Today the country is the world's leading producer and exporter of soya bean oil, the second-placed producer and the leading exporter of sunflower oil, and the third-placed producer and exporter of soya bean and sunflower, the fourth-placed exporter and producer of dried milk, among other key products. In short, Argentina stands out for its strength in the first link of the agro-industrial sector, but it is still dependent in the more advanced global value chain (Antunes 2008).

However, this structural configuration has brought about significant distortions in agrarian production, such as the concentration and centralization of capital. In terms of property, for instance, control by major landowners is still a feature. Over the last hundred years, control of the land has remained in the hands of a few families, who have expanded their lands: of the thirty-five largest landowning families in 1913, thirty still featured as such in 2010. Meanwhile smallholdings have declined to 25 per cent of the total, and nearly 85,000 properties of an average 200 hectares have disappeared. Today, 3.8 per cent of soya producers produce 60 per cent of total production, while 40 per cent of producers produce less than 4 per cent (Instituto Nacional de Estadística y Censos 2010). Another significant impact of soya conversion has been the impact on other agricultural production that is vital for the people, such as grain and livestock for domestic consumption. According to some estimates, 4 million hectares of land devoted to livestock have been converted to soya production (Reboratti 2010).

Rural reaction

In the presidential elections of 2007, Cristina Fernández enjoyed the support of the rural electorate linked to cereal production. This was despite the fact that the Kirchner administration had already increased tax on agricultural exports by more than 10 per cent and there were major conflicts over government livestock and dairy policies. For the first time, the major agrarian associations had coordinated their demands through the network known as Mesa de Enlace (literally 'linking table'). Small farmers demanded the liberalization of the export trade in livestock, as well as subsidies for the dairy industry. The government argued that regulation of the market was necessary to contain domestic prices, which have a high impact on consumption and inflation. In fact, under the Kirchner administration the underlying problem of the sector remained unresolved: the reinsertion of the Argentine economy and its agribusinesses into the world market (Antunes 2008).

On 13 March 2008, President Fernández signed Bill 125, establishing a sliding scale of export taxes on agricultural products, principally soya. The aims were to uncouple international prices from domestic, to avoid any return to hyperinflation, to guarantee availability of basic domestic food supplies and to limit soya conversion. The new system implied an increase in tax collection equivalent to 0.8 per cent of GDP – that is, between $2 billion and $3 billion. Bill 125 came as a shock to the Mesa de Enlace grouping of agri-producers, who strongly rejected it. They called on the agriculture sector to launch a national strike against it, initiating an escalating conflict that would polarize Argentine society over this and other aspects of development policy. In a nutshell, from this point on, the central objectives of the Mesa de Enlace would be to abolish any kind of agricultural export taxes and to maintain the subordination of domestic agricultural production to international prices, with the price of food on the domestic market reflecting international market forces (Ferrer 2010).

The conflict lasted four months and went through three phases. At first, it was centred on a debate about the situation of the agricultural sector. Demonstrations and failed negotiations ended in the resignation of the minister of economy, which, however, did not resolve the conflict. In the second phase, the government modified Bill 125, introducing concessions for small producers, though these were not accepted by the Mesa de Enlace group. An intensification of mobilizations fuelled confrontation in the streets with government supporters. In the third phase, the conflict was generalized and became highly politicized. When Bill 125 was sent to Congress, it was defeated, as Vice-President Julio Cobos, one of the main leaders of the governing coalition, abandoned the president.

Rural anti-government activities assumed a variety of forms: demonstrations, obstruction of the commercialization of basic foodstuffs and erection of the road blocks that were to become the central tactic of the producer groups. Previously, road blockades had been the principal means of disruption used by the *piqueteros*, who had protested against the Menem government's neoliberal policies. Unlike Menem, the Kirchner administration adopted a policy of no repression and no use of police force. Under Menem, the rural and industrial associations had denounced road blockades as a constraint on their economic rights, but now they were mounting such blockades. A distinctive feature of the protests of employers' associations was the participation of smaller producers, members of the Federación Agraria Argentina (Argentine Agrarian Federation) who radicalized the conflict with the government, deploying an uncompromising discourse based on the historical role of *el campo*, the countryside, in the life of the nation.

By pressure or persuasion, the producer groups obtained the support of municipalities and provinces with agrarian electoral bases, adding to the legitimacy of the political forces behind their demands. In an unexpected turn, these associations also received the support of opposition political parties, both left- and right-wing. Forces from the left questioned the credibility of the government because of its industrial and labour policies and because of the lack of structural reforms. Forces on the right attacked the 'populist' economic interventionism of the government, the confiscatory character of the taxes and the government's ignorance of agrarian life. However, the greatest impact on the government came from the political fracture within the *peronista* Partido Justicialista (PJ, Justice Party), which saw politicians linked to neoliberal ex-presidents Menem and Duhalde move into opposition to the government. The union of agrarian workers also came to support their employers' demands against the government. However, even though the opposition managed to bring together diverse forces, few of them would remain wedded to right-wing demands.

The more social, political and economic actors joined the new opposition, the more coherent and consistent became the discourse identifying *el campo* as the axis of the opposition, whose interests were the interests of the whole of Argentine society. Historic federalist demands for provincial autonomy, the role of the people of *el campo* in the golden era of the world's granary, authoritarianism and belief in white supremacy were all mixed in a discourse whose common components were class rage and defiance of the democratic order. The discourse of the growing agrarian revolts was accompanied by hazardous reactionary behaviour, like the parading of weapons, and attempts to dissuade the security forces from intervening against illegal activities. The conflict became a political-economic window on to phenomena that had remained concealed in recent years but now found an opportunity to reassert their lost authority and identity. However, times had changed, and these sectors no longer had control of strategic state forces. They could, however, count on the support of the larger media corporations to help them claim legitimacy for their struggle and for their claims to represent democratic common sense.

Right-wing opposition and media corporations

The principal media corporations provided wide news coverage of the conflict, in favour of the producer groups. For four months, the conflict monopolized all media and news channels, which presented a particular version of the disputes. The limited viewpoints presented can be attributed to the shared patterns of ownership and ideology that link the great media monopolies and important actors of agribusiness, particularly the powerful Clarín Group. This common outlook saw the media rapidly joining battle on the side of the agrarian sector. The role of the media focused on building an image of *el campo* and its representatives as the 'best of the Argentine identity', with country people portrayed as facing multiple adversities but continuing to get up every day to labour for 'the greatness of the nation' and 'the growth of our economy' and so on. In turbulent political waters, the large media monopolies unveiled their allegiance, taking the side of the most powerful economic interests and presenting the beliefs of the Argentine right as expressing the interests of the whole society. It constituted a Gramscian ideological construction, based on the premise that the people should defend the Argentine way of life against the tyranny of the Kirchners.

However, this experience is not a uniquely Argentine phenomenon. During the final quarter of the twentieth century, the region as a whole witnessed the consolidation of diverse oligopolies of media communication, controlled by large transnational companies. This oligopolization principally unfolded in the electronic media and television sectors. These forms of business had traditionally been characterized by the control of powerful families in the region, such as the Cisneros in Venezuela; Azcarraga in Mexico (owners of Direct TV); Marinho, Sirotsky, Saad, Abravanel and da Sílvio Santos in Brazil; Matte and Edwards in Chile (linked to the coup of Pinochet against Salvador Allende); Romay Salvo, Fontaina De-Feo and Scheck in Uruguay (García 2009); and the Noble, Saguier and Vila families in Argentina.

In Argentina media concentration accompanied the period of neoliberal transformation of the accumulation model that started with the military coup in 1976 and ended with the economic crisis of 2001. This period featured the nationalization by the military dictatorship of Papel Prensa (Press Paper), the main company producing and supplying newsprint in the country, and its partial transfer to the ownership of the three major newspapers: *Clarín*, *La Nación* and *La Razón*. The political meaning of this for the dictatorship was strategic: if you control the production of newsprint then you control the voice of newspapers. Hence the importance of control of Papel Prensa and of the military dictatorship's media regulation legislation, which limited broadcasting licences to favoured owners.

The Graviers, a Peronist family, were the owners of Papel Prensa, whose acquisition by the Grupo Clarín during the dictatorship became the subject of a heated political dispute under Cristina Fernández's administration (Sanz 2004; García 2010; Wainfeld 2010). On the one hand, the government launched an investigation and is prosecuting the Grupo Clarín, on the basis of the argument that the three newspapers had colluded with the dictatorship in the takeover of Papel Prensa – a move that was accompanied by extortion and threats to the lives of Gravier family members. On the other hand, the Grupo Clarín insists that the acquisition was legitimate and transparent, and did not feature any pressure, kidnap or torture of the Gravier family by the dictatorship. Grupo Clarín claims that the government is seeking to gag the independent media and curtail freedom of speech, and makes comparisons with media-licensing disputes in Venezuela under President Hugo Chávez. Meanwhile, in view of the history of Papel Prensa's acquisition and to avoid it being controlled by a media monopoly, President Cristina Fernández has sent a bill to Congress seeking the nationalization of the company.

In Argentina the Grupo Clarín, besides holding 267 licences for

TABLE 12.2 Key holdings of Grupo Clarín

Television	Press	Media producers and radio stations
Canal 13 (Artear)	Clarín	Pol-Ka (30% Grupo Clarín)
Señal Volver	Olé	Patagonik Film (30% Grupo Clarín)
Señal Magazine	La Razón (75% Grupo Clarín)	Radio Mitre (AM 790)
Señal TN	Genios	FM 100
Señal TyC Sports	Jardín de Genios	Gen FM 101.5
Señal TyC Max	Ñ	PRIMA – Primera Red Interactiva de Medios Argentinos (82% Grupo Clarín)
Canal 12 Córdoba	Elle Argentina	PRIMA Do Brasil
Canal 7 Bahía Blanca	Elle Decoración	Proveedor Ciudad Internet
TVC Pinamar	Elle Novias	Datamarkets
MTV Miramar	Editora de Revistas	Fullzero
TSN Necochea	Artes Gráficas Rioplatense	Clarin.com (Clarín Global; plus Edición España)
Multicanal	Arte Gráfico Editorial Argentino	Ubbi (Clarín Global)
Supercanal Holding (20% Grupo Clarín)	Impripost (Grupo Clarín and Organización Techint)	Audiotel (50% Grupo Clarín)
Trisa – Telered Imagen (50% Grupo Clarín)	CIMECO (33.4% Grupo Clarín)	Ferias y Exposiciones Argentinas Source: Sanz (2004)
Teledeportes	Revista Nueva	
Direct TV (4% Grupo Clarín, through Raven Media Investment)	Agencia Diarios y Noticias	
	Papel Prensa (36.9% Grupo Clarín)	

media communication, controls most of the business associations linked to the media, such as the Asociación de Entidades Periodísticas de Argentina (Association of Journalism Companies), the Asociación de Teledifusoras Argentinas (Association of TV Channels), the Asociación de Televisión por Cable (Association of Cable Channels) and the Asociación de Radios Privadas de Argentina (Association of Private Radio Stations). In other words, it can be argued that the Grupo Clarín controls the institutional framework of media corporations in the country. To complete the picture of the economic-political power of this monopoly, we present below a chart of significant holdings of Grupo Clarín and private media companies under its influence.

Confronting right-wing opposition

The process that followed the political defeat of the administration in the Senate over agri-export taxes was characterized by a triumphant opposition coalition deploying a defiant and aggressive discourse aimed at the next legislative elections, which were to be held in June 2009. Two opposition electoral coalitions emerged that represented the agrarian sector and its demands: the Acuerdo Cívico y Social (ACyS, Social and Civic Agreement) which gathered together such different political forces as the Unión Cívica Radical (UCR, Radical Civic Union) and the Partido Socialista (Socialist Party); and the Alianza Federal Pro (Pro Federal Alliance), which combined centre and right-wing groups of the PJ with the Propuesta Republicana (PRO, Republican Proposal) under the leadership of the 'Argentine Berlusconi', Mauricio Macri, the PRO mayor of Buenos Aires.

In the legislative elections of 2009, the government suffered a serious defeat, with a swing against it of over 12 per cent. It lost a significant number of seats, mostly in the province of Buenos Aires, where ex-President Kirchner headed the list of deputies, together with the Buenos Aires provincial governor, Daniel Scioli. In less than a year, the electoral support of the pro-government coalition Frente para la Victoria (Front for Victory) fell from 60 per cent to 30 per cent, substantially modifying the correlation of political forces and costing the pro-government coalition control of Congress. The agrarian lobby got eleven new deputies into Congress – all business association leaders, who took control of the strategic congressional commission on agriculture, defining a new political agenda based on deregulation of the agri-export sector and elimination of any form of export tax.

Despite the advance of the agrarian sector into the political system, however, the accompanying revival of the right did not produce a consolidated right-wing political coalition, but resulted in party fragmentation, driven by the rise of individual political figures. Praised by the economic establishment, Vice-President Julio Cobos was presented by the media as a presidential candidate, and there was favourable presentation of other right-wing figures, such as Francisco de Narvaez, Mauricio Macri and Carlos Reuteman, other potential presidential candidates. This support was linked to a right-wing offensive, with active leadership from key media groups, which demanded the immediate resignation of Cristina Fernández and new elections.

Nonetheless, weakened by serious electoral defeat, but with a long period before the next presidential elections, the Fernández government decided to recapture the political initiative by continuing with and deepening reforms to the neoliberal order. Some of these initiatives had started by the end of 2008. The strategic return of social security provision from private to state control, the creation of a universal child benefit scheme, the new media law and an equal civil marriage law all helped recover the electoral base of the pro-government coalition. Reversing one of the central neoliberal reforms of the last stage of the Menem administration, the social security reform led to open political confrontation with the domestic and international financial communities, which severely criticized it, as did newspapers such as *Clarín*, *La Nación* and *El Cronista*, which feared the loss of this profitable source of private-sector income. However, thanks to the reform, the government strengthened its own strategy for financing development and reducing its dependence on incomes generated by the agri-export sector.

In the 1990s, development through deregulation and privatization – the cornerstone of the neoliberal project – assumed a central role for international capital in the form of foreign direct investment (FDI). International financial institutions stressed that FDI could resolve the difficulty of generating domestic savings and capital. In Argentina, though, FDI did not follow the rule. And while FDI in the Asian economies reached 30 per cent of GDP, in Argentina it remained below 20 per cent, and most of the foreign investment went into the refinancing of public debt and into mergers and acquisitions, rather than into capital investment and technology. By contrast, between 2003 and 2008, with Argentina having departed from the international financial order by refusing to settle its international debts, the rate of investment in the country reached 27 per cent of GDP, totally financed from domestic savings, in which a strategic role was played by the new, publicly managed pension scheme (López San Miguel 2010). In a tactical financial move, pension assets equivalent to around 10 per cent of GDP were transferred to the National Social Security Administration, in order to form a public reserve fund that invests at least 50 per cent of its assets in public bonds and treasury financial instruments (International Labour Organization 2010: 10).

Up to 2009, the central critique of the new right and of the left-wing opposition had been the failure of the populist, developmentalist model to deliver social justice, particularly in a country with 8.8 per cent unemployment, with 40 per cent of workers in the informal economy and with 47 per cent of children aged under eighteen classified as poor (Instituto Nacional de Estadística y Censos 2010). The international crisis of 2008 and the agrarian conflict deepened the vulnerability of these social sectors. But this opened the door for a historic reform: the creation of Asignación Universal por Hijo para Protección Social (Universal Family Allowance for Social Protection), a social safety net for hundreds of thousands of marginalized children and adolescents. The new programme offered $47 per month per child, deposited in a savings account. The parent responsible for the child can access the cash only if the child has attended school and undergone health checks and vaccinations (in the case of children under five years of age). As a conditional cash transfer scheme, this Argentine income-redistribution measure followed similar social protection schemes in Brazil and Chile. A central feature of these redistributive policies has been the relatively small size of the social protection packages – on average below 10 per cent of total economic stimulus packages introduced by the state, and, in the case of Argentina, accounting for just 0.1 per cent of GDP. In other words, this was an income-redistribution policy based on prudent financial criteria and did not undermine the wider populist strategy for financing development (International Labour Organization 2010: 8).

A third initiative was Law 26.522, known also as the Media Law, which repealed and replaced the legislation that the military dictatorship had used to privilege its political allies. The new law limited the number of media licences each corporation could hold, allowing new media investors and actors to enter a market dominated by a handful of conglomerates. The law mainly targeted the major media corporations and multimedia monopolies which, over time, would now be obliged to sell off part of their portfolios. Opposition to the measure was led by the major media corporations, supported by the Sociedad Interamericana de Prensa (Inter-American Press Association), which represents the owners of media companies. Its central argument was that the government was violating constitutional rights and seeking to curb freedom of speech by force, like Chávez in Venezuela. Politically, the anti-Media Law campaign was headed by the UCR, ACyS with Elisa Carrió, the right-wing Peronist, and the Buenos Aires city mayor, Mauricio Macri. However, despite the right-wing alliance against the Media Law, the opposition was defeated in Congress by the government, with the support of left-wing parties. After this political setback, the political and business opposition took the matter to the courts, and following a Supreme Court ruling in 2010, the government declared its intention to implement the law from September 2011, although further challenges cannot be ruled out.

The last, but no less significant, initiative was the equal marriage rights law, which ended discrimination based on gender or sexual preference: a democratic milestone in a country with a long Catholic, conservative tradition. The measure again divided the country, this time culturally. It provoked the most sectarian and conservative groups of the Catholic Church, with some of its exponents even demanding a sort of crusade against the measure. So, by mid-2010, what the media monopolies had portrayed only two years before as a government on the verge of disintegration had become a strong coalition, which received popular support for its reform programme.

Conclusion

Those measures taken in response to the right-wing campaign enabled the Cristina Fernández administration to regain the political initiative and to resume the process of reforming Argentina's neoliberal and conservative order. Economic stability in 2009 – in clear contrast to the impact of the international crisis in other countries – undermined negative predictions about the future of the Argentine economy. By 2010, the major media corporations were recognizing the recovery of the government's electoral position and the inability of the right-wing opposition to obstruct reforms. The opposition coalition, created to undermine the Fernández government, demonstrated important weaknesses, not least in terms of its capacity to form an effective government. Left-wing parties were the first to leave the opposition bloc. The right-wing parties divided into different factions, preventing the emergence of any clear strategic perspective.

The role of the political parties in the agrarian conflict revealed the fragility and instability of the political system, when confronted by the tasks of structural reform in the context of deep inequalities. This is demonstrated by the difficulties that dominant sectors have had in building a political party capable both of reflecting their interests and of running the state. In the past, this has, more than once, turned them against the democratic system itself when they have perceived a threat to their interests. Up until 1982, conservative and neoliberal forces elected to use military force to re-establish order and progress: order for the poor and progress for themselves. But after a couple of decades of post-dictatorship democracy in the region, this option is no longer viable, given the new international, regional and domestic contexts.

Nonetheless, as the Argentine case demonstrates, processes of structural reform or transformation tend to weaken the presidential political order, because of the scale of institutional conflict (notably with the legislative and judiciary powers) – conflict that reflects the diverse interests and forces operating in the state–society complex. Rather than being simply an expression of political instability, institutional conflict is part of structural reform in any society where social justice is the major issue. The positive component of these processes of transformation is that they have reshaped the Argentine right, so that conservative and neoliberal sectors have adhered to the logic of institutional action within the democratic framework, abandoning the use of subversive force. In that sense, the most dangerous opposition to the reforms arises not in the political system itself, but in its social foundations: in the political-economic arena, where concentrations of power can have a greater impact on democratic stability.

This is apparent in attempts by powerful economic interests to subvert the democratic order through an 'institutional' coup: that is by asserting the loss of the political legitimacy of democratic government, by using media campaigns of destabilization (such as in Honduras) and by mobilizing external hemispheric and regional support. This phenomenon is not new and there is a vast academic literature, written from the US-based, positivist political science perspective, that argues that the inherent weakness of presidential systems weakens political order, which, in some cases, might justify undemocratic institutional change (Linz 1990). In this respect, a key figure is US Assistant Secretary of State for Western Hemisphere Affairs Arturo Valenzuela, a strong advocate of neoliberal development and an acknowledged specialist in US–Latin America relations. Besides expressing the US government's open support for the fraudulent elections conducted by the coup leaders in Honduras in 2009, and negotiating the establishment of seven US military bases in Colombia, Valenzuela is the leading voice of US conservative sectors proclaiming the need for strong US leadership, given the allegedly growing instability of its democracies and the presumed risks to regional security (Sabatini and Marczak 2010).

The overlap between this US hemispheric approach and the new right's domestic strategies constituted a wider scenario of institutional action for the new Argentine right, albeit with domestic restrictions. In this sense, conservative and neoliberal forces are conditioned by complex domestic structures related to the ownership of land, distribution of income, the model of accumulation and the position of large, overseas-based multinational companies within the international value chain. Beyond that, it is important to recognize that the Cristina Fernández administration was deeply unaware – even naïve – of the mobilizing capacity of the agrarian actors and of their potential to create alliances with other conservative and neoliberal forces opposed to reform. In a nutshell, the administration, with its powerful electoral position, underestimated the potential seriousness of conflict with political actors who are numerically small but economically strategic.

The agrarian conflict, which unexpectedly turned into an institutional crisis, had its roots in Argentine society, and it shook the political system, dividing the country between those for and against the regionalist, developmentalist and populist model. The opposition coalition, or the new Argentine right, has blended old and new political-economic forces, and has developed two crucial political levers: international linkages and the capacity to destabilize a government by acting within the institutional complex of the state.

13 | The Chilean right in the Concertación era, 1990–2010

PATRICIO SILVA

The victory of Sebastián Piñera in the January 2010 presidential elections marked an end to twenty years of centre-left Concertación (Reconciliation) government in Chile. It also constituted the first triumph of the Chilean right in a presidential contest for fifty-two years. In this chapter, I explore the political evolution of the right after the end of the Pinochet regime in March 1990 and throughout the two decades of Concertación government.

Following the restoration of democracy, the Chilean right managed to maintain a strong influence over the electorate and consolidated its party structures and parliamentary representation. As this study shows, however, this relative success was not just the result of its political appeal, but was aided by the Pinochet legacy, particularly some institutional and electoral regulations and the strong presence of the armed forces in the post-1990 period. The right consistently defended legislation inherited from the authoritarian era, and also sought to protect former and serving members of the armed forces who were facing possible prosecution for human rights abuses. Although right-wing parties were unable to prevent changes in both these areas, they were able to effectively obstruct them for a very long time. In this manner, and despite its failure to get into government in those twenty years, the right managed to strongly influence the pace of the democratization process in Chile.

The Chilean right and its uneasiness with party politics

The Chilean right historically found it difficult to accept that it must get involved in party politics in order both to defend its ideas and to compete with centre and left political forces (Cristi and Ruiz 1992). For a long time, the representation of right-wing ideas and interests in Chile was undertaken by powerful entrepreneurial organizations such as the Sociedad de Fomento Fabril (Society of Factory Production) and the Sociedad Nacional de Agricultura (National Agricultural Society) and by the media, particularly the influential *El Mercurio* newspaper

(Correa Sutil 2005). Until the mid-1950s, these formally non-political channels were effective in influencing government, parliament and public opinion. The right was aware that the Chilean electorate disliked blatant right-wing ideas. Thus, during the 1958 presidential election, Jorge Alessandri presented himself as an independent and apolitical figure, and during his period in government preferred to work with figures from the world of enterprise, rather than the traditional right-wing parties (Angell 1993). However, the foundation in 1958 of the Partido Democráta Cristiana (PDC, Christian Democratic Party) and the strengthening of the left following the Cuban revolution of 1959 were signals that the Chilean right needed to modernize and consolidate its organizational structures (Fleet 1985). However, this *aggiornamento* (updating) of the right only took place after the PDC's landslide victory in 1964, which propelled Eduardo Frei to the presidency and the disastrous defeat suffered by conservative and liberal parties in the parliamentary elections of the following year. This experience led to the creation of the Partido Nacional (PN, National Party), which amalgamated most of the existing right-wing parties and movements (Valdivia 2008; Soto and Fernández 2002). The PN immediately adopted a confrontational stance towards the Frei government and its socio-economic policies, particularly agrarian reform (Kay and Silva 1992). The rivalry between the PN and the PDC facilitated the electoral triumph of the Unidad Popular (UP, Popular Unity) left-wing coalition in September 1970. During the Allende government (1970–73), the PN began to adopt a putschist position: first covertly, and then in an increasingly overt manner, it encouraged the armed forces to bring the UP government down (Garretón 1989). The ultra-conservative *gremialista* (guild) movement was the main political force organizing mass opposition to the government. This originated in 1967 among conservative students at the Catholic University of Santiago, and it aimed to provide a counterweight to PDC and UP activists. In the final days of the Allende government, the *gremialistas* were responsible for huge demonstrations and long strikes in the transport and commercial sectors, by students, doctors and other groups, which practically paralysed the country (Oppenheim 2007).

Following the September 1973 coup, the military government officially prohibited political parties, but leading PN and *gremialista* politicians rapidly occupied positions in ministries, embassies and advisory committees. Jaime Guzmán, the undisputed leader of the *gremialista* movement, became one of the junta's main ideologues, nurturing it with a vast body of doctrinarian ideas, such as those reflected in the 'Declaration of Principles' of March 1974. He was one of the key architects of the legal and institutional structures of the authoritarian regime, including the 1980 constitution (Cristi 2000). Another important source of political and ideological support for the junta came from a relatively unknown group of neoliberal economists known as the 'Chicago boys'. These acolytes of Milton Friedman arrived in April 1975 and set about reordering the economy on the basis of the privatization of state assets and the introduction of orthodox free-market principles (Valdés 1995; Silva 2008). Although the *gremialistas* initially strongly resisted the ultra-liberal tenets defended by the 'boys', they recognized their relative success and gradually began to accept them. In the end, *gremialistas* and neoliberals coalesced (Huneeus 2000). A division of labour emerged, with the 'Chicago boys' responsible for the economic and financial reforms and the *gremialistas* concentrating on selling these ideas to the popular sectors, as well as on contesting the presence of clandestine left-wing activism in the shanty towns. To this end, they sought to take control of municipal governments in the poorest districts (Klein 2004). The political capital accumulated during those years would prove later to be of enormous importance for the right as a source of electoral support after 1990.

The Chilean economy underwent a strong recovery between 1977 and 1981, and many voices abroad began to talk about the 'Chilean miracle'. This created a climate of triumphalism among Pinochet's supporters, who felt that his regime was now firmly entrenched. The adoption of the 1980 constitution was an expression of that self-confidence. The constitution paved the way for the holding of a plebiscite on 5 October 1988, in which the Chilean people would say 'yes' or 'no' to another eight years of military rule. If the 'no' option prevailed, general elections would take place within a year. Pinochet and his advisers confidently believed that, by 1988, Chile would have achieved high levels of economic prosperity, which would guarantee a 'yes' victory. However, a severe crisis erupted in 1981, bringing the economy to the point of collapse. The credibility of the 'Chicago boys' evaporated rapidly, and the regime faced growing political unrest as the centre and left-wing parties re-emerged and large-scale protests demanded a transition to democracy (Silva 2003). As in the past, the Chilean right only began to act when the status quo was threatened. Thus, in September 1983, the *gremialistas* decided to organize more formally and, under Guzmán's leadership, they formed the Unión Demócrata Independiente (UDI, Independent Democratic Union), which represented the most fervent Pinochet loyalists. More moderate conservatives then founded Renovación Nacional (RN, National Renovation) in 1987. Both organizations participated in the 'yes' campaign during the run-up to the referendum.

The 1988 referendum unified all the democratic opposition forces from Christian Democrats to socialists around the 'no' option. Their victory signified the end of the military regime and the start of the restoration of democracy. The Chilean right was shocked by the defeat and the UDI and RN began a frantic search for a single presidential candidate to compete with the centre-left (grouped under the name of the Concertación) in the elections to be held on 14 December 1989. The right finally chose Hernán Büchi as its candidate. He was a young neoliberal economist who had become Pinochet's minister of finance in 1985 and, as such, was responsible for the strong economic recuperation in that period. He resigned from that post in April 1989 in order to campaign, but proved unable to turn the political tide, obtaining only 29.4 per cent of the vote. His chances were reduced by the presence of another right-wing contender, the businessman Francisco Javier Errazuriz, who ran a populist campaign and received 15.5 per cent. Patricio Aylwin, the Concertación candidate, won the election with 55.2 per cent and was sworn in as president in March 1990.

Government–opposition relations following the transition to democracy

The Chilean right lost an important battle in December 1989, but it was certainly not defeated. The fact that, after seventeen years of dictatorship, it had obtained a respectable 45 per cent of the vote demonstrated the formidable electoral strength of the right at the time of the transition. Even more important, the right-wing parties did well in the parliamentary elections that took place simultaneously with the presidential one. They received forty-eight seats (as compared to sixty-nine for the Concertación) in the Chamber of Deputies and sixteen (against twenty-two) in the Senate. The right enjoyed outright control of the Senate because of the existence of nine 'institutional senators'. These unelected politicians – former generals, government ministers and members of the Supreme Court – had been appointed by Pinochet before Aylwin's inauguration (Siavelis 2000). The right's parliamentary strength was out of proportion to the number of votes it obtained at the polls: before leaving power, the military government had introduced a binomial electoral system, which remains in place today. This compels political parties to form large coalitions to compete for seats in the Chamber of Deputies and the Senate. Each electoral coalition needs to obtain more than two-thirds of votes in a two-seat (binomial) constituency in order to take both seats – an almost impossible feat that all but guarantees the right half the seats in constituencies with a majority of left voters (Pastor 2004). For this reason, the Concertación generally obtained a similar number of seats in the Senate as the right, despite the fact that its candidates usually received 10–20 per cent more votes than their competitors. Thus one of the key aims of the UDI and the RN since the transition has been to oppose the replacement of the binomial system with one based on proportional representation, a policy desired by the Concertación. The consequence was that, so long as the right was able to maintain its large congressional presence, Concertación governments had to negotiate with the UDI and RN in order to get their legislative programmes approved.

As a result of this balance of power, the Aylwin government realized that it had to maintain both official and informal lines of consultation with the Chilean right, if democracy was to be consolidated. Aylwin and significant Concertación politicians, therefore, pursued what has been termed a 'democracy of agreements', in order to secure political and economic stability. The UDI and RN reacted differently to this governmental call for cooperation. While RN leader Andrés Allamand and most of the party's congressional representatives embraced it and facilitated the adoption of a series of important decisions on taxation, social policy and economic reform, the UDI rejected most of the Concertación's programme. The UDI demonstrated little interest in contributing to an improvement in the political climate in the country. Rather than avoiding controversial issues and moderating the tone of discussion, it fervently defended the former military regime and constantly criticized the Unidad Popular period, which was identified as the major source of most of Chile's political and institutional problems. The assassination of the UDI's founder, Jaime Guzmán, in April 1991 by a left-wing group only contributed to its intransigent stance.

The factor that most complicated the relationship between the Concertación governments and the right was undoubtedly the continued involvement of General Pinochet in Chilean politics (Fuentes 2000; Angell 2007). Under the 1980 constitution, he remained commander-in-chief of the army until 1998 and then became a senator for life. While in London in October 1998 he was arrested on human rights charges issued by a Spanish judge, but he managed to avoid prosecution (with the connivance of the British government) and returned to Chile in March 2000. Pinochet remained a controversial and divisive figure until his death in December 2006. His notoriety contributed to extremely difficult relations between government and military, which were also exacerbated by the human rights issue and the continued presence of 'authoritarian enclaves' in the country's legal and institutional framework. The UDI and RN defended the military's reputation and opposed Concertación attempts to restore democratic civilian control over it.

The Aylwin government combined decisiveness with caution when addressing the delicate question of human rights abuses during the Pinochet government. Although the latter's 1978 Amnesty Law protected the military from legal prosecution, Aylwin created the Commission for Truth and Reconciliation (also known as the Rettig Commission after its chairman) just a month after his inauguration. The commission was tasked with conducting a full investigation into abuses and then publishing a report on its findings. The right argued that its remit contradicted the amnesty provisions and denounced its report, published on 9 February 1991, as biased. The commitment of subsequent Concertación presidents Eduardo Frei, Ricardo Lagos and Michelle Bachelet to continue investigating military crimes was met with stiff right-wing opposition. Nevertheless, the judiciary gradually began to reinterpret the existing amnesty law, paving the way for the prosecution and imprisonment of a large number of former members of the armed forces and the secret services.

During the Concertación period, the right was also very active in the defence of what, in Chile, are called the *temas valóricos* (value themes), that is ethical and religious issues such as sexuality, teenage pregnancy, abortion and divorce (Blofield 2002). The UDI, in particular, strongly opposed government initiatives to enhance civil liberties in these areas. Thus, for example, the UDI, the Catholic Church and other conservative groups castigated television adverts warning young people of the consequences of HIV/AIDS and recommending that they use condoms. Similar clashes occurred over the state's decision to introduce sex education in schools and to provide educational and psychological support for adolescent mothers expelled from school because of pregnancy. The right made use of its almost total control of the Chilean mass media to discredit these policies. A particular focus of right-wing attacks was the Servicio Nacional de la Mujer (SERNAM, National Women's Agency), a specialized state agency created by the Aylwin government in January 1991 to foster gender equality in Chile. SERNAM introduced a series of programmes which aimed both to protect and to empower women in the home and at work. These included measures intended to prevent and punish domestic violence against women and children and to create legal benefits for single working mothers (Franceschet 2005). The UDI and RN regarded SERNAM as a vehicle for feminist propaganda, an unnecessary expansion of state intervention and an undesirable intrusion into family life (Baldez 1999). The single most disputed 'ethical' issue was divorce. Owing to the Catholic Church's opposition, Chile was the only western nation that lacked a legal framework for divorce. The law proposed by the Frei government in 1995 was only approved by the Chamber of Deputies in 1997, and only after the right had pushed through a series of modifications. It was then discussed for another seven years in the Senate, during which time the Concertación was forced to make further concessions, before it became law in March 2004. Once again, the approach of the UDI and RN to the divorce law differed, in that the former almost totally rejected it, while the latter's support facilitated its passage.

When Michelle Bachelet became the Concertación's presidential candidate in May 2005, as an agnostic, single mother of three and a supporter of gender equality she represented all the ideas and values conservative Chile most hated. Its fears were realized when her government proposed various policies to protect women and children, such as the right to breast-feed at work, the strengthening of penalties for men who failed to pay alimony and the establishment of nationwide shelters for victims of domestic violence. The most controversial issue was the 2006 decision to make the morning-after pill freely available at public hospitals and medical centres. This measure was intended to reduce the alarming rates of teenage pregnancy and illegal abortion, which destroyed the health and cost the lives of countless young women. Many UDI mayors, including Pablo Zalaquett, the populist mayor of the La Florida district in Santiago, saw this as a Trojan Horse designed to clear the way for the legalization of abortion, and refused to allow the pill's distribution in areas under their jurisdiction. Bachelet was forced to sign a supreme decree to guarantee the policy's implementation, but in April 2008 the Constitutional Court ruled in favour of a demand made in March 2007 by thirty-six right-wing deputies that the pill should not be available in public health centres. A protracted political and legal battle ensued between government and the right – a battle only finally won by the executive on 18 January 2010 (the day after Sebastián Piñera's election victory), when President Bachelet enacted a new law allowing the pill's distribution.

The way the Concertación governments conducted foreign policy also became a bone of contention for the right. Chile was diplomatically isolated during the military period because of the abuse of human rights. It was also isolated from the rest of Latin America owing to Pinochet's strategy of economic integration in North American, European and Asian markets (Muñoz 1986). After 1990, Chile sought to reverse this process, as well as to play a more active role in regional and global organizations (Van Klaveren 2000). It particularly tried to improve relations and resolve conflicts with its neighbours, Argentina, Peru and Bolivia. Thus, Presidents Aylwin and Frei expended great efforts to improve Chilean–Argentine relations by tackling border disputes and promoting economic integration. In August 1990, Aylwin and Carlos Menem began a review of border issues, and within a year only two of twenty-four remained outstanding, and those (in the Laguna del Desierto region) they put to arbitration. The government accepted the arbitration verdict in favour of Argentina in 1994, but the right, which had opposed arbitration in the first place, condemned Aylwin for giving away Chilean soil. It had a similar response to the agreement on Argentina selling gas to Chile, arguing that this would lead to energy dependency. When Argentina unilaterally increased the price of gas and there were frequent interruptions to its supply, voices on the right demanded that Frei break off relations with Argentina and sue it for compensation. Later, when Ricardo Lagos was criticized for not being tough enough on Argentina, he responded that it was critically important to maintain good relations despite difficult issues (Rodríguez Elizondo 2006).

Michele Bachelet's foreign policy, and particularly what were seen as her conciliatory policies towards Boliva and its leader, Evo Morales, was also attacked by the right. Bachelet and Morales enjoyed an excellent personal rapport, and the strength of the communication and cooperation between their countries increased after they were both installed in 2006. The consequence was the establishment of a bilateral agenda of thirteen points, in which, for the first time, Chile agreed to discuss the Bolivian demand for a resumption of access to the Pacific coast (which it had lost after defeat in the War of the Pacific in 1884). This provoked huge commotion within the Chilean right, which also acted as the voice of the armed forces. Influential newspapers such as *El Mercurio* and *La Tercera* constantly warned of Evo Morales' close connection to Hugo Chávez and regularly published opinion polls in which Chileans expressed their opposition to any agreement with Bolivia concerning access to the sea.

Peru's decision to define the parameters of its sea border with Chile sparked a grave diplomatic crisis, especially when the former petitioned the International Court of Justice at The Hague in January 2008. In contrast to the situation with Argentina and Bolivia, all Chilean political forces, including the right, supported the position adopted first by Lagos and then by Bachelet. However, this did not prevent right-wing politicians from attacking what they saw as weakness on the part of the government in its response to statements by Peruvian officials and newspapers. Thus, Iván Moreira, UDI deputy and member of the parliamentary foreign relations committee, demanded that the Bachelet government '*ponerse los pantalones*' ('put on its trousers', i.e. show its strength) as rumours of Peruvian spying activities spread (*El Mercurio*, 1 August 2009).

From Lavín to Piñera: the struggle for the presidency

Following its defeat in 1989, the idea of winning a presidential election appeared a very distant aspiration for the Chilean right. The fact that the Concertación had demonstrated its capacity to form competent and successful governments, which secured both economic growth and political stability, made a right-wing government highly unlikely. The right was also still identified as having played a key role in the 1973 coup and as having supported the Pinochet regime. These facts were, for many Chileans, reason enough not to vote for the right, even if they were disillusioned with the Concertación. That the right could not secure an electoral majority was shown in the results of the first two presidential elections: in 1989 Aylwin obtained 55.2 per cent of the vote, and in 1993 Frei received 57.9 per cent. This led the right to realize that it would have to distance itself both from the military regime and from Pinochet himself, if it wanted to capture the electoral support of people who would not traditionally have voted for it. However, this created a problem: by doing so, it might lose its traditional constituency. The right had to walk a political tightrope. In the early 1990s, RN leaders such as Andrés Allamand and Sebastián Piñera cautiously began to criticize aspects of the recent authoritarian past and stressed the need to democratize and modernize the Chilean right in order to focus on the country's future (Allamand 1993). At the same time, UDI and RN activists worked to augment their presence in municipal government.

The onset of the 1998 Asian financial crisis severely affected the Chilean economy and marked a turning point for the country. For the first time since the return to democracy, Chileans faced serious economic problems as the Frei government failed in its efforts to stimulate recovery. The right used this to stress the need to adopt bolder economic measures, and presented itself as the only political force capable of doing so. The crisis opened a window of opportunity for the right, and for the first time it began to believe that it could win the presidential elections scheduled for December 1999. The Concertación's electoral chances were further weakened, in that it could not decide on a single candidate. Primaries held in May 1999 between the Christian Democrat Andrés Zaldívar and the socialist Ricardo Lagos caused tensions within the coalition, which did not subside after Lagos's victory of 70.1 per cent to Zaldívar's 29.9 per cent. The support that Christian Democratic party cadres and voters would give to the Concertacíon presidential candidate appeared highly suspect.

The right's high expectations of the 1999 elections were based on the spectacular ascendancy in the opinion polls of the UDI's Joaquín Lavín. Elected mayor of the rich Las Condes county in Santiago province, his outstanding administrative record made him popular in the capital and the rest of the country. Running for re-election in 1996, he obtained an astonishing 78 per cent of the vote. This was the first indication that Lavín was able not only to reach the right-wing electorate, but also to garner the support of voters who had so far been part of the Concertación's constituency (the so-called *voto cruzado*, 'split-ticket voting'). Before becoming the right's presidential candidate, Lavín needed to win the RN's endorsement, but at the beginning of 1999 it was still planning to have its own candidate, Senator Sebastián Piñera. However, Pinochet's arrest in London facilitated rapprochement between the two parties, as they closed ranks in his defence; in early January 1999 they decided to formalize this unity with the formation of the Alianza por Chile (Alliance for Chile). A primary between Lavín and Piñera was scheduled for June of that year, but on 9 January Piñera withdrew following a poor showing in the opinion polls. Lavín became acceptable to RN leaders, who appreciated the degree of political independence he had secured from the UDI. Lagos and his advisers were slow to realize that the right now posed a serious challenge and that they needed to improve their campaign tactics. Lagos had been acting as if he were already the next president, while Concertación politicians underestimated Lavín, describing him as a *cosista*, a person concerned with practical matters who lacked a long-term vision for the country's future development. The Concertación also did not appreciate that many Chileans were fearful of electing a socialist as president (the last having been Salvador Allende) (Silva 1999).

The 1999 presidential election was the most closely contested since the restoration of democracy. Ricardo Lagos and Joaquín Lavín fought for every single vote, and for the first time since 1989 a second round would be needed to decide the result. Though the candidates were virtually level-pegging after the first round (47.95 per cent to 47.51 per cent), at the end of the second, in January 2000, Lagos managed to achieve a slight advantage (51.31 per cent to 48.69 per cent) over his right-wing rival. Once in office, the Lagos government performed well in political and economic terms, as well as in the international arena. Lavín opted to run for the politically important position of mayor of Santiago's city centre, which he easily won in October 2000. However, his attempts to resolve the district's many social and infrastructural problems were dogged by a budget shortfall; this failure affected both his standing in the city and nationally. Despite this setback, in 2004 he began his campaign for the December 2005 presidential election. His popularity was boosted during the final phase of Lagos's term because the Concertación appeared uncertain about the likelihood of a fourth victory. There was veiled criticism of Lagos, who was more concerned with his personal standing than with bolstering the chances of the coalition. Lavín campaigned with the message that another Concertación government would mean 'more of the same', whereas he would bring real change. However, the surprising selection in March 2005 of Michelle Bachelet as the Concertación candidate dented the right's prospects. Many Chileans approved of the idea of a woman as president, especially if that woman was Bachelet. She had built a strong reputation as minister of health and then of defence in Lagos's administration, and was liked for her warm and spontaneous personality. Another setback occurred when the RN chose Sebastián Piñera as its candidate and he refused to step down in favour of Lavín. So the right went into the 2005 elections divided between two candidates. In the first round of voting, Piñera narrowly beat Lavín (by 25.5 per cent to 23.2 per cent), but Bachelet trounced them both with 46 per cent; and in the second round of voting, in January 2006, she received 53.5 per cent to Piñera's 46.5 per cent. Defeat notwithstanding, Piñera had finally succeeded in displacing Lavín and ending the UDI's long hegemony over the Chilean right. Lavín largely abandoned day-to-day politics for academic life, although he did serve as a presidential adviser on some important poverty-alleviation initiatives. This closeness to the Concertación alienated many of his former supporters.

Chilean politics relaxed considerably after the death of Pinochet in December 2006, as a major source of tension between the government and the right-wing opposition disappeared. This aided Piñera's promotion of himself as a candidate of the political centre: he emphasized his upbringing in a Christian Democratic family and espoused policy positions close to that party's; he also stressed that he had not voted for Pinochet in the 1988 referendum. Pinochet's death also affected the Concertación, in that it had used him as a means of uniting its followers. Now the coalition began to fall apart. Although Bachelet's own popularity increased, her appeal did not automatically transfer to the administration; while many Chileans approved of the way she managed the effects of the international financial crisis by providing increased support to the poor, many also doubted that there would be a fifth Concertación government. This view strengthened as the Concertación went through a tortuous candidate-selection process, until finally choosing Eduardo Frei, a politician who was unable to generate much enthusiasm even among the most partisan coalition supporters. The fact that he had been president already, and that his performance was not rated highly, certainly helped Piñera's chances of victory. The Concertación's hopes were dealt a further blow by the announcement in June 2009 by the young and media-friendly socialist deputy Marco Enríquez-Ominami that he would run a separate campaign. The result of the December elections marked the end of the Concertación era. While Frei and Enríquez-Ominami received 29.6 per cent and 20.1 per cent, respectively, Piñera obtained 44 per cent of the vote in the first round and went on to win a tight victory over Frei (51.6 per cent to 48.4 per cent) in the second. Despite its being such a tight race, there was a palpable sense of disaster within the Concertación camp.

The right in power: an early assessment

After its electoral triumph, ironically the right found it more difficult to impose its political and economic agenda from the presidential palace than it had when in opposition. This was partly a consequence of the serious earthquake and tsunami that struck Chile on 27 February 2010, only days before Piñera's inauguration. This catastrophic event transformed both the political environment of the country and the agendas of its political actors. Paradoxically, the colossal task of reconstruction forced the new neoliberal government to adopt the pro-developmental stance that it had always detested ideologically. Thus, Piñera expanded state support for the thousands of citizens who had lost homes and income, and poured money into reactivating the country's economy and rebuilding its infrastructure. The earthquake did have one positive consequence for the government, in that both the Concertación and the non-parliamentary left did not adopt an oppositional role. Everyone understood that this would have been inappropriate (and politically counterproductive) given the circumstances. In reality, since the electoral debacle, the Concertación was fragmented and unable to constitute an effective political opposition.

Piñera soon came under criticism from within his own camp because of his decision – which echoed that of Alessandri in 1958 – to form a cabinet whose members came almost exclusively from the business community. Prominent leaders from the UDI and RN, such as Pablo Loneira and Andrés Allamand, were not appointed; the UDI was particularly disgruntled by the relatively minor role it was allotted. The government was also attacked by supporters and opponents alike for its lack of experience (unsurprising after twenty years of Concertación rule) and for a number of blunders it made. Piñera was forced to replace some of his new appointees after they were accused of past economic errors or criminal actions by both the Concertación and the press. Many business people turned ministers were also accused of having a conflict of interest between their public and personal roles. All of this undermined Piñera's campaign promise to deliver efficient and effective government and to put an end to corruption. Piñera himself frequently expressed his admiration for former President Aylwin and his wish to govern in a similar fashion. There were indeed similarities between the two administrations: both presidents came to power after a long period in opposition, and neither enjoyed a majority in parliament, so that they had to rely on striking deals with the opposition to get legislation through. Piñera called on the Concertación to return to Aylwin's 'democracy of agreements'. Some socialist leaders rebuffed this idea; they argued that that type of cooperation had been needed in the immediate aftermath of the transition to democracy in order to avoid a return of authoritarianism, but that nowadays Chile was a full democracy and required a proper opposition.

In the early part of his government, Piñera continued many of the domestic and foreign policies pursued by the Concertación governments. It is apparent that his previous criticism of those policies had been motivated more by electoral considerations than by ideological ones. Thus, for example, relations with Argentina and Peru remained the same, and in the case of Peru actually improved. However, Piñera's declaration in summer 2010 that Chile would not discuss the issue of Bolivia's access to the sea (although it would support full access to Chilean ports) is likely to damage relations between the two countries. The continuity which characterizes much of the current government's programme has led many commentators to describe the Piñera administration as the 'fifth Concertación government'. This continuity, and the absence of a radical reformulation of policy, might lead to a good working relationship with the Concertación. Piñera clearly recognized that the earthquake put paid to any plans he may have had to reform public policies and institutions and to reorient economic development. If, during his four-year term, he succeeds in providing adequate solutions to the most urgent social problems highlighted by the earthquake, then the Chilean right has a real chance of winning the 2013 presidential elections. This may certainly be the case if the Concertación fails to regroup its forces and regain the trust of the Chilean electorate.

Conclusion: the challenge from the right

GERALDINE LIEVESLEY AND STEVE LUDLAM

The chapters in this book have confirmed a key observation of its overview chapter (Burton above) and of previous studies (e.g. Middlebrook 2000a: 49–50): namely, the variety and historical specificity of right-wing politics in Latin America. This is not surprising. The political and party systems of Latin American states evolved at different rates and with different characteristics, even if, from a distance, they may appear to have often shared common characteristics such as 'strongman' politics and violent militarization. In recent decades, phenomena that are often treated as undifferentiated – such as the imposition of neoliberal political economy or democratization – have, of course, affected distinct polities differently. The chapters above on right-wing governments naturally reveal different compositions of political behaviour underlying electoral success, including: US-sponsored paramilitary violence in Colombia; embedded institutional powers in Mexico; ideological strength reinforced by hegemonic religious and media forces in Peru. Similarly, where the right is in opposition, it faces left-wing presidencies whose political bases have been built, in response to neoliberalism and democratization, from very different political materials, as our previous book indicated (Lievesley and Ludlam 2009a). Some, as in the case of the Peronists in Argentina and the Socialist Party in Chile, represent the survival of long-existing parties. Others have built new political parties to defeat the right, notably in the case of the Partido dos Trabalhadores (Workers' Party) in Brazil. Yet others have achieved success based on the mobilization of mass social movements, as in Bolivia's Movimiento al Socialismo (Movement towards Socialism); or around projects of political renewal led by a popular individual with, at least initially, no mass political organization under his/her control, as in Venezuela, Ecuador and Paraguay, led by Chávez, Correa and Lugo, respectively. Notwithstanding such complexities, and although this book is not a work of comparative political science, it is possible to discuss some of the general factors that may characterize right-wing politics in twenty-first-century Latin America.

The most widespread concern about the future of right-wing politics in Latin America has been the threat of a return to unconstitutional methods, including military or military-installed dictatorship (Robinson 2008: 357). In one well-rehearsed version, discussed by Middlebrook, this prospect has been linked to the consequences of an absence of effective right-wing political parties in democratized states (Middlebrook 2000b: 286–8). At the turn of the century it was also argued that the inability of right-wing neopopulism, in particular, to offer a viable alternative political economy in the face of the unpopularity of neoliberal policies implied the risk of a return to undemocratic politics on the right (Cammack 2000: 157–60). Apart from threats to the propertied classes arising from redistributive political programmes, the risk is identified that the 'wars' on terror and drugs encourage extremely right-wing politics. Livingstone, Dominguez and Raby, in their chapters above, provide plentiful evidence of this threat. Diamint has warned of the wider risks arising from the absence of a democratic culture within the armed and police services that are the main national, multi- and sub-national protagonists in such 'wars' waged in the name of security (Diamint 2004). In his chapter above, Dawson warns that the crisis of law and order in Mexico, associated above all with the militarization of the 'war on drugs', has been linked to a resurgence of extreme right-wing and fascist groups appealing to older forms of social and political control in the face of gangsterism and neoliberal fragmentation. At the turn of the century, the concerns of Middlebrook and of Cammack had not yet been borne out. Since then, however, as chapters in this volume demonstrate in relation to the successful coup in Honduras (Livingstone), the unsuccessful coups in Venezuela (Dominguez) and Ecuador, and the armed autonomism in Bolivia (Tsolakis), the willingness of right-wing forces to resort to direct and murderously violent politics has certainly not been exhausted by the process of democratization, just as one scholarly survey pessimistically concluded (Smith 2005: 344–5). Indeed, as so often in the twentieth century, in each of these four states where violent political reaction has occurred (and, in the case of Honduras, has succeeded) this violent turn in right-wing politics has been a consequence not of the failure of democratization, but of its success, insofar as it has led the left to turn to electoral politics, with consequential policy challenges to elite supremacy and wealth.

Short of unconstitutional violence, right-wing politics can retain great influence when formally in opposition, through indirect means: the domestic soft-power alternative to domestic hard power. A variety of avenues for the exercise of soft power identified in this book will continue to be open to the right. The most obvious and structurally embedded factor is the economic order, national and international, and its political implications, whether seen in terms of the emergence of a new transnational capitalist class (Robinson 2008: 171–89), or in terms of the ideological constraints on economic policymaking (Panizza 2009: 228–321). The power of capitalists to combine and obstruct a left-wing government is described in this volume, for example, in the case of agri-business in Argentina (Díaz Echenique, Ozollo and Vivares above), and even more dramatically in the case of Venezuela (Dominguez above). The right can also mobilize business interests to mount quasi-constitutional challenges to the left, as in some elements of the autonomist revolt against the national government in Bolivia (Tsolakis above). Less violent examples of right-wing power wielded within the institutions of the state have been identified above in terms of judicial power in Argentina (Díaz Echenique, Ozollo and Vivares above), and in Chile, where the Constitutional Court reversed Bachelet's contraception policy (Silva above). A particular and intense example of business power in Latin America is the private media, addressed here in the specific cases of Venezuela, Argentina and Chile (Dominguez; Díaz Echenique, Ozollo and Vivares; Silva). The role of the hierarchy of the Catholic Church in opposing progressive sex education has been noted (Silva above), and in concert with the right-wing media forms a powerful ideological force in national politics, as outlined in the case of Peru (Durand above), and is capable of inspiring right-wing extremism, as in Mexico (Dawson above). As Silva records above, the Chilean right campaigned with Church support during the years of centre-left Concertación governments, defending *temas valóricos* (value themes) in areas like sexuality, abortion and divorce. The deployment of Catholic ideological influence in the case of the Nicaraguan Sandinista government policy of extreme anti-abortionism is a striking example. The links between Catholic leaders and political parties are not confined to the right, of course, and informal links between the Catholic Church and Christian Democrat parties have become more common than direct ones; and, with the exception of Opus Dei, the torch of Christian fundamentalism is said to have passed to the Evangelical sects, whose pastors in Brazil greatly outnumber Catholic priests (Espíndola 2009: 151–3). Indirect levers of power are, of course, mutually reinforcing. In this volume, the combination of business power, media power and the exploitation of elite control of constitutional corridors of power is particularly in evidence in the case of Paraguay (Lambert above). And, it should be recalled, the clientelist method, despite the impact of neoliberal privatization on the scope for corrupt public management, remains a powerful right-wing advantage in some states with left-wing presidencies, notably Brazil (Costa Lima above). A capacity for 'reverse clientelism' is also noted in the literature, as a general instrument of business influence over politicians, the extending of material benefits to politicians in return for influence over policy and appointments (see Seligson 2008).

Within the constraints of liberal democratic politics, what are the prospects for a right-wing reconquest of the territory submerged by the 'pink tide' of left presidencies? In the two cases where the right has displaced 'pink tide' presidents – Panama in 2009 and Chile in 2010 – there are some common factors. Both of the losing centre-left candidates had histories that damaged their candidacies: Balbina del Carmen Herrera Araúz's links with the US-deposed and disgraced ex-President Noriega; Concertación candidate, Christian Democrat Eduardo Frei Ruiz-Tagle's own record in his earlier term as Chilean president. In the Chilean case, of course, the constitutional one-term limitation on presidents bequeathed by the military was crucial, with President Bachelet enjoying 80 per cent support in the polls but unable to stand again for the centre-left Concertación. Both winning candidates, Ricardo Martinelli and Sebastián Piñera in Panama and Chile, respectively, were relatively young and super-rich business tycoons, with strong personal profiles independent of their parties. It would be a mistake, though, to read this as a sign that right-wing neopopulism has returned. Neither was elected in opposition to the existing party systems. Both also were opposing presidents who occupied moderate currents in the 'pink tide', and both were elected under 'time for change' banners (Democratic Change and National Renovation), offering business experience to manage economies then faltering in the face of the world crisis. And Piñera was elected on a promise to preserve Concertación social policies, in much the same way as Mexico's right-wing Partido Acción Nacional (PAN, National Action Party) undertook a non-threatening 're-badging' of its rival's social programmes (Dawson above). Media-fuelled personalist presidentialism, conducted within the party system, is not the same as anti-systemic populism.

It is difficult to see how the neopopulism of the late twentieth century can be easily revived. Its commitment to neoliberalism hangs like an albatross around its neck, so that, even if the impact of the neoliberal world recession undermines support for incumbent left-wing presidents, it is hard to see how the populist political method could concoct a distinctive, popular alternative political economy. The PAN's success in Mexico draws on an exceptionally long corporatist tradition that has no equivalent elsewhere in the region. The left has, overwhelmingly, not made itself vulnerable by abandoning the fiscal conservatism that neoliberals successfully championed in the past (Tussie and Heidrich 2008: 62–5). And alongside this fiscal caution in their welfare policy programmes, the left-wing presidencies have not, by and large, combined criticism of neoliberalism with criticism of capitalism and trade internationalism in general (Grugel and Riggirozzi 2009: 222–4). Furthermore, the left, in its revival of nationalist political economy, however limited its radicalism in terms of direct nationalization of natural resources, has occupied the nationalist high ground, and has reinforced its position by endorsing the discourse of the new anti-imperialist, Latin American continentalism. Even in the area of historical nationalist preoccupations about territorial boundaries, the left (in Bolivia) has been at least as successful as the right (in Chile) in championing such causes. Furthermore, the progress of a new continentalism in institutions and alliances – such as the 2004 Alianza Bolivariana para los Pueblos de Nuestra América (ALBA, Bolivarian Alliance for the Peoples of Our America), the 2007 Unión de Naciones Suramericanas (UNASUR, Union of South American Nations) and the declaration in 2010 of a new Community of Latin American and Caribbean States, which will include Cuba but exclude the US and Canada – involves only a limited degree of integration and does not require the pooling of national sovereignty in transnational legislation. This does not yet give the right, or parts of it, the capacity to build a popular anti-integrationist platform of the kind attempted by some mainstream and many extreme right-wing parties and movements in the European Union in recent decades.

There do, nevertheless, remain areas of popular appeal, where the right can retain strong electoral leverage. The issues associated with social conservatism (as opposed to economic neoliberalism), such as abortion and gay rights, remain powerful tools in the hands of right-wing politicians and their religious and media allies. Further, some have argued that the underlying ideological weakness of the right, in terms of mass attitudes, is not as great as the 'pink tide' results would suggest, but rather that the left has moderated its politics to appeal to popular preferences that have not moved massively in a leftward direction (Morales 2008: 37–9). The possible general political benefit to the right of the impact of the world recession is a critical consideration. Certainly the right-wing victories in Panama and Chile may have been related to the early effect of the 2008 crisis, but we are not in a position here to unravel other contributory personal and systemic factors. And since 2008, 'pink tide' presidents have been re-elected with increased majorities (Bolivia, Ecuador), have had successor presidents elected (Uruguay, Brazil), or have won for the first time (El Salvador). What can be said here, though, is that, in any case and contrary to early predictions, Latin American economies have recovered more rapidly than those in other regions (OECD 2010: 3–5; World Bank 2011). The post-crisis decline in remittances from the US and elsewhere (Inter-American Development Bank 2009) – a crucial source of personal and national income – was also recovering in 2010 and was expected to continue to recover in 2011.

The role of the US in Latin American politics remains all-pervasive, whether it is funding 'transition' strategies in Venezuela (and, as ever, in Cuba) and coordinating support for right-wing politics in general; trying to lock national economic policy into bilateral trade agreements and financial deals; or implanting US military (and military and police training capacities) across the continent. As the chapters by Livingstone and Lievesley above make clear, the US continues to deploy massive hard and soft power in the region, and does so in ways that seek to underpin right-wing politics and undermine left-wing alternatives. It provides resources that sustain networks of right-wing support in the military and security forces, in intellectual and policy communities, and in media production. Nevertheless, its power can no longer be deployed with the same certainties of success as in the past. It has been evicted from military bases in Ecuador and Bolivia. It failed to sustain its flagship neoliberal Free Trade Area of the Americas project beyond its rejection at the historic Mar del Plata pan-American summit of 2005. It failed in 2008 to sustain the campaign of its sponsored right-wing, armed autonomists in Bolivia in the face of the defence of the Bolivian government by the member states of UNASUR. And its failure to secure support for its candidate for the secretary-generalship of the Organization of American States (OAS) in 2005 was followed, in 2009, by the unanimous OAS vote (after the US withdrew) to offer membership to Cuba. All Latin American states have opposed the US embargo on Cuba in the UN, and have diplomatic relations with a state that has been the object of half a century of US 'regime change' interventions. Many states have also called for the prosecution of anti-Cuba terrorists enjoying sanctuary in the US, and for the release of the five Cuban anti-terrorism agents imprisoned in the US. And a year after the 2009 right-wing coup in Honduras, the US had been able to persuade, of all the Latin American states, only its right-wing allies Peru and Colombia to recognize the post-coup regime. It would take an unusual diplomatic alliance in 2011, between Colombia and Venezuela, to secure a vote to readmit Honduras into the Organization of American States, along with permission for Zelaya to return to the country. Even its indirect power through the channels of foreign direct investment in Latin America, the machinery that imposed the 'Washington Consensus', has been weakened politically by the (as yet small-scale) alternative of the ALBA banks and barter deals, by the development of regional projects based on Brazilian finance, and by the much larger alternative of China's trade and investment in the continent. The World Bank has reported, indeed, that the 'China connection' has been a key factor in Latin America's rapid recovery and growth since the 2008 world crisis (World Bank 2011).

In terms of the potential challenge of the right wing in coming years, then, many political factors from past decades remain effective sources of power: a willingness to act unconstitutionally and to dispense with democracy; the indirect centres of political power among capitalists and the media, and the associated reservoirs of socially conservative ideas; the capacity of ruling classes to defend their interests within the wider institutions of the state; straightforwardly successful electoral campaigning in spite of damaged neoliberal credentials, if not necessarily in the form of neopopulism; and, of course, the pervasive (if currently less overwhelming) influence of the US in so many aspects of Latin American societies. To all of this, of course, must be added the behaviour of left-wing governments, parties and politicians in securing political office and sustaining themselves in it. A crucial question is the dilution of right-wing media domination, whether through an expansion of the impact of alternative, continental channels like ALBA's TeleSur, or by licensing and resourcing alternative and community media, as, for example, in Bolivia. In this sphere there is already a real battle for hegemony taking place that the left – whether it is in office or in opposition – cannot afford to neglect. Another area in which the reformist left can make almost unchallenged progress in securing electoral support is in the area of identity politics, the rights of women, gays and ethnic minorities, where a great deal remains to be done (UN Development Programme 2004). This is an area in which the left historically has not always been progressive (Lievesley 2009: 26–34). Yet, however shrill the opposition of social conservatives, it is an area that does not directly challenge the existence of capitalist power, but only the way in which it is exercised. The capacity of the left, as well as of the right, to defend itself at the continental level has been demonstrated in the containment of Bolivian right-wing autonomist revolt, in the reaction to the Colombian 'anti-terrorist' bombing of Ecuadorian territory in 2008, and, at least to an extent, in the attempt first to reinstate Manuel Zelaya to the Honduran presidency and then to isolate the post-coup regime. In another aspect of its new continentalism, the left's foundation of ALBA on the basis of respect for national sovereignty, rather than treaty-bound constitutional federation, as in the European Union, removes a potential target of right-wing political attack.

In our earlier work on the left in Latin America, we, like others, noted the relatively modest social democratic and orthodox programmes of most of the 'pink tide' states in economic and social policy (Lievesley and Ludlam 2009a: 220–9; Grugel and Riggirozzi 2009: 220–30). In conventional electoral terms, this can be portrayed as a workable accommodation to ideologically centrist and even right-wing voters for the purpose of assembling a majority vote (Morales 2008: 37–9). The degree of dependence of some left-wing presidential programmes on raw material exports could certainly create vulnerability in the event of world prices falling, although this vulnerability will be offset if state-initiated economic diversification proceeds with sufficient speed. But such concerns also raise the broader, and indeed historical, question of whether, to sustain their potential even for rigorous reformism, left-wing governments in a capitalist society need to avoid 'conservative possibilism' and proceed relentlessly in a socialist direction on the assumption that this is the best defence against a ruling class that will eventually move more or less violently against such a government (Borón 2008: 242–54). The history of the coup in Chile and the debates on the left about the lessons of that historic defeat, about the neutrality of the capitalist state and the commitment of its rulers to democracy and about whether radicalism is a defence against, or a guarantee of, a ruling-class revolt against an elected left-wing government have become more, not less, relevant to the fate of the 'pink tide' in the twenty-first century.

There is always the possibility of right-wing parties simply promising to sustain left-wing social policies, as in the 2010 election in Chile. Beyond considerations about economic and social policy, though, several 'pink tide' governments, notably Venezuela, Bolivia and Ecuador, have reformed their constitutions to embed forms of popular participation and administration, including ethnic rights, that can in future defend social gains in the face of right-wing government attempts to reverse progressive change.

The creation of a genuinely popular democratic culture that breaks free of the electoral paternalism of the European social democratic and socialist traditions could provide a bulwark against right-wing politics in the twenty-first century. It could also limit the risk of left-wing presidents becoming isolated from their mass electorates and undertaking policies that alienate their voters and let the right back in. There is little evidence that a coherent post-neoliberal right is emerging that offers a coherent new balance of the forces of state and market, and a new political economy – even if, in some cases, there is a willingness to sustain some social programmes inherited from the left. But, as so much of this book demonstrates, in the long battle to democratize not just political processes but also the distribution of wealth and social power, the right is still in possession of colossal resources. In the twenty-first century in Latin America, the capacity of left-wing political leaders at all levels to sustain their programmes in the face of the right's resources will determine whether the mass of Latin American people continue to have their lives blighted by poverty and exclusion, or whether they begin to enjoy not merely the periodic right to vote, but also the fruits of their labour and of the long struggle for equality.

About the contributors

Dr Guy Burton is a research associate for the Latin America Programme at the Ideas Centre at the London School of Economics. He is the author of *Building Social Democracy in Latin America* (Edwin Mellen, forthcoming); 'Brazil: Third ways in the third world' in *Reclaiming Latin America: Experiments in Radical Social Democracy* (2009); 'A textbook for the left?', *Revista Enfoques Educacionales* (2008); 'Building social democratic education', *International Journal of Contemporary Sociology* (2008); and is co-author of 'PT never again? Failure (and success) in the PT's state government in Espirito Santo and the Federal District' in *Radicals in Power: The Workers Party and Experiments in Urban Democracy in Brazil* (2003).

Dr Marcos Costa Lima is Adjunct Professor at the Universidade Federal de Pernambuco, Brazil, where he is coordinator of the Regional and Development Nuclei of Studies and Research. He is President of the Universities Forum for Mercosul, and a member of the Commission of the University of Latin American Integration. His recent books include *Dinâmica do Capitalismo Pós-Guerra Fria. Cultura tecnológica, espaço e desenvolvimento* (2008); *A atualidade do pensamento de Celso Furtado* (2008); and *Regionalismos, democracia e desenvolvimento* (2007).

Dr Alexander Dawson is an associate professor of Latin American History at Simon Fraser University in Vancouver, Canada. Along with several articles, his publications include *Latin America since Independence: A History with Documents* (2010); *First World Dreams: Mexico since 1989* (2006); and *Indian and Nation in Revolutionary Mexico* (2004). He is working on a history of peyote, indigeneity and the idea of culture, tentatively called *How Culture Became a Right*.

Dr Leonardo Díaz Echenique is Associate Professor in the Department of Political Science and Sociology at the Universidad Autónoma de Barcelona and coordinator of Public Policy Studies at the Fundació Carles Pi i Sunyer. Among his publications are: 'Argentina: reforming neoliberal capitalism' in *Reclaiming Latin America: Experiments in Radical Social Democracy* (2009); and *Lula* (2004).

Dr Francisco Durand is Professor of Political Science at the University of Texas at San Antonio. He has published several book chapters on the new right in Peruvian politics, and is author of, among other books, *El Perú fracturado: formalidad, informalidad y economía delictiva* (2008); *La mano invisible en el Estado* (*The Invisible Hand in the State*) (2006); *Riqueza económica y pobreza política* (*Economic Wealth and Political Poverty*) (2003); *Organized Business, Economic Change and Democracy in Latin America* (1998); and *Business and Politics in Peru* (1994). He has acted as a consultant to the Inter-American Development Bank, the Inter-American Center for Tax Administration and the US Agency for International Development.

Dr Peter Lambert is a senior lecturer in Latin American Studies at the University of Bath. Having worked between 1987 and 1991 in the field of politics and popular education in an NGO in Paraguay, he completed his PhD at the University of Western England at Bristol before moving to Bath. Among his publications are: 'Paraguay' in *Countries at Crossroads: A Survey of Democratic Governance* (2007); and 'Muero con mi patria! Myth, political violence and the construction of national identity in Paraguay', in W. Fowler and P. Lambert (eds), *Political Violence and the Construction of National Identity in Latin America* (2006).

Grace Livingstone is a journalist specializing in Latin American affairs. She was a reporter for the *Guardian* in Venezuela and has also worked for the BBC World Service and has written for the *Observer*, the *Statesman* and the *Tablet*. She is the author of *America's Backyard: The United States and Latin America from the Monroe Doctrine to the War on Terror* (2009); and *Inside Colombia: Drugs, Democracy and War* (2003).

Javier Ozollo is a professor at the National University of Cuyo, Mendoza, Argentina. He has also been director of cultural management in the government of the province of Mendoza, Argentina. Among his publications are: *Marx and the State. The social determinants of thought of Karl Marx* (2005), and 'Argentina: reforming neoliberal capitalism', in *Reclaiming Latin America: Experiments in Radical Social Democracy* (2009).

Dr Diana Raby is Senior Research Fellow at the Research Institute of Latin American Studies, University of Liverpool. Her most recent book is *Democracia y revolución: América Latina y el socialismo hoy* (2008), a revised version of *Democracy and Revolution: Latin America and Socialism Today* (2006). Recent articles include: 'Why Cuba is still important', *Monthly Review* (2009); 'Latin America's leftward turn', *Global Dialogue*

(2008); and 'El liderazgo carismático en los movimientos populares y revolucionarios', *Cuadernos del CENDES* (2006).

Dr Patricio Silva is Professor of Modern Latin American History at Leiden University, the Netherlands. His research focuses on democratization and the technocratization of politics in Chile. His publications include: 'Swimming against the tide? The Chilean social democratic model in historical perspective' in *Reclaiming Latin America: Experiments in Radical Social Democracy* (2009); *In the Name of Reason: Technocrats and Politics in Chile* (2008); and *The Soldier and the State in South America: Essays in Civil–Military Relations* (2001).

Dr Andreas Tsolakis is an Institute of Advanced Study postdoctoral fellow at the University of Warwick and an international relations analyst at the Fundación Secretariado Gitano in Madrid. His research interests include critical theories of the state, globalization and governance, Latin American history and politics and European integration. He is the author of *The Reform of the Bolivian State: Domestic Politics in the Context of Globalization* (2010) and has published on state theory, transnational elite formation, reforms in Bolivia sponsored by the Movement towards Socialism, the Europe 2020 Strategy, social inclusion policies and the Roma.

Dr Ernesto Vivares is Lecturer in International Political Economy at FLACSO-UNESCO, Facultad Latinoamericana de Ciencias Sociales, Quito, Ecuador. His research focuses on the political economy of South American regionalism, welfare and financing of development. Among his publications are: 'The South American semi-periphery: financing development and welfare in Brazil and Argentina', in M. Phoebe and O. Worth (eds), *Globalisation and the Semi-Periphery* (2009); and 'Toward a re-reading of the political economy of South America', IPEG Papers (2007).

Bibliography

Abente Brun, D. (1999) 'People power in Paraguay', *Journal of Democracy*, 10(3).

— (2008) 'Paraguay: the unravelling of one-party rule', *Journal of Democracy*, 20(1).

Agencia Bolivaniana de Información (2009) 'Evo Morales pondera crecimiento económico de Potosí en 2008 y considera baja este año', 29 May, www.abi.bo/index.php?i=noticias_texto_paleta&j=20090529213732&k (accessed 15 June 2009).

Alarcón Olguín, V. and F. Freidenberg (2007) 'El proceso de selección del candidato presidencial en el Partido Acción Nacional', *Revista Mexicana de Sociología*, 69(4).

Alderete, A. (2009) 'Sobre la desigualdad perfecta en la propiedad y tenencia de la tierra', *Diario ABC Color*, 29 January.

Allamand, A. (1993) *La centro-derecha del futuro*, Santiago: Editorial Los Andes.

— (2007) *El desalojo: por qué la Concertación debe irse el 2010*, Santiago: Aguilar.

Alonso Tejada, A. (1999) *Church and Politics in Revolutionary Cuba*, Havana: Editorial José Martí.

Altman, D. (2008) 'Uruguay: a role model for the left?', in J. Castañeda and M. Morales (eds), *Leftovers: Tales of the Latin American Left*, London: Routledge.

Alvarado Godoy, P. F. (2004) *Confessions of Fraile: A Real Story of Terrorism*, Havana: Editorial Capitán San Luis.

Alvarez Rodrích, A. (1986) *El poder en el Perú*, Lima: Apoyo.

American Association for World Health (1997) 'Denial of food and medicine: the impact of the U.S. embargo on the health and nutrition in Cuba: an executive summary', www.cubasolidarity.net/aawh.html (accessed 22 January 2010).

Amnesty International (2003) *Cuba: 'Essential Measures'? Human Rights Crackdown in the Name of Security*, London: Amnesty International.

— (2009) *The US Embargo Against Cuba: Its Impact on Economic and Social Rights*, London: Amnesty International.

— (2010) *USA: The Case of the Cuban Five*, London: Amnesty International.

Angell, A. (1972) *Politics and the Labour Movement in Chile*, Oxford: Oxford University Press.

— (1993) *De Alessandri a Pinochet: en busca de la utopia*, Santiago: Editorial Andrés Bello.

— (2007) *Democracy after Pinochet: Politics, Parties and Elections in Chile*, London: Institute of Latin American Studies.

Angell, A. and B. Pollack (2000) 'The Chilean presidential elections of 1999–2000 and democratic consolidation', *Bulletin of Latin American Research*, 19(3).

Antunes, J. (2008) 'Argentina: truce in three-week agricultural strike', *World Socialist*, www.wsws.org/articles/ (accessed 13 May 2009).

Aporrea (2010) 'Investigación asegura que Uribe cogobernó con narcoparamilitares durante ocho años', 22 August, www.aporrea.org/internacionales/n163868.html (accessed 3 September 2010).

Arboleya, J. (2002) *The Cuban Counterrevolution*, Havana: Editorial José Martí.

Arce, E. (2009) 'Juicio Político: sólo chantaje para sacar tajadas', *E'a Periódico de Análisis*, 30 December, http://ea.com.py/category/politica/ (accessed 14 June 2010).

— (2010) 'Paraguay: Lugo admite pocos logros', 20 April, www.bbc.co.uk/mundo/ciencia_tecnologia/2010/04/100420_1946_paraguay_lugo_aniversario_gz.shtml (accessed 17 September 2010).

Argentine Ministry of Foreign Relations (2009) 'Reunión presidencial de Brasilia: declaración conjunta y acuerdos: visita de trabajo a la República Federativa del Brasil de la Presidenta de la República Argentina, Cristina Fernández de Kirchner, Press Statement No 000/09, 18 November 2009', Buenos Aires: Argentine Ministry of Foreign Relations, www.mrecic.gov.ar (accessed 15 March 2010).

Asamblea Constituyente de Bolivia (2007) 'Nueva Constitución Política del Estado: aprobada en grande, detalle y revisión', www.laconstituyente.org/?q=node/1542 (accessed 15 October 2008).

Avilés, W. (2006) *Global Capitalism, Democracy, and Civil-Military Relations in Colombia*, Albany, NY: State University of New York Press.

Aznar, J. M. (2007) 'Latin America: an agenda for freedom', Heritage Lecture No. 1025, 27 April, www.heritage.org/Research/Lecture/Latin-America-An-Agenda-for-Freedom (accessed 20 February 2009).

Baiocchi, G. and S. Checa (2008) 'The new and the old in Brazil's PT', in J. Castañeda and M. Morales (eds), *Leftovers: Tales from the Latin American Left*, London: Routledge.

Baldez, L. (1999) 'La política partidista y los limites del feminismo de Estado en Chile', in P. Drake and I. Jaksic (eds), *El modelo chileno: democracia y desarrollo en los noventa*, Santiago: Lom Ediciones.

Banco Central de Bolivia (BCB) (2010) 'Indicadores de inflación', www.bcb.gob.bo/index.php?q=indicadores/inflacion (accessed 20 March 2010).

Bardach, A. L. (2002) *Cuba Confidential: Love and Vengeance in Miami and Havana*, New York: Random House.

Barr, R. (2003) 'The persistence of neopopulism in Peru. From Fujimori to Toledo', *Third World Quarterly*, 24(6).

Barrett, P., D. Chávez and C. Rodríguez-Garavite (eds) (2008) *The New Latin American Left*, London: Pluto Press.

Bartley, K. and D. Ó Briain (2003) *The Revolution Will Not be Televised*, http://video.google.com/videoplay?docid=5832390545689805144 (accessed 23 November 2010).

Becerra Chávez, P. (2007) 'A un año del 2 de julio, ¿hubo fraude electoral?', *El Cotidiano*, 22(145).

Beghin, N. (2008) 'Notes on inequality and poverty in Brazil. Current situation and challenges: from poverty to power', Oxfam

background paper, www.fp2p.org (accessed 5 December 2010).
Benegas, J. (2010) 'El plan golpista tiene olor a tierra', *E'a Periódico de Análisis*, 23 November, http://ea.com.py/category/politica/ (accessed 14 June 2010).
Bisang, R., G. Anlló and M. Campi (2008) 'Una revolución (no tan) silenciosa. Claves para pensar la agricultura en la Argentina', *Desarrollo Económico*, 48(190–1).
Blaiser, L. (1992) *Venezuela febrero 27. De la concertación al des-conciert*, Caracas: Cotrain.
Blofield, M. (2002) 'Guerra Santa: la izquierda y derecha frente a los temas valóricos en el Chile democrático', in M. Dávila and C. Fuentes (eds), *Promesas de cambio: izquierda y derecha en el Chile contemporáneo*, Santiago: Editorial Universitaria.
Bobbio, N. (1996) *Left and Right: The Significance of a Political Dimension*, Cambridge: Polity.
Bolender, K. (2010) *Voices from the Other Side: An Oral History of Terrorism against Cuba*, London: Pluto Press.
Boloña, C. (1993) *Cambio de rumba*, Lima: Instituto de Economía de Libre Mercado.
Bolpress (2007) 'Estados Unidos se niega a que fiscalizen la ayuda de USAID', 19 November, www.bolpress.com/art.php?Cod=2007111903 (accessed 3 October 2008).
Borges, A. (2010) 'Já não se fazem mais máquinas políticas como antigamente: Competição vertical e mudança eleitoral nos estados brasileiros', *Revista de Sociologia e Política*, 18(35).
Boris, D. and I. Malcher (2005) 'Argentinien nach dem Zusammenbruch des neoliberalen Modells', *Prokla*, 35(1).
Borón, A. (1995) *State, Capitalism and Democracy in Latin America*, London: Lynne Rienner.
— (2000) 'Ruling without a party: Argentine dominant classes in the twentieth century', in K. Middlebrook (ed.), *Conservative Parties, the Right and Democracy in Latin America*, London: Johns Hopkins University Press.
— (2008) 'Promises and challenges. The Latin American left at the start of the twenty-first century', in P. Barrett, D. Chavez and C. Rodríguez-Garavito (eds), *The New Latin American Left: Utopia Reborn*, London: Pluto Press.
Bowen, S. and J. Holligan (2003) *El espia imperfecto: la telaraña siniestra de Vladimiro Montesinos*, Lima: Ediciones Peisa.
Branford, S. (2009) 'Brazil: has the dream ended?', in G. Lievesley and S. Ludlam (eds), *Reclaiming Latin America: Experiments in Radical Social Democracy*, London: Zed Books.
Britto García, L. (2008) *Dictadura mediática en Venezuela: investigación de unos medios por encima de toda sospecha*, Caracas: Ministerio del Poder Popular Para la Comunicación y la Información.
Bromley, R. (1990) 'A new path to development? The significance and the impact of Hernando de Soto's ideas on underdevelopment, production and reproduction', *Economic Geography*, 66 (October).
Bromwich, D. (2009) 'The co-president at work', *New York Review of Books*, 22 November.
Brookings Institute (2008) 'Cuban American opinions concerning U.S. policy toward Cuba and the U.S. election, December 2008 Poll', www.brookings.

edu/events/2008/~/media/Files/events/2008/1202_cuba_poll/1202_cuba_poll.pdf (accessed 14 January 2010).

Buarque de Holanda, S. (ed.) (2006) *Raízes do Brasil*, Rio de Janeiro: José Olympio.

Buxton, J. (2009) 'Venezuela: the political evolution of Bolivarianism', in G. Lievesley and S. Ludlam (eds), *Reclaiming Latin America: Experiments in Radical Social Democracy*, London: Zed Books.

Caballero, A. (2010) 'Convicción, no coacción', *Semana* (Bogotá), 24 July, www.semana.com/noticias-opinion/conviccion-no-coaccion/142141.aspx (accessed 3 September 2010).

Calvo Ospina, H. (2002) *Bacardí: The Hidden War*, London: Pluto Press.

— (2008) *Colombia, laboratorio de embrujos: democracia y terrorismo de estado*, Madrid: Foca.

Calvo Ospina, H. and K. Declercq (2000) *The Cuban Exile Movement: An Exposé of the Cuban American National Foundation and Anti-Castro Groups*, New York: Ocean Press.

Cameron, M. A. (1997) 'Political and economic origins of regime change in Peru: the *Eighteenth Brumaire* of Alberto Fujimori', in M. A. Cameron and P. Mauceri (eds), *The Peruvian Labyrinth*, University Park, PA: Pennsylvania State University.

Cammack, P. (2000) 'The resurgence of populism in Latin America', *Bulletin of Latin American Research*, 19(2).

Campello de Souza, M. (1992) 'The contemporary faces of the Brazilian right: an interpretation of style and substance', in D. A. Chalmers, M. Campello de Souza and A. Borón (eds), *The Right and Democracy in Latin America*, London: Praeger.

Cannon, B. (2009) *Hugo Chávez and the Bolivarian Revolution*, Manchester: Manchester University Press.

Carlsen, L. (2008a) 'A primer on Plan Mexico', 26 May, www.narconews.com (accessed 10 January 2009).

— (2008b) 'Armoring NAFTA: the battleground for Mexico's future', *NACLA Report on the Americas*, 41(5).

Carter, J. (2002) 'President Carter's Cuba trip report', www.cartercenter.org/news/documents/doc528.html (accessed 22 January 2010).

Castañeda, J. (2006) 'Latin America's left turn', *Foreign Affairs*, 85(3).

Castañeda, J. and M. A. Morales (eds) (2008) *Leftovers: Tales of the Latin American Left*, London: Routledge.

Castro Fernández, S. (2008) *La massacre de los Independientes de Color 1912*, Havana: Ciencias Sociales.

Celis Méndez, L. E. (2005) 'Los protagonistas, los hechos y los tiempos. Cronología y crónica', in L. Valencia, *El regreso de los rebeldes: De la furia de las armas a los pactos, la crítica y al esperanza*, Bogotá: Corporación Nuevo Arco Iris/CEREC.

Center for Economic and Policy Research (2008) 'US should disclose its funding to opposition groups in Bolivia and other Latin American countries', 12 September, www.cepr.net/index.php/press-releases/press-releases/u.s.-should-disclose-its-funding-of-opposition-groups-in-bolivia-and-other-latin-american-countries/ (accessed 5 October 2008).

Chalmers, D. A., M. Campello de Souza and A. Borón (1992) *The Right and Democracy in Latin America*, London: Praeger.
Chávez, D. (2008) 'Uruguay. The Left in government: between continuity and change', in P. Barrett, D. Chavez and C. Rodríguez-Garavite (eds), *The New Latin American Left*, London: Pluto Press.
Chossudovsky, M. (2008) 'The destabilization of Bolivia and the Kosovo option', *Global Research*, 21 September, www.tlaxcala.es/pp.asp?lg=en&reference=6048 (accessed 6 October 2008).
Chu, M. (2005) *Accion International: Maintaining High Performance through Time*, Boston, MA: Harvard Business Review.
Cirules, E. (2004) *The Mafia in Havana: A Caribbean Mob Story*, Melbourne: Ocean Press.
Colburn, F. (2004) 'Liberalism takes root in Central America', *Current History*, 103(670).
Collins, M. (2010a) 'Arrest of alleged American spy in Cuba further sets back US–Cuban relations', *Americas Program Report*, 14 January, http://Americas.irc-online.org.am/6652 (accessed 6 March 2010).
— (2010b) 'Cuba: democracy promotion programs under fire as fall out from spy arrest continues', *Americas Program Report*, 12 May, http://Americas.irc-online.org.am/8156 (accessed 1 June 2010).
Comisión de Entes Binacionales Hidroeléctricos (2009) '*Las negociaciones del Paraguay con el Brasil sobre Itaipú*', Asunción: Ministerio de Relaciones Exteriores.
Commission for Assistance to a Free Cuba (2004) 'Report to the president, March 2004', Washington, DC: Commission for Assistance to a Free Cuba.
— (2006) 'Report to the president, July 2006', Washington, DC: Commission for Assistance to a Free Cuba.
Conaghan, C. (2000) 'The irrelevant right: Alberto Fujimori and the new politics of pragmatic Peru', in K. Middlebrook (ed.), *Conservative Parties, the Right and Democracy in Latin America*, London: Johns Hopkins University Press.
Conaghan, C. and J. Malloy (1995) *Unsettling Statecraft: Democracy and Neoliberalism in the Central Andes*, Pittsburgh, PA: University of Pittsburgh Press.
Consejo Nacional Electoral (CNE) (2009) 'Referendo aprobatorio de la enmienda constitucional', www.cne.gob.ve/divulgación_referendo enmieda_2009 (accessed 15 January 2011).
Contreras, J. (2002) *Biografía no autorizada de Alvaro Uribe Vélez (El Señor de las Sombras)*, Bogotá: Oveja Negra.
Cooker, T. O. (1999) 'Deteriorating economic and political rights in Venezuela', *Latin American Perspectives*, 108(26).
Coppedge, M. (2000) 'Venezuelan parties and the representation of elite interests', in K. Middlebrook (ed.), *Conservative Parties, the Right and Democracy in Latin America*, London: Johns Hopkins University Press.
Coronil, F. (1997) *The Magical State*, Chicago, IL: Chicago University Press.
Correa Sutil, S. (2005) *Con las riendas del poder: La derecha chilena en el siglo XX*, Santiago de Chile: Editorial Sudamericana.

Corte Nacional Electoral (2009) *Resultados Referéndum Nacional Constituyente 2009, Documento de Información Pública 4*, La Paz: Corte Nacional Electoral.

Cotler, J. and R. Grompone (2000) *El fujimorismo*, Lima: Instituto de Estudios Peruanos.

Council on Hemispheric Affairs (COHA) (2006) 'The grounds for Bolivia's new military bases', 18 October, www.coha.org/2006/10/the-grounds-for-bolivia%E2%80%99s-new-military-bases/ (accessed 15 January 2008).

— (2008) 'A closer look at recent violence in Bolivia', 19 September, www.coha.org/2008/09/a-closer-look-at-recent-violence-in-bolivia/ (accessed 4 October 2008).

— (2009) 'US-Bolivia relations: halting an avalanche', 15 June, www.coha.org/2009/06/us-bolivian-relations-halting-an-avalanche/ (accessed 17 June 2009).

Cox, R. (1992) 'Towards a post-hegemonic conceptualization of world order: reflections on the relevancy of Ibn Khaldun', in R. Cox and T. Sinclair (eds) (1996) *Approaches to World Order*, Cambridge: Cambridge University Press.

Crabtree, J. (2005) *Patterns of Protest: Politics and Social Movements in Bolivia*, London: Latin American Bureau.

— (2006) 'Bolivia stakes its claim', *Open Democracy*, 3 May, http://www.opendemocracy.net/democracy-protest/bolivia_claim_3504.jsp (accessed 10 May 2006).

— (2008) 'Bolivia's political ferment: revolution and recall', *Open Democracy*, 13 August, www.opendemocracy.net/article/bolivia-s-political-ferment-revolution-and-recall (accessed 15 August 2008).

— (2009a) 'Bolivia: new constitution, new definition', *Open Democracy*, 22 January, www.opendemocracy.net/article/bolivia-new-constitution-new-definition (accessed 3 February 2009).

— (2009b) 'Bolivia: after the vote', *Open Democracy*, 2 February, www.opendemocracy.net/article/bolivia-after-the-vote (accessed 15 February 2009).

Crawley, A. (2007) *Somoza and Roosevelt: Good Neighbour Diplomacy in Nicaragua 1933–1945*, Oxford: Oxford University Press.

Cristi, R. (2000) *El pensamiento politico de Jaime Guzmán: autoridad y libertad*, Santiago: Lom Ediciones.

Cristi, R. and C. Ruiz (1992) *El pensamiento conservador en el Chile*, Santiago: Editorial Universitaria.

Cuban American National Foundation (2009) 'A new course for US Cuba policy: advancing people driven change', www.canf.org/index.php?src=news&srctype=detail&category=Press%20Releases&refno=110 (accessed 14 January 2010).

Cupull, A. and F. González (2005) *Juan Antonio Mella y Tina Modotti contra el fascismo*, Havana: Casa Editora Abril.

Dangl, B. (2008a) 'Undermining Bolivia', *Green Left Weekly*, 542 (5 March).

— (2008b) 'Bush spending tax dollars to foment unrest in Bolivia', *The Progressive*, 10 March, www.alternet.org/story/77572/bush_spending_u.s._tax_dollars_to_foment_unrest_in_bolivia/?comments=view&cID=853416&pID=853129 (accessed 8 June 2009).

Dávila, S. (2008) 'EUA tentaram influenciar mídia brasileira sobre reforma política', *Folha de São Paulo*, 22 July.

de Bell, L. and W. Pansters (2001) 'Winners and losers: preliminary reflections on the 2000 presidential elections in Mexico', *European Review of Latin American and Caribbean Studies*, 70.

de la Torre, M. A. (2003) *La Lucha for Cuba: Religion and Politics on the Streets of Miami*, Berkeley: University of California Press.

de Soto, H. (1989) *The Other Path*, New York: Harpers & Row.

Degutis, A. (2005) 'European Parliament election observation of parliamentary elections in Venezuela', www.europarl.europa.eu/intcoop/election_observation/missions/2004-2009/20051204_venezuela_parliamentary.pdf (accessed 12 December 2010).

Democracy Now! (2008) 'US embassy in Bolivia tells Fulbright scholar and peace corps volunteers to spy on Venezuelans and Cubans in Bolivia', 11 February, www.democracynow.org/2008/2/11/us_embassy_in_bolivia_tells_fulbright (accessed 15 February 2008).

Diamint, R. (2004) 'Security challenges in Latin America', *Bulletin of Latin American Research*, 23(1).

Diario Ultima Hora (2008) 'Discurso del Presidente de la República Fernando Lugo Méndez', www.ultimahora.com/notas/145853-Discurso-del-Presidente-de-la-Republica-Fernando-Lugo-Mendez (accessed 14 June 2010).

Dieterich, H. (2006) 'Bolivia: salto cualitativo de la "Revolución Naranja", limpieza étnica y terrorismo oligárquico', *Rebelión*, 18 December, www3.rebelion.org/noticia.php?id=43319 (accessed 10 September 2008).

Dietz, H. and W. E. Dugan (1997) 'Clases sociales y comportamiento electoral en Lima: una análisis de datos agregados', in F. Tuesta (ed.), *Los enigmas del poder*, Lima: Fundación F. Ebert.

Dinges, J. (2004) *The Condor Years: How Pinochet and His Allies Brought Terrorism to Three Continents*, New York: The New Press.

Dirección General de Estadídisticas, Encuestas y Censos (DGEEC) (2008) *Anuario Estadistico 2008*, www.dgeec.gov.py/ (accessed 14 June 2010).

Do Alto, H. and P. Stefanoni (2008) *Nous serons des millions: Evo Morales et la gauche au pouvoir en Bolivie*, Paris: Raisons d'Agir.

dos Santos, W. G. (1985) 'A pré-revolução brasileira', in H. Jaguaribe, F. Iglesias, W. G. dos Santos, V. Chacon and F. K.Camparato (eds), *Brasil: sociedade democrática*, Rio de Janeiro: José Olympio.

Dugas, J. (2000) 'The Conservative Party and the crisis of political legitimacy in Colombia', in K. Middlebrook (ed.), *Conservative Parties, the Right and Democracy in Latin America*, London: Johns Hopkins University Press.

Duncan, G. (2006) *La Señores de la guerra: de paramilitares, mafiosos y autodefensas en Colombia*, Bogotá: Planeta.

Dunkerley, J. (2007) *Bolivia: Revolution and the Power of History in the Present*, London: Institute for the Study of the Americas.

Durand, F. (1992) 'The new right and political change in Peru', in D. A. Chalmers, M. Campello de Souza and A. Borón (eds), *The Right and Democracy in Latin America*, London: Praeger.

— (1996) 'El fenómena Fujimori y las crisis de los partidos', *Revista Mexicana de Sociología*, 58(1).

— (2003) *Riqueza económica y pobreza política*, Lima: Pontificia Universidad Católica del Perú.

Eaton, K. (2006) 'Bolivia's conservative autonomy movement', *Berkeley Review of Latin American Studies*, Winter/Spring, www.clas.berkeley.edu/Publications/Review/Winter2006/Winter2006-Eaton.pdf (accessed 2 February 2009).

— (2007) 'Backlash in Bolivia: regional autonomy as a reaction against indigenous mobilization', *Politics and Society*, 35(1).

— (2009) 'Conservative autonomy movements: Bolivia and Ecuador in comparative perspective', Paper presented at the Latin American Studies Association conference, June 2009, Rio de Janeiro.

Economic Commission for Latin America (2009) *Foreign Direct Investment in Latin American and the Caribbean,* Santiago de Chile: Economic Commission for Latin America.

— (2010a) *Time for Equality: Closing Gaps, Opening Trails*, June, Santiago de Chile: Economic Commission for Latin America.

— (2010b) 'Conditional transfer programmes benefit over 100 million people in the region', www.eclac.org/cgi-bin/getProd.asp?xml=/prensa/noticias/comunicados/9/42139 (accessed 21 January 2011).

Economist (2010a) 'Brazil's presidential campaign. The handover', 30 September, www.economist.com/node/17147658?story_id=1`7147658 (accessed 21 January 2011).

— (2010b) 'The campaign heats up', 30 September, www.economist.com/blogs/americasview/2010/09/brazils_presidential_election (accessed 21 January 2011).

Elizade, R. M. and L. Báez (2003) *'The Dissidents': Cuban State Security Agents Reveal the True Story*, Havana: Editora Política.

Ellis, R. E. (2009) *China in Latin America: The Whats and Wherefores*, Boulder, CO: Lynne Rienner.

Elliston, J. (1999) *Psywar on Cuba: The De-Classified History of US Anti-Castro Propaganda*, Melbourne: Ocean Press.

Ellner, S. (2004) 'Leftist goals and the debate over anti-neoliberal strategy in Latin America', *Science and Society*, 68(1).

Emmerich, G. E. (2007) 'Las elecciones de 2006 y su impacto sobre la democracia en México', *El Cotidiano*, 22(145).

Enzinna, W. (2008) 'Another SOA? A US police academy in El Salvador worries critics', *NACLA Report on the Americas*, 41(5).

Erikson, D. P. (2008) *The Cuba Wars: Fidel Castro, the United States, and the Next Revolution*, New York: Bloomsbury Press.

Escalante, F. (2004) *The Cuba Project: CIA Covert Operations 1959–1962*, New York: Ocean Press.

— (2006) *Executive Action: 634 Ways to Kill Fidel Castro*, New York: Ocean Press.

Espíndola, R. (2009) 'New politics, new parties?', in R. L Millett, J. S. Holmes and O. J. Pérez (eds), *Latin American Democracy: Emerging Reality or Endangered Species?*, London: Routledge.

European Union (1996) 'Common position of 2 December 1996 defined by the council on the basis of Article J.2 of the Treaty on European Union, on Cuba', http://eur-lex.europa.eu/LexUriServ/LexUriServ. do?uri=CELEX:31996E0697:EN:NOT (accessed 3 February 2010).

Federal Bureau of Investigation (1999) *Terrorism in the United States 1999: 30 Years of Terrorism, a Special Retrospective Edition*, Washington, DC: US Department of Justice.

Ferrer, A. (2010) 'Carta abierta a Grobocopatel', *Pagina 12*, 16 August.

Fleet, M. (1985) *The Rise and Fall of Chilean Christian Democracy*, Princeton, NJ: Princeton University Press.

Folha de São Paulo (2010) 'Veja o novo mapa do Congresso e conheça a distribução partidária', 1 November, www.folha.vol.com.br/poder/823736-veja-o-novo-mapa-docongresso-e-coheca-a-distribuicao-partidaria.shtml (accessed 21 January 2011).

Forero, S. (2005) 'Chávez tightens grip as rivals boycott vote', *New York Times*, 5 December.

Fox, M. (2007) 'US companies behind anti-reform propaganda in Venezuela', 27 November, http://venezuelanalysis.com/analysis/2904 (accessed 16 January).

Franceschet, S. (2005) *Women and Politics in Chile*, Boulder, CO: Westview Press.

Fuentes, C. (2000) 'After Pinochet: civilian policies towards the military in the 1990s Chilean democracy', *Journal of Interamerican Studies and World Affairs*, 43(3).

Fukuyama, F. (1992) *The End of History and the Last Man*, London: Penguin.

Funk, R. (2010) 'La nueva forma de triangular', *El Mostrador*, 1 June, www.elmostrador.cl/opinion/2010/06/01/la-nueva-forma-de-triangular/ (accessed 13 July 2010).

Gaitán, G. (1985) 'Orígenes de la violencia de los años 40', in Centro Gaitán, *Once Ensayos sobre la Violencia*, Bogotá: Fondo Editorial CEREC.

Gamarra, E. (2007) 'Bolivia on the brink', Council on Foreign Relations, Special Report, 24 February, www.cfr.org/publication/12642/bolivia_on_the_brink.html (accessed 27 June 2009).

García, C. G. (1996) *Havana USA: Cuban Exiles and Cuban Americans in South Florida, 1959–1994*, Berkeley: University of California Press.

García, M. (2009) 'La montaña. Concentración Oligopólica Mediática y Poder Económico', www.arbia.org/nov-detalle.php?nov=238 (accessed 22 September 2010).

— (2010) 'El grupo Clarín es una banda que se ha apoderado de los medios de comunicación', *Libres del Sur*, http://libresdelsur.org.ar/archivo/spip.php?article5867 (accessed 22 September 2010).

García Linera, A., R. Gutierrez, R. Prada and L. Tapia (2000) *El retorno de la Bolivia plebeya*, La Paz: Muela del Diablo.

Garretón, M. A. (1989) *The Chilean Political Process*, London: Unwin Hyman.

Geen, J. (2010) 'Protests as Argentina votes on gay marriage', www.pinknews.co.uk/2010/07/14/ (accessed 27 August 2010).

Gibson, E. (1992) 'Conservative electoral movements and democratic politics: core constituents, coalition building and the Latin American right', in D. A. Chalmers, M. Campello de Souza and A. Borón (eds), *The Right and Democracy in Latin America*, London: Praeger.

Gill, L., G. Grandin, D. Poole and M. Weisbrot (2009) 'Progressive policy for the Americas? A NACLA roundtable', *NACLA Report on the Americas*, 42(1).

Gill, S. (2000) 'The constitution of global capitalism', Paper presented at the International Studies Association annual conference, March 2000.

Ginden, J. and K. Weld (2007) 'Benevolence or intervention? Spotlighting US soft power', *NACLA Report on the Americas*, 40(1).

Golinger, E. (2007) *The Chávez Code. Cracking US intervention in Venezuela*, London: Pluto Press.

— (2009a) 'USAID's silent invasion in Bolivia', http://upsidedownworld.org/main/bolivia-archives-31/1865-usaids-silent-invasion-in-bolivia (accessed 18 May 2009).

— (2009b) 'The role of the International Republic Institute (IRI) in the Honduran coup', www.chavezcode.com/search?q=Fenner (accessed 5 July 2010).

— (2010a) 'Colored revolutions: a new form of regime change mode in the USA', http://venezuelanalysis.com/analysis/5139 (accessed 15 December 2010).

— (2010b) 'US interference in Venezuelan elections', *El Correo del Orinoco*, 28 September.

Goodman, A. (2008) 'Interview with Jane Meyer', 18 July, www.democracynow.org/2008/7/18/the_dark_side_jane_meyer_on (accessed 14 May 2010).

Gott, R. (2004) *Cuba: A New History*, New Haven, CT: Yale University Press.

— (2006) 'Venezuela's Murdoch', *New Left Review*, 39.

— (2009) *Hugo Chávez and the Bolivarian Revolution*, London and New York: Verso.

Gottberg, L. D. (2004) 'Mob outrages: reflections on the media construction of the masses in Venezuela', *Journal of Latin American Cultural Studies*, 13(1).

Gould, J. E. (2006) 'Venezuela's opposition concedes: Chávez is here to stay', *Time*, 5 December.

Grandin, G. (2007) 'Democracy, diplomacy and intervention in the Americas', *NACLA Report on the Americas*, 40(1).

Gray, G. (2007) 'El reto posneoliberal de Bolivia', *Nueva Sociedad*, 209 (May–June).

Grebe, H. (1983) 'Excedente sin acumulación', in R. Zavaleta (ed.), *Bolivia, Hoy*, Mexico: Siglo XXI Editores.

Grugel, J. (1999) 'Development and democratic political change in the South', *Journal of International Relations and Development*, 2(4).

Grugel, J. and P. Riggirozzi (2009) 'Governance after neoliberalism', in J. Grugel and P. Riggirozzi (eds), *Governance after Neoliberalism in Latin America*, New York: Palgrave Macmillan.

Gutierrez, F. (2007) 'Dégel et radicalisation en Colombie', in O. Dabène (ed.), *Amérique latine, les elections contre la démocratie*, Paris: Presses de Sciences Po.

Harnecker, M. (2005) 'On leftist strategy', *Science and Society*, 68(1).

Harris, D. and D. Azzi (2006) 'ALBA: Venezuela's answer to "free trade": the Bolivarian alternative for the Americas', *Focus on the Global South Occasional Papers*, 3.

Hatheway, E. (2010) 'Bolivian government negotiates internal conflict', Andean Information Network, 16 May, http://ain-bolivia.org/2010/05/bolivian-government-negotiates-internal-conflicts/ (accessed 4 July 2010).

Hedgecoe, Guy (2008) 'Ecuador's politics of expectation', *Open Democracy*, 1 February, www.open democracy.net/article/globalisation/ecuador_s_politics_ of_expectation (accessed 3 February 2009).

Heredia, B. (1992) 'Profits, politics, and size: the political transformation of Mexican business', in D. A. Chalmers, M. Campello de Souza and A. Borón (eds), *The Right and Democracy in Latin America*, London: Praeger.

Hernández, A. and A. Quintero (2005) *La familia presidencial: el gobierno del cambio bajo sospecha de corrupción*, Mexico City: Editorial Grijalbo.

Hernández Vicencio, T. (2005) 'La renovación de la dirigencia panista y el afianzamiento de la ultraderecha', *El Cotidiano*, 20(131).

Human Rights Watch (1993) 'Freedom of expression in Miami's Cuban exile community', www.hrw.org/reports/1993/WR93/Hrw.htm (accessed 8 April 2008).

Huneeus, C. (2000) 'Technocrats and politicians in an authoritarian regime: the "ODEPLAN boys" and the "Gremialists" in Pinochet's Chile', *Journal of Latin American Studies*, 32(2).

Hurtado, C. (2010) 'Venezuela and the challenge of a new democratic transition', *Florida Atlantic Comparative Studies Journal*, 12.

Hylton, F. (2006) *Evil Hour in Colombia*, London: Verso.

Hylton, F. and S. Thomson (2007) *Revolutionary Horizons: Past and Present in Bolivian Politics*, London: Verso.

Instituto Nacional de Estadística y Censos (INDEC) (2010) *National Statistics, Government of Argentina*, www.indec.gov.ar (accessed 16 November 2010).

Instituto Nacional de Estadísticas (2009) 'Inversión Extranjera Directa por Año Según Actividad Económica', www.ine.gov.bo/indice/general.aspx?codigo=40211 (accessed 15 June 2009).

Inter-American Development Bank (2006) *The Politics of Policies: Economic and Social Progress in Latin America*, Washington, DC: Inter-American Development Bank.

— (2009) *Remittances to Latin America and the Caribbean: The Impact of the Global Financial Crisis*, Washington, DC: Inter-American Development Bank.

International Institute for Sustainable Development (2007) 'Bolivia notifies World Bank of withdrawal from ICSID, pursues BIT revisions', *Investment Treaty News*, 9 May, www.bilaterals.org/article.php3?id_article=8221 (accessed 3 March 2008).

International Labour Organization (2010) *Employment and Social Protection Policies from Crisis to Recovery and Beyond: A Review of Experience*, ILO report to the G20 Labour and Employment Ministers Meeting, Geneva: International Labour Organization.

International Monetary Fund (IMF) (2007) 'Bolivia: 2007 Article IV consultation – staff report,

07/248', Washington, DC: International Monetary Fund.
— (2009) 'Bolivia: Article IV consultation – staff report, 09/27', Washington, DC: International Monetary Fund.
Jones, B. (2008) *Hugo! The Hugo Chávez Story from Mud Hut to Perpetual Revolution*, London: The Bodley Head.
Jones, H. (2008) *The Bay of Pigs*, Oxford: Oxford University Press.
Kay, C. and P. Silva (eds) (1992) *Development and Social Change in the Chilean Countryside*, Amsterdam: CEDLA.
Kingstone, P. (2001) 'Elites, democracy, and market reforms in Latin America', *Latin American Politics and Society*, 43(3).
Kirk, J. M. (1989) *Between God and the Party: Religion and Politics in Revolutionary Cuba*, Tampa: University of South Florida Press.
Kirkpatrick, J. (1982) *Dictatorships and Double Standards*, New York: Simon and Schuster.
Klaiber, J. (1996) *La iglesia en el Perú*, Lima: Pontificia Universidad Católica del Perú.
Klein, M. (2004) 'The Unión Demócrata Independiente and the poor (1983–1992): the survival of clientelistic traditions in Chilean politics', *Jahrbuch für Geschichte Lateinamerikas*, 41.
Kornbluh, P. (ed.) (1998) *Bay of Pigs Declassified: The Secret CIA Report on the Invasion of Cuba*, New York: The New Press.
Kozloff, N. (2007) *Hugo Chávez: Oil, Politics and the Challenge to the United States*, New York: Palgrave Macmillan.
La República (2010) 'La Oposición acusa al presidente Lugo de pergeñar un autogolpe', 12 January.
Lacey, M. (2006) 'Castro foe puts US in an awkward spot', *New York Times*, 8 October.
Laclau, E. (2005) *On Populist Reason*, London: Verso
Lambert, P. (2000) 'A decade of electoral democracy: continuity, change and crisis in Paraguay', *Bulletin of Latin American Research*, 19(3).
— (2007) 'Paraguay', in Freedom House, *Countries at the Crossroads: A Survey of Democratic Governance*, Washington, DC: Freedom House.
Lambert, R. (2009) 'When the "magic moment" turned to nightmare. Brazil: more dependent than ever', *Counterpunch*, 12–14 June, www.counterpunch.org/lambert06122009.html (accessed 25 November 2010).
Landau, S. (2010) 'The Alan Gross case', *Counterpunch*, 30 July–1 August 2010, www.counterpunch.org/landau07302010.html (accessed 19 August 2010).
Lander, E. (1996) 'The impact of neoliberal adjustment in Venezuela', *Latin American Perspectives*, 90(23).
Larsen, S. (2007) 'The anti-immigration movement: from shovels to suits', *NACLA Report on the Americas*, 40(3).
Latinobarómetro (2005–08) Informe Latinobarómetro 2005-8, Santiago de Chile, www.latinobarometro.org (accessed 14 June 2010).
Lauer, M. (1988) 'Adiós conservadurismo: bienvenido liberalismo. La nueva derecha en el Perú', *Nueva Sociedad*, 98.
Lendman, S. (2008) 'Grow them young, pay them well – anti-Chavistas, that is', 16 May, www.globalresearch.ca/index.php?context=va&aid=8996 (accessed 15 January 2011).
León Cotayo, N. (2006) *Crimen en*

Barbados, Havana: Ciencias Sociales.
Levine, R. M. (2001) *Secret Missions to Cuba: Fidel Castro, Bernardo Benes, and Cuban Miami*, New York: Palgrave Macmillan.
Levitsky, S. and M. V. Murillo (2008) 'Argentina: from Kirchner to Kirchner', *Journal of Democracy*, 19(2).
Lewis, T. (2006) 'Bolivia takes on the multinationals', *socialistworker.org*, 12 May, http://socialistworker.org/2006-1/588/588_12_Bolivia.shtml (accessed 25 May 2006).
Lievesley , G. (1999) *Democracy in Latin America: Mobilization, Power and the Search for a New Politics*, Manchester: Manchester University Press.
— (2009) 'Is Latin America moving leftwards? Problems and prospects', in G. Lievesley and S. Ludlam (eds), *Reclaiming Latin America: Experiments in Radical Social Democracy*, London: Zed Books.
Lievesley, G. and S. Ludlam (eds) (2009a) *Reclaiming Latin America: Experiments in Radical Social Democracy*, London: Zed Books.
— (2009b) '*Nuestra America*: the spectre haunting Washington', in G. Lievesley and S. Ludlam (eds), *Reclaiming Latin America: Experiments in Radical Social Democracy*, London: Zed Books.
Lilla, M. (2010) 'The Tea Party Jacobins', *New York Review of Books*, 29 May.
Ling Sanz Cerrada, F. A. (2008) 'El PAN en la coyuntura actual: una mirada desde dentro', *El Cotidiano*, 23(149).
Linz, J. (1990) 'The perils of presidentialism', *Journal of Democracy*, 1 (winter).
Livingstone, G. (2003) *Inside Colombia: Drugs, Democracy and War*, London: Latin America Bureau.
— (2009) *America's Backyard: The United States and Latin America from the Monroe Doctrine to the War on Terror*, London: Zed Books.
Loaeza, S. (1992) 'The role of the right in political change in Mexico, 1982–1988', in D. A. Chalmers, M. Campello de Souza and A. Borón (eds), *The Right and Democracy in Latin America*, London: Praeger.
López, C. (ed.) (2010) *Y refundaron la patria. De cómo mafiosos y políticos reconfiguraron el estado colombiano*, Bogotá: Debate.
López, S. (1989) 'La nueva derecha: refundar o refundir el Perú?', *Quehacer*, 60.
López San Miguel, M. (2010) 'Tras reunisrse con empresarios, Valenzuela cuestiono la inseguridad jurídica', *Pagina 12*, 20 June, www.pagina12.com.ar (accessed 12 September 2010).
Lovato, R. (2008) 'Building the homeland security state', *NACLA Report on the Americas*, 43(2).
Ludlam, S. (2009) 'Inside the Beast', *Cuba Sí*, summer.
Lynch, N. (1999) *Una tragedia sin heroes: la derrota de los partidos y el origen de los independientes, Perú 1980–1992*, Lima: Universidad Nacional de San Marcos.
MacShane, D. (2002) 'I saw the calm, rational Chávez turn into a ranting, populist demagogue', *The Times*, 13 April.
Mainwaring, S., R. Meneguello and T. Power (2000a) 'Conservative parties, democracy, and economic reform in contemporary Brazil', in D. A. Chalmers, M. Campello de Souza and A. Borón (eds), *The Right and*

Democracy in Latin America, London: Praeger.
— (2000b) *Partidos conservadores no Brasil contemporâneo*, São Paulo: Paz e Terra.
Márquez, H. (2010) 'Brazil's capitalist invasion builds socialism a la Venezuela', *IPS News*, 20 November, http://ipsnews.net/news.asp?idnews=53623 (accessed 3 December 2010).
McGee Deutsch, S. (1999) *Las Derechas: The Extreme Right in Argentina, Brazil, and Chile, 1890–1939*, Palo Alto, CA: Stanford University Press.
McSherry, J. P. (1998) 'The emergence of "guardian democracy"', *NACLA Report on the Americas*, 32(3).
Medina, M. (2010) 'Doscientos años, el cuadriculado número redondo', www.razonpublica.com/index.php?option=com_content&view=article&id=1294:doscientos-anos-el-cuadriculado-numero-redondo&catid=167:articulos-recientes- (accessed 3 September 2010).
Méndez B. and H. Luis (2008) 'Neoliberalismo y derechización en México (1983–2008)', *El Cotidiano*, 23(149).
Merkel, W. (2004) 'Embedded and defective democracies', *Democratization*, 11(5).
Middlebrook, K. (2000a) 'Introduction: conservative parties, elite representation, and democracy in Latin America', in K. Middlebrook (ed.), *Conservative Parties, the Right and Democracy in Latin America*, London: Johns Hopkins University Press.
— (2000b) 'Conclusion: conservative politics, the right, and democracy in Latin America', in K. Middlebrook (ed.), *Conservative Parties, the Right and Democracy in Latin America*, London: Johns Hopkins University Press.
— (ed.) (2000c) *Conservative Parties, the Right and Democracy in Latin America*, London: The Johns Hopkins University Press.
— (ed.) (2004) *Dilemmas of Political Change in Mexico*, London: Institute for Latin American Studies.
Miliband, R. (1982) *Capitalist Democracy in Britain*, Oxford: Oxford University Press.
— (1989) *Divided Societies: Class Struggle in Contemporary Capitalism*, Oxford: Clarendon Press.
Ministerio de Hacienda (2010) *Impuesto a la renta personal: imperativo de la democracia*, Asunción: Ministerio de Hacienda.
Ministerio del Poder Popular para la Comunicación y la Información (2004) *La Guerra mediática contra Venezuela desde el diario español El País*, Caracas: Ministerio del Poder Popular para la Comunicación y la Información.
Moncada, A. (2006) 'Opus Dei over time', *ICSA E-Newsletter* 5(2).
Morales, M. A. (2008) 'Have Latin Americans turned left?', in J. Castañeda and M. A. Morales (eds), *Leftovers: Tales of the Latin American Left*, London: Routledge.
Moreno, A. (2008) 'La opinión pública Mexicana en el contexto postelectoral de 2006', *Perfiles Latinoamericanos*, 31.
Moses, C. (2000) *Real Life in Castro's Cuba*, Wilmington, DE: SR Books.
Movimiento al Socialismo (MAS) (2008) 'Programa de gobierno', www.masbolivia.org/mas/programa/pgsmatrizp.htm (accessed 10 June 2008).

Mullin, J. (2000) 'The burden of a violent history', *Miami New Times*, 20 April.

Muñoz, H. (1986) *Las relaciones exteriores del gobierno militario chileno*, Santiago de Chile: Ediciones del Ornitorrinco.

Mychalejko, C. (2009) 'Dirty business, dirty wars: US-Latin American relations in the 21st century', http://upsidedownworld.org (accessed 9 February 2009).

National Assembly of Cuba (2006) 'Summary of the main terrorist actions against Cuba (1990–2000)', www.parlamentocubano.cu/ (accessed 16 June 2008).

National Security Archive (2002) 'The Cuban missile crisis: the documents', www.gwu.edu/~nsarchiv/nsa/cuba_mis_cri/docs.htm (accessed 13 October 2005).

— (2005) 'Luis Posada Carriles: the declassified record. CIA and FBI documents detail career in international terrorism; connection to U.S.', www.gwu.edu/~nsarchiv/NSAEBB/NSAEBB153/index.htm (accessed 5 May 2008).

— (2006) 'Bombing of Cuban jetliner: 30 years later', www.gwu.edu/~nsarchiv/NSAEBB/NSAEBB202/index.htm (accessed 5 May 2008).

Navarro, E. J. (2004) 'Venezuela, crónicas de la corrupción', 9 August, www.voltairenet.org/article121729.html (accessed 16 January 2011).

Nickson, R. A. (2009) 'Paraguay: Fernando Lugo vs the Colorado machine', *Open Democracy*, 28 February, www.opendemocracy.net/article/democracy_power/politics_protest/paraguay_fernando_lugo (accessed 14 June 2010).

Nickson, R. A. and P. Lambert (2002) 'State reform and the privatized state in Paraguay', *Public Administration and Development*, 22.

Nogueira, M. A. (2009) 'Uma crise de longa duração', *Estudos Avançãdos*, 23(67).

Noriega, R. (2009) 'Heading off another "lost decade" in Latin America', www.aei.org (accessed 17 March 2009).

Ó Loingsigh, G. (2002) 'La estrategia integral del paramilitarismo en el Magdalena Medio de Colombia', www.sinaltrainal.org/anterior/Textos/parasmagda2004.pdf (accessed 11 November 2010).

O'Donnell G. (1978) 'State and alliances in Argentina, 1956–1976', *Journal of Development Studies*, 15(1).

— (1994) 'Delegative democracy', *Journal of Democracy*, 5(1).

O'Donnell, G. and P. Schmitter (1986) *Transitions from Authoritarian Rule: Tentative Conclusions and Uncertain Democracies*, London: Johns Hopkins University Press.

O'Shaughnessy, H. (2009a) 'Democracy hangs by a thread in Honduras', *Independent on Sunday*, 19 July 2009.

— (2009b) *The Priest of Paraguay: Fernando Lugo and the Making of a Nation*, London: Zed Books.

OECD Development Centre (2010) *Latin American Economic Outlook 2010*, Paris: OECD Development Centre.

Oppenheim, L. H. (2007) *Politics in Chile: Socialism, Authoritarianism, and Market Democracy*, Boulder, CO: Westview Press.

Ortega, L. (1998) *Cubanos en Miami*, Havana: Ciencias Sociales.

Ortiz, F. A. (2010) 'Entrevista con el "colombianólogo" Marc Chernick' por Fernando Arellano Ortiz, 23 August, http://alainet.

org/active/40346 (accessed 2 September 2010).

Ortiz, S. (2009) 'Cómo inflar "globos" mediáticos para debilitar un gobierno', *E'a Periódico de Análisis*, 21 October, http://ea.com.py/category/politica/ (accessed 14 June 2010).

Otero Prada, D. (2010) 'Listos para la Guerra de las Galaxias', *Razón Pública*, 16 August, www.razonpublica.com/index.php?view=article&catid=21 (accessed 19 August 2010).

Oxford Analytica (2008) 'Paraguay: land reform pressures test Lugo', 13 October.

— (2009a) 'Paraguay: guerrilleros in the north?', 9 January.

— (2009b) 'Paraguay: congress wages fiscal war on executive', 10 June.

— (2009c) 'Lugo's first anniversary', 20 August.

Oxhorn, P. (2003) 'From Allende to Lula: assessing the legacy', *NACLA Report on the Americas*, 37(1).

Palacios, A. (2002) *Asedio a una embajada*, http://video.google.com/videoplay?docid=1352185964025828251 (accessed 23 November 2010).

Palacios, M. (2006) *Between Legitimacy and Violence: A History of Colombia, 1875–2002*, Durham, NC: Duke University Press.

Palma, E. and R. Balderas (2007) 'Desarrollo electoral y estrategia del PRD en el 2006', *El Cotidiano*, 21(141).

Panizza, F. (2005) 'Utopia Unarmed revisited: the resurgence of left-of-centre politics in Latin America', *Political Studies*, 53.

— (2008) 'Economic constraints and strategic choices: the case of the Frente Amplio of Uruguay's first year in office', *Bulletin of Latin American Research*, 27(2).

— (2009) *Contemporary Latin America: Development and Democracy beyond the Washington Consensus*, London: Zed Books.

Paredes, C. and J. Sachs (eds) (1991) *Estabilización y crecimiento en el Perú*, Lima: GRADE.

Pastor, D. (2004) 'Origins of the Chilean binominal election system', *Revista de Ciencia Política*, 24(1).

Pearce, J. (1990) *Colombia: Inside the Labyrinth*, London: Latin America Bureau.

Peñaloza Díaz, M. A. (2010) 'Análisis: la abstención es activa, por eso en Colombia no decide', *Vanguardia Liberal*, 20 June, www.vanguardia.com/politica/nacional/65447 (accessed 27 August 2010).

Pérez, L. A. (1995) *Cuba between Reform and Revolution*, Oxford: Oxford University Press.

Pérez Roque, F. (2003) 'Press conference by Foreign Minister of the Republic of Cuba, Felipe Pérez Roque on the mercenaries at the service of the Empire who stood trial on April 3, 4, 5 and 7, 2003, Havana City, April 9 2003', http://europa.cubaminrex.cu/English/PressConferences/Articulos/2003/C2.html (accessed 7 August 2003).

Petras, J. (1999) *The Left Strikes Back*, Oxford: Westview Press.

— (2005) 'Latin American strategies: class-based direct action versus populist electoral politics', *Science and Society*, 68(1).

Petras, J. and H. Veltmayer (2003) *Cardoso's Brazil: A Land for Sale*, New York: Rowman & Littlefield.

Philip, G. and F. Panizza (2011) *The Triumph of Politics: The Rise of the Left in South America*, Cambridge: Polity Press.

Pine, A. (2010) 'Message control: field notes on Washington's golpistas', *NACLA Report on the Americas*, 43(2).

Planas, P. (1996) 'Existe un sistema de partidos en el Perú?', in F. Tuesta (ed.), *Los enigmas del poder*, Lima: Fundación F. Ebert.

Portes, A. (2007) 'The Cuban-American political machine: reflections on its origins and perpetuation', in B. Hoffman and L. Whitehead (eds), *Debating Cuban Exceptionalism*, New York: Palgrave Macmillan.

PressTV (2009) 'Chávez says coup attempt thwarted', 13 February, www.presstv.ir/detail.aspx?id=85534§ionid=351020704 (accessed 15 January 2011).

Przeworski, A. (1986) 'Some problems in the study of the transition to democracy', in G. O'Donnell, P. C. Schmitter and L. Whitehead (eds), *Transitions from Authoritarian Rule: Comparative Perspectives*, Baltimore, MD: Johns Hopkins Press.

Rabello, M. L. (2009) 'Brazil senators approve Venezuela entry into Mercosur', Bloomberg TV, 15 December, www.bloomberg.com/apps/news?pid=newsarchive@sid=aKMNCEFXqsq4 (accessed 21 January 2011).

Raby, D. L. (2006) *Democracy and Revolution: Latin America and Socialism Today*, London: Pluto Press.

Ramírez Mercado, M. (2007) 'La distribución del voto en las entidades federativas. Análisis sobre las elecciones presidenciales en México, 1988–2006', *El Cotidiano*, 21(141).

Reboratti, C. (2010) 'Un mar de soja: la nueva agricultura en Argentina y sus consecuencias', *Revista de Geografía, Norte Grande*, May.

Reid, M. (2007) *Forgotten Continent: The Battle for Latin America's Soul*, New Haven, CT & London: Yale University Press.

Reinhardt, N. and F. Peres (2000) 'Latin America's new economic model: micro responses and economic restructuring', *World Development*, 28(9).

Republic of Cuba (1992) *Constitución de la República de Cuba*, Havana: Editora Política.

Reyes del Campillo, J. F. (2007) 'Resultados electorales 2006', *El Cotidiano*, 21(141).

Reyes García, L. (2005) 'La coalición dominante del Partido Revolucionario Institucional: auge, crisis y recomposición', *El Cotidiano*, 21(133).

Richards, D. (2001) 'The poverty of democracy in Latin America', *Review of Radical Political Economics*, 33(2).

Richardson, N. (2009) 'Export-oriented populism: commodities and coalitions in Argentina', *Studies in Comparative International Development*, 44(3).

Right Web (2007) 'National Endowment for Democracy', www.rightweb.irc-online.org/profile/National_Endowment_for_Democracy (accessed 20 July 2007).

— (2008) 'Project for the New American Century', www.rightweb.irc-online.org/profile/Project_for_the_New_American_Century (accessed 20 June 2008).

Roberts, K. M. (1996) 'Neoliberalism and the transformation of populism in Latin America: the Peruvian case', *World Politics*, 48(1).

Robinson, W. I. (1996) *Promoting Polyarchy: Globalization, US*

Intervention, and Hegemony, Cambridge: Cambridge University Press.
— (2007) 'Democracy or polyarchy?', *NACLA Report on the Americas*, 40(2).
— (2008) *Latin America and Global Capitalism: A Critical Globalization Perspective*, Baltimore, MD: Johns Hopkins University Press.
Rocha Menocal, A. (2001) 'Do old habits die hard? A statistical exploration of the politicisation of Progresa, Mexico's latest federal poverty-alleviation programme, under the Zedillo administration', *Journal of Latin American Studies*, 33(3).
Rodríguez, J. C. (1999) *The Bay of Pigs and the CIA*, New York: Ocean Press.
Rodríguez Cruz, J. C. (ed.) (2005) *Cuba: The Untold History*, Havana: Editorial Capitán San Luis.
Rodríguez Elizondo, J. (2006) *Las crisis vecinales del gobierno de Lagos*, Santiago de Chile: Random House Mondadori.
Romero, M. (2003) *Paramilitares y autodefensas, 1982–2003*, Bogotá: Universidad Nacional de Colombia.
Rouquié, A. (1986) 'Demilitarization and the institutionalization of military-dominated politics in Latin America', in G. O'Donnell, P. C. Schmitter and L. Whitehead (eds), *Transitions from Authoritarian Rule: Comparative Perspectives*, Baltimore, MD: Johns Hopkins Press.
Rueschmeyer, D., E. H. Stephens and J. D. Stevens (1992) *Capitalist Development and Democracy*, Chicago, IL: University of Chicago Press.
Sabatini, C. and J. Marczak (2010) 'Obama's tango: restoring U.S. leadership in Latin America', *Foreign Affairs*, 13 January, www.foreignaffairs.com/articles/65923/christopher-sabatini-and-jason-marczak/obamas-tango (accessed 19 September 2010).
Sader, E. (2005) 'Taking Lula's measure', *New Left Review*, 33.
Sánchez, R. (2008) 'Venezuela, turning further left?', in J. Castañeda and M. A. Morales (eds), *Leftovers: Tales of the Latin American Left*, London: Routledge.
Sánchez Gudiño, H. (2008) 'Mediocracia, dinero y elección presidencial en México 2006', *Revista Mexicana de Ciencias Políticas y Sociales*, 202.
Sánchez Murillo, L. F. and F. de Jesús Aceves González (2008) 'Campañas políticas y configuración del voto electoral en 2006. Encuestas electorales y publicidad política', *Revista Mexicana de Ciencias Políticas y Sociales*, 202.
Sanders, T. G. (1989) 'The fall of Stroessner: continuity and change in Paraguay', *Field Staff Reports*, 2.
Sanz, C. (2004) 'El grupo Clarín y los medios cómplices: nuevos despidos y conductas oscuras', *Periódico Tribuna*, www.periodicotribuna.com.ar/954-el-grupo-clarin-y-los-medios-complices.html (accessed 17 July 2010).
Sawyer, M. Q. (2006) *Racial Politics in Post-Revolutionary Cuba*, Cambridge: Cambridge University Press.
Seligson, A. L. (2008) 'The right in Latin America: strategies, successes, and failures', *Latin American Politics and Society*, 45(1).
Semana (2010) 'En el clóset', 21 August, www.semana.com/noticias-nacion/closet/143355.aspx (accessed 31 August 2010).

Shifter, M. (2010) 'Santos y Washington: ¿una época diferente?', *El Colombiano*, 6 July.
Shirk, D. (2000) 'Mexico's victory: Vicente Fox and the rise of the PAN', *Journal of Democracy*, 11(4).
Siavelis, P. M. (2000) *The President and the Congress in Post-Authoritarian Chile: Institutional Constraints to Democratic Consolidation*, University Park, PA: Penn State University Press.
Silva, C. G. (2010) 'Santos' massive coalition', *Colombia Reports*, 28 June, http://colombiareports.com/opinion/gustavo-silva-cano/10508-santos-massive-coalition.html (accessed 13 July 2010).
Silva, P. (1999) 'Collective memories, fears and consensus: the political psychology of the Chilean democratic transition', in K. Koonings and D. Kruijt (eds), *Societies of Fear: The Legacy of Civil War, Violence and Terror in Latin America*, London: Zed Books.
— (2003) 'Democratisation and state–civil society relations in Chile, 1983–2000: from effervescence to deactivation', *Nordic Journal of Latin American and Caribbean Studies*, 32(2).
— (2008) *In the Name of Reason: Technocrats and Politics in Chile*, University Park, PA: Penn State University Press.
Smink, V. (2009) 'Peligra el futuro de Lugo en Paraguay?', BBC News, 6 November, www.bbc.co.uk/mundo/america_latina/2009/11/091105_0111_paraguay_futuro_gm.shtml (accessed 14 June 2010).
Smith, P. H. (2005) *Democracy in Latin America: Political Change in Comparative Perspective*, Oxford: Oxford University Press.
Smith, W. S. (2006) 'Center for International Policy. New Cuba Commission report: formula for continued failure', www.ecdet.org/Commission_Response.pdf (accessed 17 February 2007).
Smith, W. S., S. Harrison and S. Adams (2006) *Sanctuary for Terrorists: US Tolerance of Anti-Cuban Terrorism*, Washington, DC: Center for International Policy.
Sonntag, H. (1992) *Venezuela: 4F 1992: un análisis sociopolítico*, Caracas: Nueva Sociedad.
Soto, A. and M. Fernández (2002) 'El pensamiento político de la derecha chilena en los 60: el Partido Nacional', *Bicentenario Revista de Historia de Chile y América*, 2(1).
Spronk, S. and J. R. Webber (2007) 'Struggles against accumulation by dispossession in Bolivia. The political economy of natural resource contention', *Latin American Perspectives*, 34(2).
Stephens, S. and A. Dunscomb (eds) (2009) 'Center for Democracy in the Americas: 9 ways for US to talk to Cuba and for Cuba to talk to US', http://democracyinamericas.org/9-ways-us-talk-cuba-and-cuba-talk-us-new-report (accessed 14 January 2010).
Stokes, D. (2005) *America's Other War: Terrorizing Colombia*, London: Zed Books.
Sullivan, M. P. (2009) 'Venezuela: political conditions and U.S. policy', *Congressional Research Service*, 28 July, www.fas.org/sgp/crs/row/RL3488.PDF (accessed 16 January 2011).
Tanaka, M. (1999) 'Del movimientismo a la media-política: cambios en las relaciones entre la sociedad y la política en el Perú de Fujimori', in J. Crabtree and J. Thomas (eds), *El Perú de*

Fujimori, Lima: Instituto de Estudios Peruanos and Universidad del Pacífico.

Teubal, M., D. Domínguez and P. Sabatino (2005) 'Transformaciones agrarias en la Argentina. Agricultura industrial y sistema alimentario', in N. Garriacca and M. Teubal (eds), *El campo en la encrucijada. Estrategias y resistencias sociales, ecos en la ciudad*, Buenos Aires: Alianza Editorial.

Thomas, H. (2001) *Cuba or the Pursuit of Freedom*, Basingstoke: Picador.

Tickner, A. B. (2010) 'De la Plaza de Mayo a Soacha', *El Espectador*, 17 August, www.elespectador.com/node/219625 (accessed 18 August 2010).

Tokatlion, J. G. (2008) 'A new doctrine of insecurity? US military deployment in South America', *NACLA Report on the Americas*, 41(5).

Torreira Crespo, R. and J. Buajasán Marrawi (2000) *Operación Pedro Pan: un Caso de Guerra Psicológica contra Cuba*, Havana: Editorial Política.

Transparency International (2002) *Corruption Perceptions Index*, www. transparency.org/policy_research/surveys_indices/cpi/2002 (accessed 14 June 2010).

Tsolakis, A. (2008) 'Evo Morales, the MAS and elite resistance to change', *Global Dialogue*, 10(1).

— (2010) *The Reform of the Bolivian State: Domestic Politics in the Context of Globalization*, Boulder, CO: Lynne Rienner/First Forum Press.

Tussie, D. and P. Heidrich (2008) 'A tale of ecumenism and diversity: economic and trade policies of the new left', in J. Castañeda and M. A. Morales (eds), *Leftovers: Tales of the Latin American Left*, London: Routledge.

UN Development Programme (2004) *Democracy in Latin America: Towards a Citizen's Democracy*, New York: UN Development Programme.

— (2008) *Informe nacional sobre desarrollo: equidad para el desarrollo*, Asunción: United Nations.

UN Habitat (2010) *State of the World's Cities 2010/11. Bridging the Urban Divide*, London: Earthscan and UN Habitat.

United Nations (2005) *UN Working Group on Arbitrary Detention (Human Rights Commission) 'Opinion No. 19/2005 (United States of America) 27 May 2005'*, New York: United Nations.

— (2008) 'Compilation prepared by the High Commissioner for Human Rights – Cuba', http://lib.ohchr.org/HRBodies/UPR/Documents/Session4/CU/A_HRC_WG6_4_CUB_2_E.pdf (accessed 22 January 2010).

Uprimny, R. (2010) 'En el Día Internacional del Desaparecido', *El Espectador*, 30 August, www.elespectador.com/node/221825 (accessed 31 August 2010).

Uribe, M. (2008) 'La ultraderecha en México: el conservadurismo moderno', *El Cotidiano*, 23(149).

US Congress (2009) 'Department of Airforce, military construction program, fiscal year (FY) 2010 budget estimates, justification data submitted to Congress, May 2009', Washington, DC: United States Congress, www.justf.org/files/primarydocs/091104pal.pdf (accessed 15 July 2010).

— (2010) 'Testimony of the Honorable Otto J. Reich, President, Otto Reich Associates, LLC, former Assistant Secretary of

State for the Western Hemisphere, to the House Committee on Foreign Affairs, Subcommittee on the Western Hemisphere, March 10, 2010', Washington, DC: United States Congress, http://foreign affairs.house.gov/111/rei031010.pdf (accessed 15 July 2010).

US Court of Appeals for the Eleventh Circuit (2005) *United States of America v Gerardo Hernández et al, 9 Aug 2005*, Atlanta: United States Court of Appeals for the Eleventh Circuit.

US Department of Defense (2009) 'White Paper, Air Mobility Command, global En Route strategy, preparatory document for Air Force Symposium 2009—AFRICOM', Washington, DC: United States Department of Defense, www.latinreporters.com/colombieBasesWhitePaperAirMobilityCommand.htm (accessed 15 July 2010).

US Department of State (2002) 'A review of U.S. policy toward Venezuela November 2001–April 2002', Report Number 02-OIG-003, July 2002, Washington, DC: United States Department of State and the Broadcasting Board of Governors, Office of Inspector General, http://oig.state.gov/documents/organization/13682.pdf (accessed 15 March 2010).

— (2003) 'On certain counternarcotics activities in Colombia', report submitted to Congress by the Secretary of State, pursuant to section to 694 (b) of the Foreign Relations Authorization Act, Fiscal Year 2003, (Public Law 107–228)

US Government Accountability Office (2006) 'U.S. democracy assistance for Cuba needs better management and oversight', http://ftp.resource.org/gpo.gov/gao/reports/d07147.pdf (accessed 22 January 2010).

— (2007) 'Economic sanctions: agencies face competing priorities in enforcing the U.S. embargo on Cuba', www.gao.gov/new.items/d0880.pdf (accessed 22 January 2010).

— (2008) 'Continued efforts needed to strengthen USAID's oversight of U.S. democracy assistance for Cuba', www.gao.gov/new.items/d09165.pdf (accessed 14 January 2010).

US Senate (2009) 'Changing Cuba policy – in the United States national interest: a report to the Committee on Foreign Relations', http://lugar.senate.gov/sfrc/pdf/Cuba.pdf (accessed 14 January 2010).

— (2010a) 'Annual threat assessment of the US Intelligence Community; for the Senate Select Committee on Intelligence, by Dennis C. Blair, Director of National Intelligence, February 2, 2010', Washington, DC: United States Senate.

— (2010b) 'Cuba: immediate action is needed to ensure the survivability of Radio and TV Marti: a report to the Committee on Foreign Relations', http://foreign.senate.gov/imo/media/doc/56157.pdf (accessed 6 July 2010).

US Southern Command (2008) 'Command Strategy 2018. Partnership for the Americas. December 2008', Miami, FL: United States Southern Command, www.southcom.mil/AppsSC/files/0ui0i1177092386.pdf (accessed 15 July 2010).

— (2010) 'Posture statement of General Douglas M. Fraser, United

States Air Force Commander, United States Southern Command before the 111th Congress House Armed Services Committee, March 18 2010', Miami, FL: United States Southern Command, www.southcom.mil/AppsSC/files/634038960550937500.pdf (accessed 15 July 2010).

USAID (2007) 'USAID/Bolivia, FY 2007 program summary', Washington, DC: United States Agency for International Development, http://jeremybigwood.net/BO/2008-BO-USAID.htm (accessed 15 July 2010).

— (2008) 'USAID/Bolivia, planned FY2008 program overview', Washington, DC: United States Agency for International Development, http://jeremybigwood.net/BO/2008-BO-USAID.htm (accessed 15 July 2010).

Valdés, J. G. (1995) *Pinochet's Economists: The Chicago Boys in Chile*, Cambridge: Cambridge University Press.

Valdivia, V. (2008) *Nacionales y gremialistas: el parto de la nueva derecha política chilena, 1964–1973*, Santiago de Chile: Lom Ediciones.

Van Klaveren, A. (2000) 'Chile's international integration', in C. Toloza and E. Lahera (eds), *Chile in the Nineties*, Stanford, CA: Stanford University Press.

Vargas Llosa, M. (1993) *El pez en el agua*, Barcelona: Seix Barral.

Vivares, E., L. Díaz Echenique and J. Ozorio (2009) 'Argentina: reforming neoliberal capitalism', in G. Lievesley and S. Ludlam (eds), *Reclaiming Latin America: Experiments in Radical Social Democracy*, London: Zed Books.

VTV (2009) 'José Vicente Rangel denuncia presencia de 9 grupos paramilitares en Venezuela', 2 February, www.vtv.gov/ve/noticias-nacionales/13988 (accessed 16 January 2011).

Wainfeld, M. (2010) 'Ganarle al miedo en buena ley', *Pagina 12*, 25 August.

Webber, J. (2008) 'Rebellion to reform in Bolivia, Part I: domestic class structure, Latin American trends and capitalist imperialism', *Historical Materialism*, 16(2).

Weffort, F. C. (1984) *Por que democracia?*, São Paulo: Editora Brasiliense.

Weisbrot, M. (2008a) 'Is Washington undermining democracy in Latin America?', *Alternet*, 16 February, www.alternet.org/story/77256/ (accessed 3 March 2008).

— (2008b) 'Poverty reduction in Venezuela: a reality-based view', *Harvard Review of Latin America*, autumn.

— (2010) 'Brazil wins with Dilma Rousseff', *Guardian*, 1 November, www.guardian.co.uk/commentisfree/cifamerica/2010/nov/01/brazil-republicans (accessed 1 November 2010).

Weyland, K. (2001) 'Clarifying a contested concept: populism in the study of Latin American Politics', *Journal of Comparative Politics*, 34(1).

Wilpert, G. (2003) 'Collision in Latin America', *New Left Review*, 21.

— (2007) *Changing Venezuela by Taking Power*, London and New York: Verso.

Wolff, J. (2007) 'Argentinien – mit links aus der Krise? Zur Verortung der Regierung Kirchner im lateinamerikanischen "Linksruck"', *Lateinamerika Analysen*, 17.

World Bank (2000) *Bolivia: From*

Patronage to a Professional State – Bolivia Institutional and Governance Review, Vol. II: Annexes, 25 August, Washington, DC: World Bank.

— (2005) *Bolivia Country Economic Memorandum. Policies to improve growth and employment.* Report No. 32233-BO, 31 October, Washington, DC: World Bank.

— (2011) 'Latin America and the Caribbean regional brief', web.worldbank.org/WBSITE/EXTERNAL/COUNTRIES/LACEXT/0,,contentMDK:20340156~menuPK: 258561~pagePK:146736~piPK:146830~theSitePK:258554,00.html (accessed 25 January 2011).

Young, K. (2008) 'Colombia and Venezuela: testing the propaganda model', *NACLA Report on the Americas*, https://nacla.org/node/5344 (accessed 15 January 2011).

Zavala Echavarría, I. (2008) 'Factores sociales agregados de la elección presidencial mexicana de 2006', *Revista Mexicana de Ciencias Políticas y Sociales*, 202.

Zibechi, R. (2008) 'The new Latin American right: finding a place in the world', *NACLA Report on the Americas*, 41(1).

Index